WETLAND DRAINAGE IN EUROPE

The effects of Agricultural Policy in four EEC countries

DAVID BALDOCK
with Ben Hermans

Patricia Kelly

Laurent Mermet

The Institute for European Environmental Policy

The International Institute for Environment and Development

Published by the International Institute for Environment and Development and the Institute for European Environmental Policy

© IEEP/IIED 1984   631·62

ISBN No. 0-905347-52-8

Printed by Russell Press Ltd, Nottingham

Cover design by Graham Whatley

Maps by John McCormick

CHAPTER 1:   INTRODUCTION

The Seeds of Conflict

For centuries the drainage of wetlands has been seen as a progressive, public-spirited endeavour, the very antithesis of vandalism. It has been a way of counteracting disastrous floods, reclaiming new land and adding to food production, a means of controlling mosquitoes and other unwelcome denizens of the marsh. It is only recently, as wetlands have become scarcer and more polluted, that their loss has been regretted, and the benefits of their destruction considered more carefully. It is now unusual for these sometimes inhospitable zones to be seen as a threat to human welfare and the struggle to protect them receives increasing public support. The kind of drainage work which traditionally has been admired may now be seen as an act of destruction and self-interest.

This re-evaluation of wetlands and the merits of draining them is a recent and far from universal phenomenon. Concern for the protection of wetlands has grown markedly over the last two decades, fuelled by scientific interest, a series of international meetings and, perhaps more importantly, by a wider movement in support of environmental conservation.

The protection of wetlands was the subject of a Council of Europe campaign in the mid 1970s and the Council has chosen 1984 as the year of a second international effort focussed on "The Water's Edge". In northern Europe there has grown up a vigorous organisation concerned with the protection of the Waddensee which stretches from western Denmark to the Netherlands. Wetland drainage, previously an obscure topic in the UK, has become increasingly controversial and shown itself capable of igniting considerable passion and media attention.

The growth of concern is probably most marked in northern Europe but it can be expected to spread throughout the European Community (EC) and become an issue of increasing importance to farmers, the rural community and agricultural authorities.

In a now familiar pattern, the demise of a once plentiful resource has been accompanied by a growing understanding and appreciation of its value. This value is not purely ecological;

1

wetlands have an economic worth as a source of fish, wildfowl, peat and reed, not to mention grazing for livestock. They offer distinctive landscapes and places for peaceful recreation as well as facilities for people in search of fishing, shooting and water sports. They have a part in our history and cultural life and a role in education.

The ecological functions of wetlands are many and varied. The natural biological productivity of many lowland sites is remarkably high, sometimes greater than that of the intensively managed arable land into which they may be converted after drainage. Europe's wetland ecosystems make a significant contribution to genetic variety and support many threatened plant and animal species. They are identified as an area of priority in the "World Conservation Strategy", published in 1980 (1). In them can be found a characteristic fauna and flora including many of our most familiar waterfowl and fish.

Wetlands are important not only for animals which are permanently resident, but also for those which spend part of their life cycle in other habitats. These include many fish which use rivers and estuaries for spawning and maturation and birds which may use a site simply for winter feeding or moulting or as a passage halt in their annual migration. Many of the rarer species of European waterfowl depend on a small number of wetland sites for their survival.

One of the most significant but least studied aspects of wetlands is the role which they play in the regulation of water regimes. This varies greatly, according to the particular characteristics of a wetland and its surrounding watershed, but areas of marsh for example may aid flood control and assist in the assimilation of wastes. Studies in the United States suggest that if wetlands and lakes comprise 15 per cent of the area of a watershed, the flood peaks may be as much as 60 to 65 per cent lower than they would be in the absence of any wetland or lake area (2).

The threats to European wetlands are by no means confined to drainage. Wetlands are also damaged or destroyed by urban development, pollution, water supply schemes, recreation, tourism, waste disposal, shooting and many other human activities. Nor is all drainage agricultural. Some schemes are designed primarily to improve urban flood control or to reclaim land for industrial development. Nonetheless, agricultural improvement is probably the single most important reason for drainage work and in almost every European country it is a large scale highly organised activity, attracting government grants and subsidies. Stronger measures to protect wetlands cannot be achieved without some conflict with agricultural interests and new drainage schemes are likely to be at the centre of dispute.

Behind the issue of wetland drainage lies a potentially wider conflict between modern agriculture and the environment and a more general question about how we wish to manage the resources

The study on which this book is based was funded by World Wildlife Fund International, World Wildlife Fund - Netherlands, World Wildlife Fund - United Kingdom and the Ernest Cook Trust.

CONTENTS

PREFACE

This book arose from a study of agricultural drainage and wetlands in four countries undertaken by the Institute for European Environmental Policy and the International Institute for Environment and Development in 1982-84. It brings together the results of four separate national studies and the efforts of five different people.

Laurent Mermet and Michel Mustin prepared the report on France and Patricia Kelly the one on Ireland. The report on the Netherlands was compiled by Ben Hermans of Stichting Natuur en Milieu and that on the UK by myself.

The report on France, "Assainissement Agricole et Regression des Zones Humides en France" by Laurent Mermet and Michel Mustin has been published in French by the Institute for European Environmental Policy.

In writing this book I have drawn very heavily on these reports and on the help of all the different authors. Each of them has come to meetings, read drafts and made many helpful suggestions. In a few places there are explicit references to their work but for the most part the chapters on France, Ireland and the Netherlands have grown directly from their reports and detailed acknowledgement in the text would be impractical. There are many places where I have elaborated on their reports, drawn my own conclusions or taken a slightly different view and it need scarcely be said that they are not responsible for what I have written here.

This book could not have been written without the help of a large number of people in each of the countries concerned. Not only have I received help and support from people in the UK and elsewhere in Europe, but so also have the four other contributors. In acknowledgement of all this assistance, special mention must be made of some of the people directly concerned with the preparation of this book.

The original idea for the project came from Nigel Haigh, the head of IEEP's London office and from Professor Timothy O'Riordan from the University of East Anglia. I must also thank Nigel Haigh for his support at all stages of the project and for innumerable insights into the workings of the European Community.

In France I would like to thank particularly Professor Claude Henri and Peter Nowicki. In Ireland, both Tony Whilde and Professor Frank Convery made invaluable contributions and Patricia Kelly introduced me to many wetlands and their inhabitants as well as preparing a national report. In the Netherlands special thanks are due to Graham Bennett and to Dr de Molenaar from the Research Institute of Nature Management.

In the United Kingdom I received help from many quarters including the various Ministries of Agriculture and I would particularly like to thank Dr Trafford and Mr Buxton in London, Mr Kerr and Mr Ingram in Northern Ireland and Mr Dalgleish in Scotland for answering so many long and sometimes tedious inquiries. Gwyn Williams of the Royal Society for the Protection of Birds was particularly generous with his time and I also had invaluable discussions with Tony Long from Council for the Protection of Rural England and Dr Penning-Rowsell and others at Middlesex Polytechnic. At the beginning of the project F.H.W. Green from Oxford University gave me a first flavour of the European drainage scene and I am one of many who regret his recent death.

I am particularly grateful to the World Wildlife Fund and the Ernest Cook Trust for providing financial support for the research project on which this book is based.

Thanks are also due to all those involved in the production of the book, especially Kate Partridge and Dawn Webster for typing drafts at a speed which I could never keep up with, Graham Whatley for designing the cover, John McCormick for the maps and Annie Petrie for the organisation.

Finally I would like to thank Maria for such patience during the two years in which I have been immoderately interested in drainage.

David Baldock
London, May 1984

of the countryside. For many generations good husbandry and care of the countryside were seen as largely synonymous and it is only in the last three decades that the advent of new farming techniques has forced a reappraisal and revealed a divergence of aims. As the countryside undergoes rapid change it is vital to recognise that agricultural policy does more than regulate farming and food production; it is an important determinant of the quality of the rural environment.

This report is primarily concerned with agricultural drainage in four EC countries, the way in which it is organised and financed and the kind of effects which it has on wetlands. However, it is also an attempt to show, in a very preliminary way, that agricultural policy, at both national and EC levels, is of great significance for the future of the European environment.

Wetlands

From the marshy corners of upland farms to the coastal mudflats which only appear between tides, there is a great variety of habitats which can be described as "wetlands". The term is often used to cover almost all the ecosystems in which water predominates, including marsh, bog, fen, streams and rivers, water meadows, estuaries and shallow bays. Strictly speaking, only some of these wetland habitats, such as certain raised bogs, are distinct ecosystems in their own right, others are more properly "transition environments"(3). In general these lie somewhere between open water and the dry uplands and are often links in the chain of natural succession whereby shallow water gives way to fringe vegetation and swamp, later drying to marshland and ultimately woodland.

The definition of wetlands is a somewhat arbitrary business. No single definition is universally accepted but perhaps the most widely used internationally is the one embodied in the Convention on Wetlands of International Importance, adopted at Ramsar in Iran in 1971. The Convention defines wetlands as

"areas of marsh, fen, peatland or water, whether natural or artificial, permanent or temporary, with water that is static or flowing, fresh, brackish or salt, including areas of marine water the depth of which at low tide does not exceed six metres".

This is a broad definition and is intended to include those areas within wetlands, such as bodies of water deeper than six metres, islands and coastal zones immediately bordering wet areas, which do not themselves meet the criteria. It does, however, appear to exclude wet or periodically flooded lowland pasture and areas of reclaimed marsh where the water table is permanently high, typically within 20 cms of the surface. Such sites are often thought of as wetlands and will be treated as such in this report.

3

This generic use of the word is important, but in every day use "wetlands" often refers to a much smaller range of habitats, including marsh, fen, bog, wet meadows, places with saturated and often flooded soil. Precisely where these habitats begin and end may be difficult to determine, sometimes water levels may sink temporarily to as much as half a metre below the surface on reclaimed marsh, which is still thought of as "wetland". Such areas are often of botanical and ornithological interest and are especially vulnerable to agricultural drainage.

Wetlands are often divided into two basic types, saltwater and freshwater. This report is concerned principally with freshwater wetlands, especially rivers, streams, ditches, lakes, marshes, fens, peatland and bogs. However, reference will also be made to estuaries, salt marshes, brackish lagoons and other coastal sites.

In evaluating wetlands and setting goals for their management, a number of attempts have been made to select those of "international importance". This is not a particularly easy exercise, since our inventory of the world's wetlands is far from complete and much remains to be learned about the properties and functioning of even the more familiar sites.

In practice, the most widely appreciated and closely observed residents of wetlands are often the birds, and the ornithological interest of a site is a convenient, albeit imperfect, indicator of its overall value. The number and variety of birds found on a site has become an increasingly common measure of its importance, nationally or internationally. For example, the International Waterfowl Research Bureau (IWRB) is responsible for one of the most authoritative and most referred to lists of European wetlands. This is entitled "A Preliminary Inventory of Wetlands of International Importance for Waterfowl in West Europe and Northwest Africa" (4).

More than one definition of international importance is in use, but the latest set of criteria agreed by Ramsar Convention countries now commands the greatest authority. These criteria were adopted by the International Conference on Conservation of Wetlands and Waterfowl in 1980 at a meeting in Cagliari in Sardinia and superseded an earlier set adopted at the 1974 conference in Heiligenhafen. The criteria are set out here in full (see page 6) and it can be seen that quantitive criteria are supplied for birds, while the other guidelines are much less specific. The criteria provide a useful, but not infallible, guide to international importance; they are more appropriate for some bird species than for others, for example.

The use of wildfowl numbers as an indicator of importance is not ideal, as it fails to take into account the myriad other aspects of wetlands, such as their botanical interest, and hydrological functions. However, a more complete appraisal of sites is not really practical in the forseeable future and bird populations are a useful indication of the fauna and flora likely to be

4

present. Birds attract particular interest, they are visible,
their numbers can be counted relatively easily, and volunteers
from ornithological societies, shooting clubs, etc., are willing
to undertake this task. Where counts are held regularly, changes
in a habitat may become apparent quite quickly. Since many
waterfowl are migratory species, often they visit several different sites in the course of their annual cycle. The habitat
required for breeding, for wintering, for moulting, for passage
halts, may be varied and spread over thousands of miles but the
migrants tie them together in a kind of natural chain. In this
sense, wetlands are frequently inter-dependent, a truly international resource, requiring management on an international
scale.

The Ramsar Convention

This special feature of wetlands has led to a number of
efforts to conserve sites of international interest. A series of
meetings held in the 1960s culminated in February 1971 at the
International Conference on the Conservation of Wetlands and
Waterfowl, held at Ramsar in Iran. This was attended by 18
countries and led to the adoption of a "Convention on Wetlands of
International Importance especially as Waterfowl Habitat". The
Ramsar Convention was one of the earliest and most significant of
a recent series of international conventions concerned with the
environment. It is also one of the first attempts to impose
external obligations on the land use decisions of independent
countries. Inevitably, it treads cautiously, binding signatories
more to the support of general principles rather than to tight
conditions.

The essential aim of the Convention is to "stem the
progressive encroachment on and loss of wetlands now and in the
future" and the strategy adopted is to combine "far sighted
national policies with co-ordinated international action". The
main obligation for each contracting party is to designate at
least one wetland of international importance for inclusion in a
formal list. Sites should be selected "on account of their
international significance in terms of ecology, botany, zoology,
limnology, or hydrology. In the first instance, wetlands of
international importance to waterfowl at any season should be
included". Contracting parties agree to promote the conservation
of the wetlands which they have listed and to aim at the wise use
of all wetlands in their territory. There are exhortations to
establish nature reserves, make provision to warden them adequately, to increase waterfowl populations on wetlands through
management, encourage research and train personnel. None of the
obligations is too heavy or too specific and the Convention
relies on persuasion and moral pressure rather than legal powers.

CRITERIA FOR IDENTIFYING WETLANDS OF INTERNATIONAL IMPORTANCE

Adopted by the International Conference on Conservation of Wetlands and Waterfowl, Cagliari, Italy, November 1980

(1) Quantitative criteria for identifying wetlands of importance to waterfowl

A wetland should be considered internationally important if it:

(a) regularly supports either 10,000 ducks, geese and swans; or 10,000 coots; or 20,000 waders, or

(b) regularly supports one per cent of the individuals in a population of one species or subspecies of waterfowl, or

(c) regularly supports one per cent of the breeding pairs in a population of one species or subspecies of waterfowl.

(2) General criteria for identifying wetlands of importance to plants or animals

A wetland should be considered internationally important if it:

(a) supports an appreciable number of rare, vulnerable or endangered species or subspecies of plant or animal, or

(b) is of special value for maintaining the genetic and ecological diversity of a region because of the quality and peculiarities of its flora and fauna, or

(c) is of special value as the habitat of plants or animals at a critical stage of their biological cycles, or

(d) is of special value for its endemic plant or animal species or communities.

(3) Criteria for assessing the value of representative or unique wetlands

A wetland should be considered internationally important if it is a particularly good example of a specific type of wetland characteristic of its region.

6

By the end of 1982, 35 states had become contracting parties, including six EC Member States: Greece, the UK, the Federal Republic of Germany, Italy, Denmark and the Netherlands, each of which had designated a number of sites, typically between 10 and 30. Ireland and Belgium had both signed the Convention, but not ratified it. The original text of the Convention was in English and this proved a barrier to France and other francophone countries interested in signing. However, in 1982 a Protocol of Amendment was agreed in Paris, introducing equivalence of languages and an amendments clause. This Protocol is expected to come into force in 1984 and this should pave the way for France to become a contracting party.

Given the very modest progress towards international cooperation on controversial environmental issues, the achievements of the Convention are not to be dismissed. Wetlands have been singled out for special attention and their international importance recognised, however tentatively. Research and the exchange of information have been stimulated and designation has helped to protect a number of sites. For example, at the Cagliari conference, delegates from Greece, Sweden, Italy and both German Republics stated that the Convention had been a positive influence in efforts to protect individual sites. Unfortunately, a number of listed sites have been damaged, but the very fact that many governments are reluctant to list sites which are not fully protected, suggests that they have some respect for the obligations entailed.

Turning to the other side of the balance sheet, it must be stated that the limitations of the Convention are considerable and few of the contracting parties appear impelled by a great sense of urgency. The vast majority of wetlands of international importance are not listed, either because the countries concerned have not signed or because they have listed only a small number of sites, usually those already protected. There is a general reluctance to accept new conservation obligations even in the more affluent nations and relatively few developing countries have the funds to participate. Little money is available to the Secretariat, which is provided by the International Union for Conservation of Nature and Natural Resources (IUCN) with help from the IWRB and, unavoidably, this inhibits the development of the Convention.

The authors of the "World Conservation Strategy", who were otherwise temperate in such judgements, commented that the Convention "lacks force, requiring only that states select at least one wetland for conservation, but not providing adequate criteria to guide selection, guidelines for management or adequate safeguards for delisting" (5). The Cagliari criteria now provide some guidance and most signatories have listed more than one site, but the Convention has yet to prove a strong countervailing force against the sustained pressure on many important sites. Frustration at this weakness is likely to grow, but it is probably more important to secure real changes in national policy than to seek nominal consent to a stronger Convention.

7

The position of the four countries considered here is symptomatic of the prevailing caution with regard to listing. Only the Netherlands and the UK are contracting parties. By the end of 1983, the Dutch government had listed only 12 sites, half of them in the Netherlands Antilles (in the West Indies), although there are probably 50 or 60 of international importance in their European territory alone. The United Kingdom began with 13 sites and then listed another six in 1981, although the Nature Conservancy Council, the statutory body concerned, have furnished the Department of the Environment with a list of 129 sites which meet the Cagliari criteria. Until recently the government has only been prepared to designate sites which are already largely protected. No more than nine additional sites were subject to consultation in late 1983, although many more are now expected to follow.

This reluctance to list sites of established international importance is one of the most eloquent statements of the vulnerability of wetlands and the limited commitment to conservation even in two of the most extensively drained and traditionally more environmentally conscious European countries. To appreciate their vulnerability a little more fully, reference must be made to some of the basic characteristics of wetlands.

Wetland Characteristics

Many wetland sites are either continuously submerged or are intermittently inundated by seasonal river flooding or normal tidal action. Most are readily identifiable by the presence of typical emergent vegetation − such as plants which are rooted in the soil but are thrusting through the surface of the water − or by varying amounts of submerged and floating plant life. The depth, duration, chemistry, temperature of the water and, in coastal marshes, the reach of the tide, greatly influence the types of plant life found in a given wetland. The same physical and chemical features affect not only the vegetation, but the wide array of fish, molluscs, birds, crustaceans, insects, worms and tiny organisms which find food and shelter in the substrata and within the vegetation (6).

Many of these plants and animals are dependent on particular hydrological conditions and are sensitive to changes in the depth and temperature of water, the frequency of flooding or drying out, the pattern or change in water conditions and the chemical quality of the water itself. Because they depend on highly particular conditions, the natural inhabitants of wetlands are exceptionally vulnerable to change and many are likely to be eliminated by a significant alteration in conditions, whether induced by man or nature.

Wetlands are not only vulnerable to human intervention in water management, they are also subject to some of the more

8

extreme natural events. Wetland ecosystems can be shaped and destroyed by floods, drought, winter ice, high winds, waves, violent storms and hurricanes, and although some wetland habitats take centuries to develop fully, there are others which are more transient features of the landscape.

Many of the wetlands of western Europe are not "natural" in the sense that they have appeared and survived independently of human action. Man has played a part in creating as well ·as destroying these habitats. There are many wet meadows in the floodplains of major European rivers which for centuries were farmed in a traditional and consistent way, each year hay was cut and the remaining sward used for grazing livestock. "As a result of this regular and uniform system of management, they developed a characteristic assemblage of plants and animals that are of particular interest to ecologists studying the dynamism of plant populations and to those interested in the mechanisms which regulate or stabilize systems of great age. For these reasons, the destruction of these wetland sites has had a particularly catastrophic effect, leading to the decline and local extinction of such species as the snake's head fritillary (Fritillaria meleagris) in Britain...and in Belgium...over the past 80 years" (7). Not only are such sites of great ecological value, they also form an important element in what has now become the traditional landscape of many river valleys.

Even drainage itself can produce new wetland habitats of interest. The gently sloping banks of older or well-designed drainage ditches can sometimes offer suitable conditions for a remarkable variety of plant species. Wetlands now include both ancient natural sites and the new "artificial" habitats. These include reservoirs, abandoned quarries, farm ponds and even the ditches which were dug to drain the original and far more extensive wetlands of Europe.

There are several different ways of classifying wetlands for scientific purposes, but these will not be defined in a systematic fashion in this report. The aim is to provide no more than an overall sketch of the relationship between drainage and the many types of wetland found in north west Europe and words such as "marsh" will be used in their familiar every day sense rather than as scientific terms. As a bare minimum, however, it must be mentioned that freshwater wetlands can be categorised by their degree of alkalinity.

The alkalinity of water is measured by the quantity of calcium carbonate dissolved in it. This is closely correlated with the pH of the water and with the amount of dissolved nutrients it contains, but is regarded as a somewhat better means of characterising freshwater than either of the other two. Water which is highly alkaline usually contains a relatively large supply of nutrients, the most important of which are nitrogen and phosphorous in different forms, and consequently supports an abundance of plant and animal life. Conversely, acid waters contain fewer nutrients and support less life. Acid wetlands are

9

often identifiable by the sparseness of the fringe vegetation and clarity of the water.

Alkaline waters are known as "eutrophic" and relatively acid waters as "oligotrophic". Typically the former are found in the fertile lowlands and include many of the slow moving rivers, lakes and pools which enrich the agricultural landscape. The more acid "oligotrophic" waters are common in the less fertile and upland regions, the Scottish lochs are one example. These two basic categories are the most important, but between them lies a third group of waters, known as "mesotrophic". Where alkalinity is exceptionally high, carbonate may be precipitated out to form a bottom layer, known as "marl". At the other end of the scale, waters with a very low level of calcium carbonate are known as "dystrophic". These support little flora or fauna and are mainly found on peat, which is responsible for staining the water a characteristic brown.

Since the basic character of many freshwater habitats greatly depends on their alkalinity and fertility, changes in water chemistry can be of great significance. Such changes often arise from human activities, particularly the discharge of sewage wastes and the run-off from farm land of water enriched with nitrates and phosphates. Excessive enrichment can lead to "eutrophication", a process whereby the growth of algae and other vegetation is stimulated to the point where the amount of dissolved oxygen available in the water falls to a level which renders it uninhabitable for fish and many other forms of life. Of all the consequences of modern agriculture for wetlands, the shedding of surplus nutrients and agrochemicals into the aquatic environment is one of the most important and should not be forgotten in the subsequent discussion of drainage.

Agricultural Drainage

"Drainage" like "wetlands" is a generic term, covering a variety of activities, such as the removal of surplus water from the land, flood protection, sea defences and, in a different context, the disposal of sewage. The concern of this report is agricultural land drainage but it cannot be separated entirely from other forms of water management. The links between different forms of water management may be hydrological, economic or, indeed, administrative, especially where water authorities are organised on a catchment basis. Improvements in agricultural drainage in one part of a river catchment may cause flooding downstream, the alleviation of which may require a second separate scheme. Conversely, sea defence works may provide a level of protection which makes drainage inland financially worthwhile for the first time. Many projects are multi-purpose. For example, the reclamation of a polder in the Netherlands may be partly to create new agricultural land, partly to provide new space for urban expansion and recreation.

The removal of excessive soil moisture from the land in order to improve its agricultural potential is the primary reason for drainage works in all the countries covered in this report. Wetlands are sometimes drained for other purposes, such as peat exploitation, irrigation improvements or the reclamation of land for industrial development, but the large-scale lowering of water tables and regulation of river systems is mainly for the benefit of agriculture.

Land drainage has been taking place for several centuries in Europe and techniques have been developed to fit local soils and local conditions. Once an arduous and extremely labour intensive undertaking, drainage is now achieved relatively fast with sophisticated machinery. This has allowed a continued increase in standards on previously drained land and a growing ability to tackle sites until recently thought difficult or too expensive to drain, some of which are important wetlands.

Although there are significant differences between countries, agricultural drainage schemes employ broadly the same principles throughout Europe. The natural drainage system is amended by a catena of artificial modifications and additions, ranging in size from small pipes installed under the field surface to major alterations to main rivers. F.H.W. Green, who was a notable expert on European drainage, likened this interlocking system of drainage channels to a road network (8). He subdivided the key elements in the network as follows:

"(i)   field under-drainage

(ii)   minor surface channels
       (a)   for agricultural field drainage
       (b)   to drain hill land to improve rough grazing
       (c)   for forestry purposes
       (d)   for building and other purposes

(iii) improvement of natural stream channels, and construction of ditches to supplement them

(iv)   major works on rivers and on sea defences to accommodate satisfactorily water outflowing from the above."
       (9)

This basic system may be supplemented by irrigation systems, the extraction of water for urban or agricultural consumption, the disposal of urban wastes and other complications, but it forms the backbone of land drainage. The terminology for different parts of the system varies between countries, but there is a useful fundamental distinction between field drainage and arterial drainage.

Arterial works are concerned with the regulation of rivers and large drainage channels. This may involve deepening a channel, widening it, straightening or diverting it, changing its profile, constructing weirs and dams, installing pumps or building flood banks and other related operations. Sometimes major arterial works are multi-purpose, designed for example to improve urban flood control and navigation as well as agricultural drainage.

Intermediate between major arterial schemes and field drainage are a series of smaller works; the construction and improvement of drainage ditches, the canalisation of streams, the clearing out of small channels, etc. These may be seen as an extension of field drainage work or as a form of minor arterial works, partly depending on who is responsible for them. Arterial works are usually carried out by public authorities, while farmers are generally responsible for field drainage, usually employing a contractor to do the work. Minor channel works are often the concern of more than one farmer and may be tackled by a local group of some kind, if not by a public authority.

Field drainage is the foundation of the entire network. Its basic aim is "to remove surplus water rapidly from a soil profile, thus enabling the land concerned to be more fully utilised" (10). In order to create the best environment for the germination, rooting and growth of crops, it is desirable to attain a suitable balance between air and moisture in the soil. Excessive moisture can restrict the depth of root penetration and the aeration of the soil, the effects of which may include reduced resistance to drought and poor respiration. Wet soils warm up more slowly in the spring, retarding germination and resulting in a shorter growing season. They are more vulnerable to poaching by livestock and may also have a lower bearing capacity, meaning that machinery cannot be brought onto the land until later than otherwise desirable. This factor is probably of increasing importance as farm machinery becomes heavier and more frequently used. The other penalties of surplus moisture vary, but may include increased risks of disease for crops and livestock and poor take up of fertiliser, especially nitrogen.

For these and other reasons, the agricultural potential of certain soils can be improved by drainage. In particular, farmers can expect a longer growing season, higher yields, higher stocking densities, fewer disease and pest problems and greater freedom to use machinery. A major fall in the water table may allow a farmer to switch a field from grass, which is relatively tolerant of moisture, to arable production, which generally produces a larger income. Similarly, drainage may permit a marshy pasture made up of low yielding grasses, sedges and reed to be ploughed, reseeded with high yielding varieties of ryegrass and cocksfoot and turned into intensively managed grassland. Drainage designed to relieve periodic flooding may also open the way for new forms of management as several valuable crops can survive only limited periods of complete waterlogging.

Adequate drainage, in short, is one of the essential conditions for the full application of modern agricultural techniques. Its benefits are stressed by agricultural advisers in almost every European country and usually grants or cheap loans are offered as an additional incentive. Not surprisingly, drainage nearly always increases the value of a field and for small farmers unable to acquire additional land it may be one of the few practical means of intensifying production and increasing output. As one of the main planks of land improvement and the restructuring of fragmented land holdings, drainage has played a key part in the abandonment of traditional farming practices and the adoption of new technology.

Some drainage schemes are designed to bring land into agricultural production for the first time, and these tend to have the most adverse effects on the natural environment. Much more common, however, are works aimed at improving the water regime on existing agricultural land. In the four countries covered here, the wetter soils and those with the poorest drainage tend to be pasture or rough grazing, relatively lightly stocked with cattle or sheep. These are often the subject of drainage work, for example in the west of Ireland. However, the productivity of this land is often restrained by other factors and the costs of drainage can be high. The economic returns are usually greater on fertile soils in drier areas where crop yields can be improved by up-grading the existing drainage system. This explains why field drainage is more common in many parts of northern and central France than in the wetter regions of the west, such as Brittany, and more extensive in East Anglia than in the dairying regions in the west of Britain.

Excessive moisture may arise from a high water table or from the presence of soil layers with poor permeability or because the land is subject to flooding. Field drainage systems are designed to regulate the soil water regime in such a way as to benefit the soil structure and the crops to be grown. On porous soils this may be done by digging surface ditches, which are common in the Netherlands, for example, where fields are often divided into thin strips, separated by ditches.

More usually, under-drainage is installed. This involves inserting a series of parallel drains at regular intervals, under the soil surface, work now done with specialist heavy machinery. The drains normally feed into appropriately constructed ditches or naturally occurring streams and rivers. In most cases the system works by gravity, but occasionally pumps are installed, especially on low flat land. Originally the field drains themselves were often made from stone and later from clay pipes, but recently cheaper plastic pipes have become increasingly popular. On land with a poor soil structure under-drainage alone may not be sufficient. It may need to be supplemented by other techniques, such as subsoiling or using a mole plough to create transverse channels between the drains and the soil surface.

Often, water tables are lowered by drainage, particularly if they are considered too high at important periods for cultivation and crop growth. The single most crucial time of year is usually the spring. The British Ministry of Agriculture, for example, in a leaflet for farmers about draining grassland advises "Grass becomes sensitive to periods of waterlogging once growth starts in spring. Yields fall very rapidly if the water table is less than 450 mm from the surface in spring. Maximum yields are obtained where the water table is kept at a depth of 450-900 mm in summer and rising to not more than 200-300 mm in winter" (11).

The design of drainage schemes varies according to the local circumstances, the objectives chosen and the amount of money it is thought worthwhile to spend. Nowadays, under-drainage ·is often installed about a metre below the surface, although sometimes it may be as deep as two metres, especially on arable land, or as little as 300 mm on impervious soils. If conditions permit, there are often strong agricultural arguments for deep drainage and a relatively low water table. This may be particularly helpful in increasing the bearing capacity of the soil in the spring, allowing cultivation to begin earlier. In parts of the Netherlands it is now thought worthwhile to lower water tables to the extent that water shortage and crop dessication becomes a problem in the middle of the summer and this creates the need for costly irrigation systems.

Another important aspect of a scheme is the distance between parallel sub-surface drains. Ideally, these should be close together, perhaps only one or two metres apart in heavier soils, in order to achieve rapid drainage. In practice, such close spacing is usually prohibitively expensive and a distance of perhaps 10-30 metres apart is more typical.

To allow any under-drainage system to operate properly, it must be able to discharge reasonably freely into a larger drain or ditch and thence into a series of bigger channels. If the water level in the ditches is high enough to cover the drain outfalls for an appreciable period of time, it will considerably reduce the efficiency of the system. In practice, ditch improvement and arterial works may be essential preconditions for field drainage and the two operations are closely connected. River improvement projects often involve the creation of a straighter and deeper channel, which may reduce flooding in neighbouring fields, lower the surrounding water table, permit ditches to be dug deeper and increase the speed of run-off. When the economic benefits of such schemes are calculated, the resulting improvements in local field drainage are often the single biggest factor.

As new field drains are installed and old ones replaced, usually at a lower depth, the existing network of ditches and natural streams is often altered to suit the needs of the new system. Some ditches may be eliminated altogether, and replaced by pipe drains. This is particularly common in the Netherlands and to a lesser extent in France, since drainage improvements in both countries are often part of land consolidation projects in which the landscape is rearranged and fields made larger and reallocated between farmers. . Other ditches may be deepened and the channel profile made steeper and narrower in order to provide a better outfall for the field drains. This process can involve the elimination of much of the bankside vegetation and an impoverishment of the habitat which it provided. Regular maintenance is required to keep the ditches functioning properly and this also can mean that bankside vegetation is severely controlled.

Drainage of all kinds is expensive and it is highly desirable to try to estimate the costs and benefits of a scheme before embarking on it. The design of a scheme should reflect this evaluation and, leaving aside environmental considerations, there are usually several options worth considering. A modest, inexpensive scheme may prove preferable to what appears the best solution in engineering terms. Perhaps partly for this reason and because they absorb significant amounts of public money, larger drainage schemes in the four countries covered here are usually subject to some form of cost-benefit assessment. The evaluation procedures are often unsatisfactory and frequently display a bias towards agricultural improvement, but it is still significant that the technique is more often applied to drainage schemes than to most other forms of public investment.

Estimating the benefits of drainage schemes is not particularly easy, as there are a large number of uncertainties. Even the effects of field drainage can be rather unpredictable. In the UK, for example, there is little experimental data about the response to drainage and what there is "serves only to illustrate that there is no 'norm' and that the benefits may range from nil to very substantial, depending upon the specific circumstances" (12). The weather is one important variable, with many schemes only showing large benefits in wetter years. The number of uncertainties multiplies with larger projects. For example it may be difficult to predict how many farmers in the locality affected by a river improvement project will take advantage of the opportunity for field drainage, or how many years it will take for them to do it.

Larger publicly funded projects are subject to methodological problems of their own. What degree of immunity from flooding is worth aiming for? Is it satisfactory to measure the benefits of drainage improvements by changes in land values? Should the additional output of wheat that may be expected from a drained field be valued at its market price, which is what the farmer gets? If this is unsatisfactory, which it is, how do we determine an appropriate price to reflect the fact that wheat prices are artificially high because of the operation of the Common Agricultural Policy? As surpluses continue to mount, how does one judge the true value to society of a marginal increase in wheat production?

Despite these difficulties, methods of evaluating drainage schemes are improving and there is every reason to apply them with increasing vigour. A proportion of projects has always been ill-designed or executed and a number have failed completely. However, as the more promising and accessible sites are drained and the previously neglected ones are tackled, these risks increase. Costs may be driven higher, while the benefits often become more speculative. Furthermore, as agricultural prices enter a period of new uncertainty and quotas are applied more widely, new drainage investments are correspondingly less likely to produce the kind of returns expected in the past and will require careful scrutiny. Thorough evaluation will also be encouraged by public expenditure cuts which have caused several governments to review their agricultural grant systems and reduce the support offered to drainage work.

An economic assessment is, of course, only one of the evaluation procedures which should precede the start of a new project. A thorough examination of the likely environmental effects, although rarely attempted, is also of crucial importance.

Drainage and the Environment

No two drainage schemes are exactly alike and nor are the places in which they have been constructed. For this reason alone it is difficult to provide a satisfactory general picture of the effects of drainage. Furthermore, there is a shortage of good case studies to tell us precisely what has happened at individual sites. The environmental impact assessment is a relatively new idea and it has yet to be applied on a significant scale to drainage projects in north-west Europe. In very few cases has there been a full study of an area prior to drainage, followed by a close monitoring of the effects of the scheme during construction and in the following years. Where records exist, it is possible to reconstruct the past with some success, but our knowledge of historic wetlands prior to their drainage is inevitably partial.

This failure to study the effects of drainage in detail leaves us with general impressions and rules of thumb, but it makes it more difficult to predict the outcome of future schemes or to understand the precise ecological functions of certain wetlands. Traditionally many of the environmental effects of drainage have been disregarded and the lack of scientific studies has impeded the abandonment of this habit.

Some references to the ways in which drainage affects the environment have been made earlier in this chapter, but some slightly more detailed comments may also be useful. Unfortunately, this description must be brief and highly generalised — it must be stressed that there is no substitute for evaluating schemes individually.

One of the most thorough reviews of the subject is that by A.R. Hill (13). He distinguishes a number of general effects:

(a) The removal of surface water or lowering of the water table can lead to a reduced area of certain types of permanent wetlands, such as marshes, swamps and bogs.

(b) The draining of permanent wetlands affects the plant and animal communities dependent on these habitats and can also cause changes in the water chemistry, sediment load and discharge of rivers.

(c) Channelising natural streams and digging artificial drainage ditches can directly affect the fauna and flora of the adjacent area.

(d) Ditching work and field under-drainage affect water courses by altering channel form, discharge, water chemistry and temperature, changes which in turn affect aquatic organisms.

Over the centuries, drainage has resulted in a very substantial reduction in the area of European wetlands. Indeed this has been the purpose of innumerable schemes. Many of those which remain are remnants of what were once much larger areas. Only small fragments of natural fen still survive in the Netherlands, for example. In Scotland and Northern England, a recent survey of 120 raised bogs showed that their total area had declined by 87 per cent between 1850 and 1978. Only 34 raised bogs remained in 1978 and half of these had been reduced in size to less than 10 hectares (14).

Many former wetlands have been destroyed in the process of reclaiming land for agriculture and this remains one of the principal threats to some types of habitat such as the extensive areas of coastal marsh in France. Both fresh and saltwater marshes often have considerable agricultural potential. Very large areas have been reclaimed from the sea in the Netherlands and reclamation continues on a smaller scale on the east coast of England.

In Ireland a combination of peat exploitation, agricultural improvement and afforestation have caused the rapid removal from the landscape of large areas of raised and blanket bogs. This once plentiful resource has been reduced to the point where intact raised bogs are now extremely rare. Drainage is also responsible for the decline of a once common type of wetland now close to extinction in Ireland and extremely rare elsewhere. This is the turlough, an unusual kind of temporary lake found in carboniferous limestone areas in the west. Turloughs are drained and usually filled by subterranean passages, largely drying out in the summer. With their varying water level they provide a valuable habitat for many species of waterfowl.

It is not only the larger areas of fen, marsh and bog which can be wholly eliminated by drainage. Individual lakes and ponds can be drained, either directly or as a result of a general lowering of the water table. Farm ponds are no longer seen as an asset on many modern holdings and their removal is considered an improvement. Similarly, farm ditches are often filled in or radically altered, and water meadows eliminated in the course of agricultural drainage improvements leading to a larger area of intensively farmed landscape. Wet pasture, which may be

seasonally flooded and is not worth improving or regularly ferti-
lising, is becoming rarer and is one of the wetland types most
threatened by drainage in the four countries looked at in this
book.

River improvement schemes may involve a variety of different
works, such as dredging, channel straightening, the construction
of flood banks, etc. The character of the river and its ecological value is often altered in the process, for example by the
removal of pools, shallows and bankside vegetation, the disturbance of spawning grounds, and increases in sediment flows. However, the greatest impact may be felt in the surrounding land,
where water tables will usually fall as a consequence of changed
river levels. This may eliminate some habitats, and reduce the
area or wetness of others, with important consequences for the
plants and animals adapted to the previous water table. With a
reduced water level in farm ditches, field drainage can be
installed for the first time or improved. This in turn may
result in the elimination of regular flooding or wet patches and
may permit the ploughing and reseeding of previously unimproved
pasture, often a valuable habitat for birds.

Even where there is no loss of wet meadows, the general
effect of new field drainage usually is to allow a further intensification of agriculture. This may involve the conversion of
pasture to arable production, the increased use of fertilisers,
heavier applications of pesticides, herbicides and other agrochemicals, higher stocking densities for cattle, etc. Drainage
may also permit heavier machinery to be used on the land and
there is often a tendency to increase field size and remove old
boundaries such as hedges at the same time so as to make more
efficient use of new equipment. This is particlarly so when
drainage is part of a package of other improvements, as it often
is in land consolidation schemes in France and the Netherlands.

The whole process of agricultural intensification has profound effects on the rural environment, one of which is the
growth of agricultural pollution. Increased applications of
nitrate fertiliser, for example, can result in the leaching of
substantial quantities of nitrates into the groundwater and subsequently into drinking water supplies. Many important wetlands
are threatened by eutrophication which, as we have already seen,
is often caused by fertiliser run-off from adjacent farmland.

The role of drainage in stimulating agricultural intensification should not be exaggerated. Conditions in Europe vary
enormously and there are many areas where little or no reduction
in the water table is required in order to permit greater
mechanisation, the heavier use of agrochemicals and so forth.
Furthermore, intensification has already taken its course on most
of the better land in the Community, with or without drainage.
However, there do remain areas, such as the Halvergate Marshes in
England, where lack of drainage is the main obstacle to intensification and lower water tables could result in a transformation
of the farmed landscape and its peripheral habitats. Drainage in

fact may be the key to the future character of the area.

The extent to which a drainage scheme lowers water tables is one of the main determinants of its environmental impact. This varies enormously and depends on the nature of the scheme, local hydrogeological conditions, soil properties and other factors. In a blanket peat bog, for example, it is possible to dig a ditch a metre deep without much effect on water levels only eight metres away. In other situations, water tables may fall 50 metres away (15). When water tables do fall, which is often the intention, this may not only affect wetland habitats, but may also cause lower summer flow levels in streams, reduced levels of groundwater recharge and other hydrological changes.

The precise hydrological and ecological functions of wetlands are very imperfectly understood and vary to such an extent that broad levels of generalisation are rather unsatisfactory. In certain situations, wetlands may have a significant role in regulating flood patterns, in the control of erosion, in the recycling of nutrients and in the recharging and purification of groundwater, possibly helping to break down water pollutants or acting as a chemical sink, for example. These and other functions are likely to be affected by drainage. Where drainage causes the removal of wetlands from a catchment and a faster rate of water discharge, heavy rain may lead to a more rapid rise in river levels and a danger of flooding downstream. In these circumstances, the reduced water retention capacity in the drained area leads to higher flood peaks downstream, although floods are likely to be less frequent. Effects of this kind are often difficult to measure, but there is some evidence of their importance, for example in the UK (see Chapter 5).

More readily observed and recorded is the impact of drainage on the fauna and flora of wetland habitats. Wetland species are likely to be affected by the removal of permanent or temporary areas of open water, the reduction of water tables, the disturbance of river beds, the filling in of ponds and ditches, and the direct destruction of vegetation, all of which may occur in the course of drainage works. Subsequent alterations in the management of neighbouring agricultural land, changes in the flow, chemistry and temperature of river water will also affect wildlife, as will routine maintenance work in the years that follow. Regular dredging to maintain river depth and the use of aquatic herbicides to control vegetation can be particularly damaging to species which survive the original works.

Many permanent wetlands, such as fens, support a rich and varied flora and drainage is usually associated with a loss of species diversity and often a reduction in productivity. Aquatic plants and those dependent on very moist soil for at least part of the year are particularly sensitive to changes in the water regime. Most of the plants on the Council of Europe's list of rare and threatened species are found in wetland habitats and several are aquatics. "Analysis of individual country lists would support the view that wetlands and their characteristic species are under threat throughout much of Europe and especially in the more industrialised countries" (16).

Insects, fish, amphibians, otters and wildfowl are among the animals affected by drainage works. Otters, for example, are usually found in quiet and unpolluted stretches of river, with ample vegetation and plenty of mature trees along the banks. The roots are often a source of suitable sites for holts, while the ground cover provides a place to lie up during the day. When rivers are denuded of such features during improvement schemes, otters tend to be confined to small patches where the vegetation remains.

Fish too benefit from bankside vegetation and the insect life which it supports. They can be affected by changes in water chemistry and temperature and the heavy sediment loads which can result from dredging, ditch cleaning and the re-profiling of banks. Fast flowing streams in the uplands are often valuable game fisheries, containing salmon and trout, but works further downstream may affect coarse fish and possibly coastal fish stocks as well. Where channels are dredged and straightened and shallow patches, pools and spawning areas are destroyed, fisheries are likely to be damaged and several studies have shown that fish populations tend to be higher in streams which have not been channelised (17).

Fish vary in their requirements but where drainage schemes are well designed and executed with care, it may be possible to reduce the impact on fish populations considerably. For example, it is possible to protect spawning areas, carry out works to short reaches only, moving fish stocks in between if necessary, construct low weirs across the river bed at irregular intervals, and to avoid working during the spawning season (18).

Best known and most studied of all the wetland fauna are the waterfowl, many of which are migrants, dividing their lives between different sites, as we have already seen. Among the requirements of "field" nesting species, such as redshank, snipe, shoveler and yellow wagtail is a high water table "at or within 0.3 metres of the soil subsurface, with some areas of permanent water from March to June. The elimination of summer flooding and the lowering of the water table may create conditions that are too dry to retain wintering birds and attract passage birds to breed. Conditions may also become too dry to meet feeding requirements, since duck take most of their food in water, and waders such as snipe can only probe into damp soil" (19). Such species also require unimproved grazing land for nest cover and a plentiful supply of invertebrates as food, both of which may be in short supply in the aftermath of drainage works.

Wintering wildfowl, which occur in large numbers in all four countries are more dependent on extensive areas of shallow water and flooded grassland (20). Such habitats provide a safe refuge as well as feeding grounds, but are particularly vulnerable to lowered water tables and flood relief schemes. Other aspects of drainage can affect the many other birds which use wetlands, such as kingfishers, but it is not necessary to make a full inventory of species to observe that many birds have suffered a substantial loss of habitat and some have become rare, confined mainly to nature reserves.

All of these effects of drainage can be grouped together as ecological changes but for many people the greatest cost of drainage is probably the changed appearance of the countryside. Lakes, rivers and streams often form the centrepiece of a landscape and attract people both because of their visual beauty and also for the various forms of recreation which they can provide. A straight and relatively featureless drainage channel is no substitute for a long meandering river, overhung by trees and fringed with reed and flowering plants.

Unfortunately, many of the features which make a river bank attractive can be a direct impediment to the drainage engineer who seeks an efficient discharge channel, with an even gradient, stable, neatly graded banks and no sharp bends (21). Trees and bankside vegetation are often removed during improvement works, partly because they may create blockages and trap debris and partly because it allows easier access for machinery. Meanders, riffles and pools are better eliminated. Vertical banks may be unstable and shallow ones susceptible to flooding. Spoil from dredging is often deposited next to the river, sometimes in unsightly heaps.

Many of the worst characteristics of a river improvement scheme can be eliminated by forward planning, a willingness to give conservation some priority and sensitivity to the local environment by the team who do the actual work. This may involve some compromises over the design of a scheme, such as avoiding improvements at particularly sensitive points and some additional expense may also be incurred. Old features, for example, can be retained and new ones created, machinery can be used from only one bank, bank profiles can be varied, native trees and wild flowers planted and spoil spread thinly over neighbouring fields.

Conservation has undoubtedly become a subject of growing importance for river engineers over the last decade and a new approach has been established in some authorities. Considerable effort has gone into improved landscaping for major projects in the Netherlands in recent years and guidelines for integrating conservation principles into drainage schemes have been produced in the UK (22). Examples of good schemes have become more common although there remain plenty of bad ones.

River improvement schemes are perhaps one of the forms of drainage work in which compromise with environmental consider-ations is most feasible. There will be certain rivers or stret-ches of river in which no form of improvement will be acceptable from a conservation viewpoint, but others where sensitive management can greatly reduce the impact of a scheme. However, greater difficulties occur when it is proposed to lower water

21

tables, whether by arterial works or by local farm schemes. This may threaten flood plains and permanent wetlands such as bogs, fens or flower-rich meadows. High water tables are essential for the survival of many wet habitats and drainage is often synonymous with destruction.   A small area can be selected as a nature reserve, but if water tables in the vicinity are lowered it may be difficult to retain the original level inside the reserve, even with special management.   Furthermore, drainage may be the first step towards agricultural improvement and the subsequent changes which it entails.

The Four Countries

This book is concerned with four countries in north west Europe: France, Ireland, the Netherlands and the United Kingdom. Together they contain about 230 wetlands of international importance for waterfowl (which is more than half of those listed for the European Community) and hundreds of other sites of national or local importance (23).

Amongst the many and varied threats to this resource, agricultural drainage is one of the most important and most widespread.   Each of the four countries has pursued an expansionist agricultural policy over the past 30 years and each has built up an extensive drainage programme. For more than a decade they have been bound together in the European Community and drainage activities have been subject to the presiding influence of the Common Agricultural Policy.

In the four chapters which follow, each country is considered separately but in a European context. Each chapter is divided into six sections.   The first is a general introduction to the agriculture and wetlands of the country concerned.   The second section describes the current drainage programme and how it has developed. The third and fourth sections are devoted to a rather more detailed look at the organisation and finance of drainage work, while the fifth section is a review of some of the ways in which wetlands have been or are likely to be affected by drainage.   Finally, there is a short concluding section which includes some comments on the influence of the Common Agricultural Policy.

These four chapters are intended to stand alone and can be read quite independently. They are not identical; but while there are differences in emphasis and in detail, the approach is broadly the same. In each case heavy use has been made of a specifically commissioned report prepared by a consultant from the country concerned and these contributions constitute the heart of the book.

Some of the common threads are drawn together in the final chapter, where some brief conclusions are presented.

References

1. IUCN, 1980, World Conservation Strategy, IUCN, UNEP, WWF, Geneva
2. See Carter, V., Bedinger, M.S., Novitzki, R.P. and Wilen, W.O., 1978, Water Resources and Wetlands paper presented to National Symposium on Wetlands, Florida, USA and Novitzki, R. P., 1978, "Groundwater recharge and related hydrologic values of wetlands" in National Wetlands Technical Council, 1978, Scientists' Report, Washington DC, USA
3. Newbold, C., 1974, "Wetlands and agriculture" in Conservation and Agriculture edited by Davidson and Lloyd, London
4. Scott, D.A, 1980, A Preliminary Inventory of Wetlands of International Importance for Wildfowl in West Europe and Northwest Africa, IWRB, Slimbridge, UK
5. IUCN, 1980, op. cit.
6. This description was formulated in Patricia Kelly's national report on Ireland
7. Sheail, J., and Wells, T.C.E., 1983 "The Fenlands of Huntingdonshire, England: A case study in catastrophic change" in Gore, A.J.P., (Ed) MIRES: Swamp, Bog, Fen and Moor, B. Regional Studies, Amsterdam
8. Green F.H.W., 1979. Field drainage in Europe: a quantitive survey. Institute of Hydrology, Wallingford, U.K.
9. Ibid.
10. Ministry of Agriculture, Fisheries and Food 1977. Drainage in the Economy of the Farm; ADAS Technical Management Note No.23. London
11. Ministry of Agriculture, Fisheries and Food 1977 (a) Drainage of Grassland; ADAS Field Drainage Leaflet No. 18 London.
12. Ministry of Agriculture, Fisheries and Food 1977 op. cit.
13. Hill, A.R. 1976 "The Environmental Impact of Agricultural Land Drainage" Journal of Environmental Management 4. 251-274
14. Goode, D. "The threat to wildlife habitats", New Scientist 22.1.81
15. Hill 1976 op. cit.
16. Lucas, G.L., and Walters, S.M. 1977. List of Rare, Threatened and Endemic Plants for the Countries of Europe. Nature and Environment Series 14. Council of Europe. Strasbourg
17. Hill. 1976 op. cit.
18. Water Space Amenity Council 1980, Conservation and Land Drainage Guidelines London.
19. Royal Society for the Protection of Birds, 1983. Land Drainage in England and Wales: an Interim Report. Sandy. England
20. Ibid.
21. Newbold, C. Pursglove, J. and Holmes, N. 1983. Nature Conservation and River Engineering. Nature Conservancy Council, London.
22. Water Space Amenity Council, 1982. op.cit.
23. Scott, 1980, op. cit.

CHAPTER 2:   FRANCE

Introduction

France is one of the largest countries in Europe and perhaps the most varied. It contains about a third of all the agricultural land in the European Community and has regions in which almost every form of western European farming can be found. Regional differences are founded not only on climate and topography but also on history and wealth and there remains a remarkable diversity in social and economic conditions today. The range and variety of geography, vegetation and human activities clearly distinguishes France from the three other countries considered here.

In agricultural terms, conditions range from the prosperous fertile plains of the Paris basin, Champagne and the north to the drier, warmer areas of Provence and Languedoc-Roussillon in the south where wine, fruit and vegetable production predominates. The wetter regions in the western parts of the country tend to be devoted to dairying and other forms of livestock farming. Fairly small family farms predominate in this part of the country, but there has been a marked growth in intensive livestock units in recent years. Arable farming is more common in the north and in the east where incomes have been traditionally higher and farms larger. By contrast, there are extensive areas, notably in the Auvergne and southern Alps, where it is extremely difficult to make a living from farming and abandonment of land and sometimes whole communities is not uncommon.

Agriculture, it need scarcely be said, occupies a salient position in French society and the French economy. 1.8 million people continue to work on the land and they exert an influence even greater than their numbers suggest. Approximately 7 per cent of the French GNP is derived from agriculture and about 21 per cent of the country's exports. With a relatively generous allowance of land per capita, relatively low dependence on imports of food, and a strong tradition of small family holdings, the pressure to modernise and intensify agriculture came later in France than in the Netherlands and the UK. Nonetheless, there has been a revolution in farming in the last 30 years and the full panapoly of modern techniques, already established on the intensive arable units in the north, has now made a visible impact on almost all kinds of farming. A dramatic increase in drainage has recently become an important part of this rural transformation.

Separated by mountains from its neighbours to the south and to the east, France is divided into six major river basins. The flood plains of these and other rivers form an important group of wetlands, including for example the valleys of the Loire and Maine. A second major category of inland wetlands is a group of naturally poorly drained areas containing woods and agricultural land as well as extensive lakes and marsh. There are small patches of such **zones humides** scattered all over the country, but there are also major expanses such as Les Dombes near Lyon and La Sologne near Orléans. A third category comprises the very extensive wetlands of the Atlantic coast, comprising a complex network of estuaries, mud flats, brackish water, dunes, grazing marsh and bog, a significant portion of it in agricultural use. On the Mediterranean coast is a further network of wetlands containing large areas of salt marsh, brackish ponds and lagoons, open water and fresh water marshes. Of these the largest and most famous is the Camargue. Finally, there is a group of hill and mountain bogs and peatlands most heavily concentrated along the eastern frontier and in the Auvergne.

One of the striking features of French wetlands is their great size; there are many extensive individual areas containing pockets of great ecological interest. La Sologne, for example, is listed by the IWRB as being 300,000 hectares, containing 30,000 hectares of lakes. The IWRB's authoritative Inventory of Wetlands of International Importance for Waterfowl contains sites in France together covering rather more than 1,300,000 hectares, a little less than the entire agricultural area of Belgium (1).

Agricultural Drainage

There are three French terms which cover the spectrum of different drainage activities. The first, **le drainage agricole**, refers to all operations designed to remove excess water from a field and especially to underground drains. It is broadly equivalent to the English term "field drainage". The second, **l'assainissement agricole**, is a broader concept which refers to the process of transferring water from drained fields to the main river or other outlet through a network of ditches, channels, streams, etc. Some works on large rivers may also be included in this category which broadly corresponds to the English term "main drainage". Finally, river works, whether capital schemes or maintenance, are referred to as **l'aménagement de rivière**, which thus covers a large slice of what is meant by "arterial drainage" in English. Both **le drainage** and **l'assainissement agricole** can be used in a general sense to describe the drainage of a large area, and on some occasions the words are used almost interchangeably.

In the past agricultural drainage in France has proceeded more slowly than in other parts of north west Europe. In the mid-nineteenth century, a period of peak activity on both sides of the Channel, the area drained in France is unlikely to have exceeded half a million hectares, compared with perhaps 5 million in Britain (2). Progress then reverted to a rather slower pace until the early 1960s when mid-nineteenth century levels were regained for the first time. Since then the acceleration of effort has been spectacular, particularly during the last decade.

Figures for early years are not reliable, partly because field drainage was not subsidised by the state and was wholly the responsibility of landowners. The available estimates suggest that perhaps 100-140,000 hectares of field drainage took place this century prior to 1972, although this excludes the roughly equal volume of private drainage works undertaken quite independently of the Ministry of Agriculture. Ministry aided schemes amounted to about 31,000 hectares in the decade 1956-65 and the pace then doubled, 36,100 hectares were covered between 1966 and 1969. Figures for the years since are shown in the Table below.

Table 2.1:   ANNUAL AREA OF DRAINAGE IN FRANCE 1970-82

Year	hectares	%
1970	8,780	(collective schemes only)
1971	8,689	(" " ")
1972	20,000	(collective and individual works)
1973	28,661	+ 43%
1974	32,815	+ 14%
1975	44,297	+ 35%
1976	46,834	+ 6%
1977	50,524	+ 8%
1978	63,135	+ 25%
1979	74,400	+ 18%
1980	105,000	+ 42%
1981	115,000	+ 10%
1982	130,000	(estimate)

Source: Le Service de l'Hydraulique, quoted in Mermet and Mustin (3)

As the Table shows, the annual rate of drainage has grown about 6.5 times since 1972. This pattern is rather less pronounced for river improvement works and surface drainage. The tradition of river management has been stronger than that of under-drainage in France and in some parts of the country, especially the coastal plains of the south and south west, minor arterial works were quite extensive by the mid 1960s when the boom in under-drainage began. Regional differences were quite pronounced; by 1966 the regulation of **non-domainaux** rivers (ie local rivers not owned by the state, which controls all major navigable water courses) extended to more than 60 kilometres in about a third of French **départements**, between one and 60 kilometres in another third and less than one kilometre in the remainder (4). There has been an upward trend in the rate of river improvement works in the last four years, with about 2,000 kilometres being covered annually.

The overall effect of these efforts is that the total drained area in France is in the region of one to two million hectares. The influential Sabin report (5) estimated that about 1.9 million hectares had been drained by the late 1970s but this is regarded as rather optimistic by many observers and the area of land with good artificial drainage may still be less than this. However, there is little doubt that France has drained a much smaller area than most of her neighbours and consciousness of this fact and a conviction that France has fallen far behind in this particular aspect of farm modernisation is a major spur to the current programme. Table 2.2, or variants of it, appears in many French reports on drainage and is often presented as a key justification for accelerating contemporary efforts.

Table 2.2: PERCENTAGE OF AGRICULTURAL LAND DRAINED BY COUNTRY

Northern France	10.4%
France (total)	10%
UK	60.9%
Germany	37.1%
Italy	24.2%
Belgium	22.5%
Netherlands	65.2%

Source: Manuellan (6)

These figures may not be wholly accurate and they do not allow straight-forward comparisons. There are major differences between the countries concerned, including rainfall, altitude, topography, soil types and the proportions of agricultural land in arable use. These explain some of the discrepancy; soils, for example, vary extensively. However, it has probably been social and economic factors which have held back drainage more than technical considerations. Drainage is only effective if organised on an appropriate scale, so that water levels in neighbouring fields are compatible and there are adequate channels for the removal of surplus water to a river or suitable outlet. The fragmentation and small scale of many French farms has probably been the chief restraint on drainage in the past, one overcome more successfully elsewhere, particularly in countries such as the UK and Netherlands where extensive restructuring has already taken place. The regional pattern of drainage rather supports this view.

A map of the area reported as drained by the time of the 1970/71 Census of Agriculture shows that earlier efforts had been concentrated on the polder lands near the Belgian border, on the arable farming area around Paris where farms have traditionally been larger and less fragmented than elsewhere and also in parts of the south and in Normandy. During the decade that followed the main foci of activity were the **départements** with the largest farms and the better arable land where returns from drainage could be expected to be relatively high.

The surge of new drainage work since the 1960s would not have been possible without a policy of active government support. Although policy is not simply defined in any one official document, the thinking behind it is clearly set out in an advisory report from the powerful **Conseil Economique et Social** dated May 1979 (7). Often referred to as the Sabin report, this document deals with all aspects of agriculture's water needs and is widely quoted. It identifies drainage and irrigation as crucial areas for the development of French farming and suggests some targets. With an estimated 1.9 million hectares already drained, the report suggests that there is an urgent need to drain a further area of about 3 million hectares and in the long term there is scope for draining up to a maximum of about 10 million hectares. To cover the former area by the year 2,000, an annual rate of 165,000 hectares is put forward, almost three times the area being covered at the time the report was written. It is further proposed to broadly double river improvement and maintenance work to 3,700 kilometres per year and to increase annual state support for drainage from 300 million FF to 1,000 million FF. The irrigation proposals are also ambitious and include a suggestion that dams should be constructed at six times the then current rate in order to create storage for 150 million cubic metres of water a year.

For both river works and field drainage, there has been some progress towards the Sabin report's targets. The philosophy behind it stresses not only the agronomic benefits of drainage, such as a longer growing season, but a number of broader considerations. Conspicuous amongst these is the argument that

France has fallen behind her competitors, although when making this point the Sabin report recognised the importance of different soil conditions. Other arguments relate to the need to maintain a regular level of output, to help combat world hunger and to improve the conditions of those working on the land. Both irrigation and drainage are regarded as an important way of helping the Mediterranean areas of France to compete with imports from Greece and, in due course, Portugal and Spain. Two further arguments are perhaps of particular significance. First, the report suggests that better drainage is an indispensable precondition to the adoption of modern agricultural practice in a number of areas. Second, it argues that drainage raises farm incomes and therefore benefits employment not only directly, but also by allowing small farms to compete more effectively with larger units and thus to remain viable without having to expand so much themselves. In other words, it is an important aid to intensification.

The probability is that drainage operations will continue to expand in France, although the exact rate of progress will depend on the economics of individual schemes and the availability of public subsidies. New drainage is likely to form a large proportion of this work, affecting most parts of the country. Official bodies are giving drainage a greater priority, especially now that slightly less effort is being directed to promoting **remembrements** (the restructuring of small farms to create more compact and, often, fewer units). A substantial drainage industry has been built up with contractors using modern machinery capable of high work rates. PVC pipes are used almost universally for field drainage and the technical revolution has opened up much greater horizons than could have been contemplated 20 years ago when much slower labour-intensive methods were still widespread. If these factors are added to the general pressure for intensification and the existence of large areas of undrained land, the momentum behind the programme is quite apparent.

The Organisation of Agricultural Drainage

To do full justice to the intricacies of the French system of organising and administering water resources would require a short book of its own and only the barest of outlines can be considered here.

Nine or ten different ministries have some involvement in water affairs, with the Ministry of the Environment having an overall role as co-ordinating agency and principal source of technical support. Tight liaison is maintained between the different ministries and there are three top level national co-ordinating bodies, of which the most senior is the **Comité interministériel de la qualité de la vie.** By this means it is possible to maintain a coherent policy, but with four different levels of administration and a large number of different functions to cover there is a complex web of responsibilities and relationships, linked together at appropriate stages by co-ordinating bodies and consultative committees.

The Ministry of Agriculture is responsible for all of agriculture's water requirements, including drainage, and also takes charge of the great majority of rural rivers. Among the ministries with which it interacts is the Ministry of Transport which is also involved in rivers, being responsible for the **domainaux** and **navigables** rivers referred to earlier, as well as predominantly urban water courses. Several different ministries have responsibilities for pollution, including the Ministry of Health and the Mines Service of the Department of Industry. Water supplies to towns are within the remit of the Ministry of the Interior, which is also concerned with flooding on non-navigable rivers.

France is divided into six major river basins, each with its own **Agence Financière de Bassin.** These are mainly concerned with the financial aspect of water supply, waste waters and pollution control, including irrigation, but have little involvement with drainage. One tier down are the 22 **régions** and at this level there are a number of bodies or officials concerned with drainage. At the lowest level are the 96 **départements** which directly administer both drainage and river works.

Within the Ministry of Agriculture is a Directorate of Planning within which is the **Service de l'Hydraulique Agricole** which is responsible for agriculture's water needs, including drainage. This body is in overall charge of drainage activities, the apex of a pyramid of which the 96 **Directions départementales de l'agriculture** (DDAs) form the base. The DDA providesthe Ministry's local service in each **département** and are the principal actors in a decision-making process which reaches up through intermediate levels to the Ministry in Paris. Although there are a number of other bodies with an interest indrainage, the main axis of policy and finance is located within the Ministry.

Relativeto the UK or Ireland, drainage powers are notably decentralised. It is the departmental administration which assesses local needs, draws up plans, liaises with local organisations, develops and often designs schemes, has discretion over financial allocations, commissions environmental studies and has responsibility for the satisfactory completion and subsequent management of schemes. In executing these tasks, the DDA liaises with a number of local bodies with an official or semi-official status, known collectively as **collectivités publiques.** Day to day management of local water courses and drainage channels is in the hands of these local organisations which range from the smallest farmers' associations, containing perhaps as few as 10 farms, up to more substantial **syndicats inter-communaux** which may regulate the whole of a river basin containing several thousand farms. The **syndicats,** which usually group together several **communes** (the lowest level of local authority in France) are admini-

. stered by a committee which is elected. Their powers and responsibilities are carefully defined by legal codes, under the relevant articles of the **Code Rural** and the **Codes des Communes.**

The emphasis of field drainage policy is on collective
rather than individual efforts and the administration is not
unnaturally concerned to organise drainage in the most rational
and efficient way. Collective work is supervised and substantially funded by the state and is strongly encouraged, whereas
purely individual schemes, which may or may not be well designed
or compatible with DDA plans for the local river basin, are
independent of the state and qualify for relatively little aid.
In order to organise field drainage on the appropriate scale, the
DDA encourages farmers to form local associations, **associations
syndicales,** purely for the purpose of establishing and maintaining a drainage scheme. Such associations can then acquire
legal status, most often as **associations syndicales autorisées,**
which allows them to negotiate a scheme with the DDA, receive
finance for it, execute and subsequently maintain it. Once
legally established and equipped with an elected **Conseil
syndical,** these associations acquire powers and access to funds
but also become subject to the control of the DDA and the financial supervision of the Ministry of Finance. These associations
are the basic tools of drainage policy and the main recipients of
public funds. They have the additional advantage from the DDA's
point of view of providing greater leverage over local farm
structure, sometimes providing opportunities to promote **remembrements.**

To illustrate the way in which the system works we can trace
the evolution of a scheme, ignoring all but the most important
steps. A farmer or group of farmers may begin by identifying an
area of their land which they think would benefit from drainage.
They approach the DDA for help directly, through the **Syndicat
inter-communal,** or perhaps through a local farmers' organisation,
often the **Chambre d'Agriculture.** Engineers in the DDA will then
examine their needs, discuss the technical and economic aspects
with them, possibly design a scheme for them and, if they are not
already part of a **collectivité publique,** advise them of the legal
structure which they should form. If advised that the prospects
for public finance are reasonable, the group will then adopt an
appropriate structure and prepare a dossier on the proposed
scheme. This is submitted to the DDA and shows the design,
technical details, expected cost and timescale, anticipated rate
of return, finance arrangements, implementation and subsequent
management plans.

Scrutiny of the dossier then begins, involving the DDA and
other competent authorities, for example the **Direction départe-
mentale de l'équipement** (DDE), an important body at the level of
the **département,** combining responsibility for transport and urban
planning, including the management of some rivers. Finance for
drainage schemes is available from the **département,** the region
and from the Ministry of Agriculture. The DDA acts as local
agent for all these bodies and makes recommendations about the

31

appropriate level of funding to all three sources of finance. If the scheme is approved and funds made available, then these are paid out by the DDA to the **Association, Syndicat** or individuals undertaking the scheme.

The system is basically operated to stimulate collective schemes, some of them on a large scale. Big schemes, suchas those on the extensive individual marshlands of the Atlantic coast, require more sophisticated procedures and may be planned over a number of years. As the area drained has grown over the years, the Ministry's Hydraulic Service has felt the need to increase its co-ordinating role and to intensify its control. Since 1978 there have been a number of circulars from the Ministries of Agriculture and the Environment which have instituted more specific guidelines and procedures providing a tighter framework for the DDAs. Amongst the most important of these was a 1978 circular from the Ministry of Agriculture, **sur les schémas régionaux de développement de l'hydraulique agricole** setting up regional water schemes, requiring DDAs to institute a positive planning procedure.

Under this circular, the DDAs were asked to consolidate local drainage and irrigation requirements for three different time horizons. First, they had to produce a short-term programme, based on the local schemes which are ready or almost readyfor funding, and an assessment of the **département's** needs. In a second, medium-term programme, schemes are shown which are at a much earlier stage but where needs have been identified, either by farmers or the DDA's engineering staff. The third, long-term programme shows the scope for possible further projects, potential problems and wet areas where no initiatives have yet been taken.

Since drainage activity has traditionally been on rather a small scale in France, previously the DDAs have had relatively little knowledge of the precise drainage needs of different areas or the likely technical difficulties. They are now building up such knowledge rapidly and there is an expanding research effort, including detailed mapping projects and attempts to build up a zoning system for undrained land. A few **départements** have employed zoning in some of their larger river basins for about five years and its wider use was advocated in a Ministry of Agriculture directive of May 1981. The objectives are to document the areas where drainage is required, to identify suitable parcels into which land can be divided for this purpose and the obstacles which may be encountered in the process, to estimate the potential benefits of drainage to agriculture, and to indicate the sort of schemes which would be appropriate showing, for example, the need for new channel works. This exercise usually involves close co-operation with the local farming community and, through new contacts and an exchange of information between farmers and officials, bolsters confidence in the drainage programme as well as aiding planning.

Zoning could potentially be used for assembling detailed

information on wetlands, classifying areas ecologically as well as agriculturally. This, however, is not being done and the opportunity to build up an inventory of sites is being lost. Indeed, it is notable that all drainage planning is firmly in the hands of agricultural authorities and the Ministry of the Environment does not have its own offices at the level of the **département** where so much of the power resides. There are offices at the regional level and these are likely to become involved in the larger schemes involving major works and special expenditure, but they are remote from the majority of more routine drainage.

The most remarkable figure in the administration of agricultural drainage is the DDA's chief engineer, who is a member of the higher civil service rather than purely a technician. He or she is always a member of the **Génie Rural des Eaux et des Forêts,** one of the elite Corps of Engineers trained in very small numbers in Paris for a lifetime career in the higher echelons of public administration. The engineer supervises all the activities of the DDA's hydraulic service and must sign all drainage schemes submitted for funding. In some cases he combines the roles of initiator, advisor, administrator and financial arbitrator. Many schemes are designed in the engineer's office at the DDA and he is responsible for ensuring an adequate quality of work at all stages. He assesses the schemes and recommends appropriate levels of public subsidy and may commission environmental impact assessments in some cases. He is the pivot of the system with a unique influence on the eventual environmental impacts of any scheme.

Finance for Drainage

Both field and arterial drainage benefits from substantial public funding in France, derived from several different levels of the administration. Schemes submitted to the DDA for funding will vary from purely field drainage proposals to relatively large river improvement schemes but the basic procedure is the same for all but the largest. For these, the extensive programme in the Marais de l'Ouest for example, a vote of special funding is usually required and there may be several **départements** involved, as well as more active participation at the regional level. Ordinarily, however, it is the DDA's chief engineer who is responsible for assessing schemes and recommending the level of subsidy.

Although the chief engineer has considerable discretion, maximum and minimum levels of subsidy were set by the Ministry of Agriculture in 1972 and more specific recommendations were made in a circular of 1979. For river works, which include both capital projects and some maintenance schemes, a range of 20–80 per cent was permitted by the decree of 1972 and the recommended subsidy was set at 50 per cent. For river schemes containing an urban as well as an agricultural element, the DDE would be expected to contribute also and a maximum grant of 30 per cent from the agricultural budget is recommended.

For **assainissements,** the provision of ditches and other channels for moving water from drained fields to river outlets, the limits are between 30 and 80 per cent and the currently recommended level is 60 per cent, although more may be available for very large schemes. The policy is to actively promote and aid collective works of this kind, since they are indispensable for field drainage in many areas and, once completed, they make it financially attractive for farmers to drain their own fields with little or no support from the state. Aid for field drainage alone is thus much more limited. In principle, purely private field drainage may not qualify for a grant at all, unless experimental in nature, and the grant for draining fields within group schemes (usually organised through **associations** or **syndicats**) is fixed between 10 and 30 per cent, with a recommended level of 10 per cent since 1979. The aim is to phase out subsidies for field drainage altogether, but it is interesting to note that in 1981 it was still attracting an average grant of 27 per cent, as against about 58 per cent for group works (8). In early 1984 farmers were still able to get grants for field drainage. In the Département of Orne in Basse Normandie, for example, individual schemes attracted a 10 per cent grant and group schemes 20 per cent. Low interest loans were also available in both cases (9).

In addition to these principal sources of funding, grants are available for local farmers' co-operatives for the purchase of drainage equipment. The decree of 1972 allows grants of 20-50 per cent for this purpose and the maximum recommended level is currently 50 per cent.

Some indication of the pattern of subsidies for drainage in recent years can be gained from Table 2.3, although many of the figures are provisional and should be used with caution. The categories used do not precisely coincide with the distinction between field drainage and group works, but they are sufficiently close to show the more favourable treatment given to the latter.

In selecting an appropriate level of grant, the engineer scrutinises the dossier which accompanies each application and assesses the likely economic return and the overall value of the project. Benefits are assessed on expected returns from drained fields rather than on increased land values and subsidies are set with an eye to helping farmers towards a reasonable level of income. To some degree, subsidies are sensitive to pay-back periods, and where schemes are likely to produce a high rate of return for the farmers concerned, subsidies should be correspondingly low.

For both river works and agricultural drainage, the Ministry of Agriculture is the largest source of public funds, providing about half the total for each in 1981. It can be seen from Table 2.4 that Ministry expenditure has risen significantly in recent years and this trend seems set to continue. Once a **département**

34

Table 2.3: DRAINAGE EXPENDITURE – FRANCE 1979–81 (million French Francs)

Year	Ditching and Sur-face Channels (1)	Infrastructure for Drainage (2)	Field Drainage (3)	Total
A.	**Ministry of Agriculture Subsidies**			
1979	16.2	11.2	40.1	67.2
1980	11.0	15.8	32.3	59.1
1981	17.6	24.8	55.2	97.6
B.	**Total Public Subsidies** (including Ministry of Agriculture Expenditure)			
1979	33.4	28.1	78.3	139.8
1980	27.0	36.4	70.4	133.8
1981	27.2	36.9	86.7	150.8
C.	**Provisional Total Cost of Works** (public and private)			
1979	64.5	67.4	249.0	370.9
1980	50.8	64.7	254.8	370.3
1981	66.1	91.7	396.6	554.4
D.	**Provisional Total Area Covered** (in '000 hectares)			
1979	*	*	*	*
1980	129.2	39.2	37.9	n/a (4)
1981	102.6	100.6	63.5	n/a (4)

Notes

(1) Assainissement superficiel par réseaux des fossés
(2) Infrastructure de drainage collectif enterré (collecteurs et émissaires)
(3) Drainage souterrain à la parcelle
(4) These figures are not mutually exclusive and should not be totalled
 *   Unknown

Source: Mermet and Mustin (3)

has established a regular level of expenditure on drainage it is difficult for the Ministry to try to cut this back and the easiest way for Paris to control overall expenditure on drainage is by regulating the larger schemes. Money from the Ministry is transmitted to the DDA via the **région** and, within his particular **région**, a **Préfet** can supervise the way in which the cake is cut between **départements**. Even with Ministry subsidies, local political factors can have a bearing on the distribution of finance between schemes.

This is even more true of funding from the departmental and regional levels, which is already almost as great as that from Paris and likely to become a larger proportion as decentralisation takes its course. There are elected representative bodies at each level, and they provide the subsidies from their annual budgets. Traditionally the **Préfets** have had a strong influence over the disposition of such budgets, but their power has been somewhat reduced by recent moves towards decentralisation which have given the chairmen of the elected bodies a much greater say in the use of local finances. With the administration undergoing rather fundamental changes it is difficult to foresee exactly how drainage will be affected, but as local politicians acquire greater powers there may be a yet stronger emphasis on drainage which provokes much less conflict than the other major form of investment in farming infrastructure - **remembrements**.

Table 2.4: SOURCES OF SUBSIDIES FOR DRAINAGE AND RIVER WORKS - 1981

(000's of FF)

	Field Drainage, Ditches etc(1)	River Works(2)
Ministry of Agriculture	97,654	61,613
Department	44,589	35,586
Region (des Etablissements publics Régionaux)	39,785	23,606
FEOGA	10,549	3,822
Other	504	2,481
Total subsidies	197,802	128,350
Total cost of works	554,417	251,124

Notes

(1) Assainissement (fossés, drainage collectif, drainage au champ)
(2) Aménagement de rivières

Source: Mermet and Mustin (3)

36

Table 2.4 shows the breakdown of different sources of funding for drainage in 1981. It can be seen that FEOGA, the fund of the Common Agricultural Policy, contributed about 5 per cent of the total public expenditure on drainage and about 3 per cent of expenditure on river works. These figures come from Ministry sources and unfortunately it is not clear exactly what types of Community expenditure are involved. What is clear, however, is that the FEOGA contribution is now extremely small. It is no longer possible for French drainage projects to qualify for capital grants direct from Brussels under Regulation 17/64 as it was until the late 1970s.

Under the old system, the Guidance Section of FEOGA was occasionally used as a source of direct aid for larger schemes, such as the drainage of the Marais des Echets, discussed in the next section. It was not unknown for the chief engineer in charge of such a scheme to go directly to Brussels himself in search of this form of funds. In such cases, 25 per cent might be made available by FEOGA under Regulation 17/64 and the Ministry of Agriculture would provide a counterpart contribution, with the net effect of boosting the overall level of subsidy by 10 per cent relative to schemes funded purely nationally. FEOGA grants were around 5 million FF in 1975, 10 million in 1976 and 43 million in 1977 when aid was obtained for a large scheme at Wateringues in the north.

Funds are still available from FEOGA for drainage purposes under a number of structural Directives, which apply throughout the Community. In the UK, for example, Directive 72/159 on the modernisation of farms is used to help finance some field drainage because many of the "development farms" qualifying for aid under the Directive include improved drainage as part of their modernisation plans. Higher rates of grant are available to development farms in Less Favoured Areas which, in France, cover about 35 per cent of the land area. This mechanism accounts for some of the current FEOGA contribution to French drainage, since plans for "development farms" were being approved at around 4-6,000 a year in 1978–80 and 34 per cent of these involved some investment in land improvement (10). FEOGA money may also be spent on drainage through other channels, such as the Less Favoured Areas Directive and the proposed Integrated Development Programme for Lozère, which will include measures for land and pasture improvement. Forty per cent of the agricultural part of the Lozère programme will be repaid by FEOGA at an estimated cost of 12 million ECU.

Although they are able to obtain subsidies from an impressive range of public institutions, French farmers still have to meet a substantial proportion of drainage costs themselves. In doing so they have recourse to another institution, the **Crédit Agricole.** This semi-public organisation provides farmers with 70 per cent of all their credit, and probably helps to finance most drainage schemes. The **Crédit Agricole** offers farmers loans at a lower interest rate than is available from elsewhere and for many purposes subsidised interest rates are available, with the cost being reimbursed to the bank by the government. The **Crédit Agri-cole** thus constitutes another source of public funds for drainage, although the size of their contribution is difficult to gauge. A recommendation in the Sabin report that a clearly iden-tified credit line for drainage schemes should be set up within the bank, so that the cost of loans would become more explicit, has yet to bear fruit.

Impact on Wetlands

The great leap forward in drainage over the last 20 years has undoubtedly had a major impact on wetlands in France and the extensive plans for further work pose an even more serious threat. In a recent report for the **Office National de la Chasse**, Catherine Chantrel estimated that of 25 wetlands of major impor-tance for wildfowl, a dozen were already subject to agricultural drainage affecting their habitat value and a further eight were vulnerable to such works (11). Past drainage work has affected about two million hectares, and while we can only guess what impact this has had on wetlands, it is certain that a number of important sites have either been destroyed or badly damaged (12). To take just one example, 80 per cent of the marshes of the Landes de Gascogne, an important migration staging post for crane, have been drained for agriculture. As we have seen, there are a further 3-10 million hectares which may be subject to drainage in future, and within this total there are probably around 600,000 hectares of wetland at risk (13).

Agriculture is by no means the only threat to French wet-lands. In the Camargue, for example, there are also threats from tourist development, industrial projects, the use of agro-chemicals and air pollution. The famous Lac Leman (Lake Geneva) is subject to heavy metal pollutants and the risk of eutrophica-tion. A number of sites are threatened by urban development, such as a plan to build a motorway across the middle of the Etangs du Forez on the upper Loire in the east. France already has a large hydro-electric capacity and there are plans to con-struct further dams, not only for hydropower but also for irriga-tion purposes. Such schemes are often environmentally insensi-tive. **Electricité de France** wished to build a dam 100 miles west of Nice in the Grand Canyon of the Verdon river, one of the most beautiful canyons in Europe, and were only forced to drop the proposal after a bitter confrontation with local interests, including the Regional Assembly (14). Wetlands near to towns are often regarded as being of little value or even a menace and may be used for rubbish disposal. Another use of wetlands is as poplar plantations, usually requiring drainage. A number of peat bogs in the Pyrenees have been employed for this purpose by **l'Office National des Forêts**.

Even where wetlands survive, wildlife is often under intense pressure from shooting and hunting. The French waterfowl shooting season is frequently criticised for starting earlier and continuing longer than in neighbouring countries and intensive night shooting is also a problem. The record of 13 coastal **départements** where night shooting is practised was recently compared with that of 12 other coastal **départements** where it is not. In the first group the annual bag was double that of the other, 600,000 birds as against 340,000, while the mean duck population revealed in organised counts was seven to ten times higher in the areas without night shooting (15).

Agricultural drainage and the intensification which follows it still remains perhaps the greatest single threat to several categories of French wetland. Those most susceptible are wet pasture, flood meadows, grazing marsh, certain areas of bog and wet marsh where afforestation is feasible, coastal marsh, the valleys and estuaries of major rivers where large flood control schemes and other big projects are most often located and, finally, the smaller rivers where little management has taken place in the past. There are some low-lying valleys, for example adjoining the Rhine in the east, where field drainage is difficult to achieve, but networks of ditches and surface channels have been installed, allowing farmers to convert pasture to arable land, destroying many sites of botanical and ornithological interest.

In France, as elsewhere, there has been no systematic attempt to examine the impact of drainage on wetlands and, although there is now increasing knowledge of the location and importance of different kinds of wet zone, many have been destroyed before being studied in any detail. It is only in the last few years that detailed investigations and the preparation of lists of important sites, for example for the EC Birds Directive, have made an adequate appreciation of the resource possible. Much more information is still required urgently if France is to develop a positive management plan for the remaining wetlands, as they are now under intensive pressure, both from drainage and other activities. Changes in the coastal wetlands of Brittany were recently the subject of one of the few regional studies to have been undertaken. It showed that about 40 per cent had been lost altogether over the last 20 years and 67 per cent of the remaining area had been adversely affected by drainage or other activities (16).

Many wetlands are already in use for agricultural purposes and few of these sites can be regarded as wholly "natural". The interest of many of them depends on the continuation of a traditional form of management, most often extensive grazing by cattle, geese and other livestock. Much of the grazing marsh bordering littoral wetlands on the Atlantic coast is a product of this form of management and, while the wildfowl potential is considerable, there may only be small pockets of real botanical interest within quite large areas. Gradual improvements in drainage and a general tendency towards intensification may not have an immediately perceptible effect on the value of a site, and it is often difficult to object to such developments individually. However, the cumulative effect of these changes can be as disastrous as a more sudden and dramatic transformation. The close relationship between ecological value and traditional forms of management characterises many of France's larger wetlands and here the need is not simply to control drainage but to introduce detailed local management plans in order to preserve some kind of balance between agricultural and conservation requirements.

Drainage can have a variety of different impacts on wetlands, a point illustrated by Mermet and Mustin (17). They sketch the fate of six different wetlands affected by agricultural change, each characteristic of a certain approach.

-   The Marais des Echets, part of Les Dombes, was a site of international importance both botanically and for wildfowl but it was drained with the aid of a FEOGA subsidy in the late 1960s and early 1970s, despite vociferous protest by scientists and opposition from the Ministry of the Environment. The scheme was pushed hard by an important local politician but the agricultural benefits have yet to be properly established.

-   After this setback, the **Préfet** and DDA agreed with environmental interests to protect the 2,200 hectares Marais de Lavours in the same **département**. However, this has been progressively nibbled away by local farmers, leaving only 450 hectares and a dispute as to whether this should be made a nature reserve or used more intensively for farming.

-   The problems of gradual change on large sites, alluded to above, can be seen in the 300,000 hectare Marais de l'Ouest, on the coast between the Gironde and the Loire. The ecological value of sites is uneven and there are extensive drainage schemes in progress. A management plan has been prepared and an environmental impact study commissioned by the Ministry of Agriculture. This study is useful in identifying the most interesting and fragile sites, but it takes no account of the broader ecological functions of the wetland; further work is required to show the effect of drainage on water chemistry and local hydrology. There is dispute, for example, over whether drainage will cause biological changes affecting fishing, especially for shellfish, on the adjoining coast. Although local negotiations may lead to the conservation of some important sites, there is currently a fierce legal battle over one scheme and the functions and value of the wetland as a whole may never be evaluated.

-   More successful compromises between drainage and conservation are easier to achieve on small sites, such as the Marais de Silligny in Haute-Savoie, where there were considerable engineering problems. The DDA instituted **remembrements** (restructuring) on the marsh, but only after detailed and well informed discussions and the preparation of a managment plan taking account of the environment. In the end, drainage took place, but only to a level already attained in a neglected scheme installed a century earlier.

- Wetland drainage is not always worthwhile agriculturally. Some schemes fail and the land may even be abandoned. This happened at the Marais Vernier in Normandy where the shrinkage of peaty soils after drainage created unanticipated difficulties. Farmers stopped using the land for grazing and this led to intervention by the regional **parc naturel**,which was concerned about the impact of this change of management on the flora and fauna. An experiment is being conducted on a 100 hectare site within the marshes. This is based on the introduction of new breeds from outside the area better adapted to the relatively poor herbage remaining. Small highland cattle, Shetland sheep and horses from the Camargue appeared amongst much scepticism from both locals and experts, but they survived and went on to breed successfully. There is now the prospect that they might produce a commercial return – horse meat remains popular in France.

- Experiments are also being undertaken by the DDA and one of these, in the Marais de Carentan in Normandy, is being supported by the EC, not through FEOGA, but from the funds of DG XI, the Directorate-General of the Commission concerned with the environment. DG XI is paying a substantial share of the cost of a typical drainage scheme to remove water from permanently wet and periodically flooded land, on the grounds that some special conservation measures have been built into the scheme, for example management plans for the most sensitive areas. It is hoped that this will be a useful demonstration project, although the design has been heavily criticised by some environmentalists and it is not particularly clear whether it is a good scheme. Indeed, the approach whereby essentially conventional designs are subject to slight modifications in the interests of the environment may not be the most useful one to try to replicate. If, as seems likely, DG XI commissions an evaluation of the scheme some of these questions may become clearer.

One point that emerges from these and many other examples is that drainage is firmly in the hands of agricultural interests, particularly the DDA. When appraising schemes, the DDA is concerned with the agricultural dimensions of the proposal, with an emphasis on technical and economic factors rather than on ecological ones. There are a number of protected areas in national parks, nature reserves and the more numerous but less conservation-oriented hunting reserves, but otherwise the DDA is little restrained by ecological requirements. Zoning is not used to identify important wetlands.

The results are very variable, with some DDAs ignoring the environment altogether and others devising sensitive management schemes. Much depends on the attitude of the chief engineer and the interplay of the various local forces concerned. These range from the regional **Préfet** and the Ministry of the Environment to the promoters of the scheme and the local environmental groups. Politicians at any of the various levels involved may also choose to intervene.

There are arrangements for some public participation in the planning of drainage and irrigation works and there is evidence that the DDA will usually respond when there is local pressure for conservation. However, this system is somewhat arbitrary and reactive and is particularly poorly suited to consideration of the overall ecological value of wetlands, which requires painstaking research and is unlikely to be the focus of public attention in the same way as the fate of an individual site.

Formal responsibility for wetlands is vested in the Ministry of the Environment. This is represented at the regional level only by the local office of the **Délégué Régional à l'Architecture et à l'Environnement** (DRAE) which is not a powerful body, mainly providing information and advice. At the level of the **département** the DDA is the administrative agency representing the Ministry of Environment with regard to water projects, fishing and shooting. The weaknesses of this arrangement are self-evident, especially for smaller projects, and reinforce the need for more formal conservation procedures reducing the discretion of the DDA and clearly identifying sites of importance.

At present wetland conservation depends largely on either strong pressure from local people and organisations or the relatively drastic and unusual step of creating a new reserve. Larger projects tend to attract more interest from environmental authorities, and in principle have the additional protection of the law of 1976 which made Environmental Impact Studies mandatory for projects costing more than FF 6 million. In practice, this provides little defence for wetlands, as most large schemes are phased over a period of several years and expenditure in any one year is usually below this threshold. For example, it is estimated that 95 per cent of river management works involve an expenditure of less than FF 5 million (18). Furthermore, where an impact study does take place, its recommendations are not binding.

Recent work undertaken by the Ministry of the Environment, the **Office National de la Chasse** (a semi-public body) and other organisations has provided a much clearer picture of French wetlands and the threats which they face. For example, the **Institut Européen d'Ecologie** has prepared an inventory of 900 important peat bogs in France, classifying them by conservation value, identifying 81 sites of major importance (19). The Ministry of Environment is preparing an inventory of sites of ecological importance for fauna and flora and a directory of French wetlands will be compiled, followed by work on the impact of drainage. At the same time, France is preparing to become a contracting party to the Ramsar Convention, following a special meeting in Paris in December 1982. The Camargue has been designated as France's first Ramsar site.

A year or so earlier France deposited with the EC Commission a list of 114 sites for which special protection measures were proposed under the Community's Bird Directive 79/409. This broadly corresponds with independent estimates of the number of French sites of international importance, about half of them wetlands. These developments put the Ministry of the Environment in a much stronger position to identify important sites ahead of drainage plans, to anticipate the effects of the works and to prepare and defend appropriate conservation measures.

The magnitude of the task should not be underestimated, however. Table 2.5 and the accompanying Figure 1, taken from the recent report of the **Office National de la Chasse** referred to earlier, show the major wildfowl sites in France and the large proportion threatened by drainage.

Conclusions and Impact of the Common Agricultural Policy

For social and historic reasons rather than technical ones, the proportion of agricultural land drained in France is less than in most other parts of north west Europe. This 'backwardness' is probably not as great as it is often perceived to be, but is an important element in the recent acceleration of publicly supported drainage works.

Much drainage work probably takes place on arable land and other areas already in intensive agricultural use. However, it is clear that wetlands form a significant proportion of the area drained annually and many important sites have been lost and others damaged. As in most other countries, the agricultural statistics do not distinguish wetlands from other drained areas and there is insufficient information available to permit a full analysis of the impact of drainage on wetlands.

The regulation of water affairs in France is a complex matter, but decisions on drainage and local river works are primarily in the hands of the Agricultural Ministry and, more particularly of its local offices, the DDAs. The concentration of power at this level allows for some flexibility and sensitivity to local conditions and makes positive planning possible. However, safeguards for the environment such as environmental impact studies are inadequate, the Ministry of Environment is remote from most of the decisions and the information required to devise satisfactory management schemes for wetlands is rarely collected. Under these conditions the prospective increase in the rate of drainage to a level likely to be the highest in the EC can only inflict considerable further damage on wetlands, including several of international importance. Since wetlands comprise a highly significant proportion of the area yet to be drained, stronger protection measures are required urgently.

Table 2.5: WETLANDS OF MAJOR IMPORTANCE FOR WILDFOWL

Site	Breeding	Important for Migratory Birds	Wintering Birds	Area of Site (ha)
1. Baie de Somme*	X	X	X	/
2. Baie de Seine		X	X	20,000
3. Baie de Veys*		X	X	20,000
4. Baie du Mont-St-Michel	X	X	X	
5. Baie de St-Brieuc		X	X	
6. Rade de Brest			X	18,100
7. Golfe du Morbihan		X	X	28,000
8. Estuaire de Loire*		X	X	45,000
9. Lac de Grand-Lieu	X	X	X	6,300
10. Littoral vendeen		X	X	165,000
11. Littoral charentais*		X	X	170,000
12. Bassin d'Arcachon		X	X	15,500
13. Etangs du Languedoc Roussillon		X	X	29,600
14. Camargue*	X	X	X	140,000
15. Lac Leman		X	X	23,400
16. Vallée du Rhin*	X	X	X	30,000
17. Etangs de Champagne et Région Parisienne*		X	X	13,100
18. Dombes*	X	X	X	100,000
19. Plaine d'Allier*			X	
20. Brenne	X	X	X	80,000
21. Forez*	X			50,000
22. Etangs de Lorraine*	X	X		
23. Sologne*	X	X	X	490,000
24. Vallée du Maine		X	X	
25. Etang de Biguglia		X	X	1,600

* Sites containing agricultural land

Source: Chantrel (11)

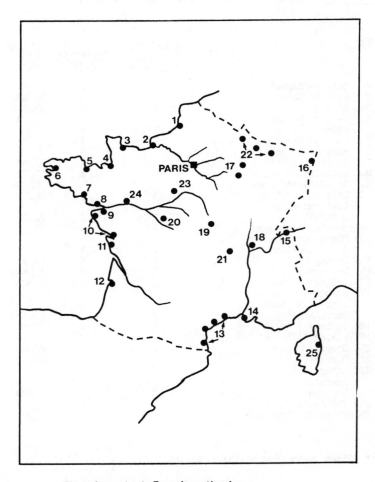

Fig.1: Important French wetlands

France was a founder member and principal architect of the CAP and, as the biggest agricultural producer in the Community, derives considerable benefit from it. Most of this benefit comes from price guarantees and export refunds, especially from cereals, milk products and sugar. Direct grants from FEOGA for drainage schemes have been on a modest scale, particularly since 1978, and do not appear to constitute a significant proportion of public support for such works in France. Money for drainage is available from FEOGA through structural measures such as Directive 72/159 on farm modernisation and 75/268 on less favoured areas, but France does not seem to draw significantly on either of these channels for drainage purposes at present. When the Integrated Development Programme for Lozère gets under way this may also be used to aid local drainage projects which will attract grants at the higher rate of 70 per cent, but the sums involved are likely to be small.

More significant, but more difficult to gauge, is the effect of the CAP price support system on French agriculture. The security provided by the CAP, the relatively high prices for most products and the generous provision of export refunds have almost certainly encouraged a rise in output. The volume of agricultural production grew at a little over 1 per cent a year between 1973 and 1980, although this was below the Community average. France has become an important agricultural exporter, producing twice as much wheat and sugar as she consumes, but without export refunds most French exports would not be competitive in the world market. The availability of an export market and the stable price regime have created a suitable climate for agricultural investment and this has been one of the reasons for intensification and a general process of modernisation, of which drainage is a part.

The balance between livestock and cereal prices is an important element of the CAP, with cereal prices receiving rather more favourable treatment in recent years. French cereal production grew at 2.3 per cent a year between 1973 and 1980, slightly faster than livestock production, and the areas devoted to cereals expanded slightly (20). This almost certainly contributed to increased prosperity and intensification in the arable areas of the north and east where drainage operations have been most concentrated. On the other hand, support for beef and other products of extensive grazing has been relatively weak.

Finally, the recent grant from DG XI for a more environmentally sensitive drainage scheme in the Marais de Carentan makes a new departure in Community influence. The scheme itself may not have been well chosen but it is a first attempt to redress the colossal imbalance in expenditure between agricultural production and the environment.

References

1. Scott, D.A, 1980, A Preliminary Inventory of Wetlands of International Importance for Wildfowl in West Europe and Northwest Africa, IWRB, Slimbridge, Glos, UK
2. Green, F.H.W, 1979, Field Drainage in Europe: a quantitive survey, Institute of Hydrology, Wallingford, UK
3. Mermet, L, and Mustin, M, 1983, Assainissement Agricole et Regression des Zones Humides en France, IEEP
4. Green, 1979, op. cit.
5. Conseil Economique et Social, 1979, L'eau et les besoins de l'agriculture. Avis adopté le 9 mai 1979
6. Manuellan, G., undated, Problèmes de la maîtresse des eaux dans les zones humides continentales et litorales. Ministère de l'Agriculture, Service de l'Hydraulique. Mimeo
7. Conseil Economique et Social, op. cit.
8. Mermet and Mustin, 1983, op. cit.
9. "Role of the Chambres", Farmers' Weekly, 9 March 1984
10. Commission of the European Economic Communities, 1983 The Agricultural Situation in the Community: 1982 Report, Brussels
11. Chantrel, C, 1982, Eléments d'étude pour un bilan économique de la transformation des zones humides par l'agriculture, Office National de la Chasse
12. Délégation à la Qualité de la Vie, 1979, Report of an internal working group on Gestions des espaces naturels
13. Lesaffre, B, 1982, Assainessement Agricole, Environnement et Economie: Approche technique et institutionelle en France, paper presented to seminar at L'Ecole Polytechnique, 2nd February 1982
14. Henry, C, 1983, Public Economics and the Conservation of Natural Environments, Laboratoire d'Econometrie, Ecole Polytechnique, Paris, 1983
15. Tamisier, A. and Saint-General, T, 'The impact of night shooting on water birds", Alauda 49, pp 81-93, quoted in IWRB Bulletin No 47, December 1981
16. Mermet, L., personal communication
17. Mermet and Mustin, 1983, op. cit.
18. Cacas, J, 1983, (CEMAGREF), L'Aménagement des Rivières: Lois et Contraintes, paper presented to a seminar at L'Ecole Polytechnique, January 1983
19. Institut Européen d'Ecologie, 1981, Inventaire des tourbières de France, Ministère de l'Environnement
20. Commission of the European Economic Communities, 1983, op. cit.

CHAPTER 3 : IRELAND

Introduction

Ireland, lying on the western edge of Europe, has an unusual saucer-shaped configuration, with most of the hills located around the coastal perimeter, leaving a broad area of lowland in the centre. The climate is temperate and moderately wet, with a mean annual rainfall of 750-1,250 mm per year, high relative humidity and low evaporation rates. This combination, together with the poor drainage characteristics of many soils, makes the discharge of excessive water a major preoccupation in Ireland and helps to explain why many of the rivers are slow and meandering in their natural state, providing little relief from waterlogging and flooding. Almost a third of the country's farmland is covered by wet mineral soils and about 8 per cent is peat bogs.

Agriculture is at the heart of the Irish economy, providing a large slice of GNP, just under 20 per cent of employment and around 46 per cent of exports. Climate and soil dictate the use of most farmland for pasture and production is centred on dairying and beef cattle - about 70 per cent of all output consists of milk products, beef and veal. It is too wet for growing cereals on a large scale and less than a fifth of farmland is in arable use. Nonetheless Ireland now produces a small surplus of barley for export.

Farming conditions in the central and eastern areas are not unlike those in the west of England, except for the size of holdings. Although there are some large estates, most farms are small family units, averaging about the same size as in France.

Traditional methods of farming still predominate over large areas, especially in the west, where the landscape is among the most beautiful in Europe, but farm incomes are exceptionally low. The advent of modern intensive techniques is relatively recent and still largely confined to the better land, but it has accelerated sharply since Ireland joined the EC. The CAP introduced a higher level of farm prices, an extended export market and new sources of finance. Farmers enjoyed four years of boom, with land prices rising precipitously and a great deal of new investment. To take a small example - there were 32 pigs in the average herd in 1973, 114 by 1979. This bubble has now burst and farmers have suffered a sharp decline in income since the late

1970s. Remote from the main European market and heavily dependent on dairy and beef production, Ireland is under considerable pressure to raise farm productivity and make the most of its extensive pastures.

Ireland is well endowed with wetlands. Five hundred and one separate sites with significance for ornithological, botanical or zoological reasons were identified in a recent survey of Areas of Scientific Interest (1). There are several different estimates of the number of sites of international importance, but the IWRB report, which covers only sites for waterfowl, lists 36, including islands, estuaries, loughs, rivers, freshwater marshes, peat bogs, mires, wet meadows and salt marshes (2). One type of habitat which is rare internationally and is particularly threatened by drainage is the turlough. This is a shallow intermittent lake, disappearing in dry conditions and found only in carboniferous limestone areas in the west of Ireland.

Wetlands are to be found around almost all parts of the Irish coast, but there is a marked concentration of inland sites of importance to wildlife in the north western half of the country. The most westerly European island south of Iceland, Ireland is the last refuge in cold weather for many birds before they turn south. As well as a passage halt, it is a major wintering area, often harbouring 20 per cent or more of the north west European populations of teal, wigeon and shoveler, about 70 per cent of the Greenland race of white-fronted goose and important populations of Bewick's swans, redshanks, black-tailed godwits and golden plover.

Agricultural Drainage

Wet soils and slow flowing rivers with a tendency to silt up ensure that poor drainage is a recurrent problem in Ireland. Improvement works are clearly divided into arterial drainage and field drainage, which are organised and financed independently.

Most arterial drainage is concerned with deepening and widening the channels of main rivers and their larger tributaries in order to increase channel flow. Contemporary designs generally aim at immunity from the three-year flood and a reduction in the water table sufficient to improve drainage in the surrounding area. A lower water table provides farmers with an adequate outfall for ditches and field drains and is an important precondition of field drainage work in many areas, especially in the west. Originally, arterial drainage was done entirely by hand, around 40,000 people were employed at the time of the famine, when the first big public scheme was launched. Now, however, it is highly mechanised, employing less than 1,000 people operating large dragline excavators and floating dredges (3).

Originally undertaken by private landowners in a piece-meal fashion, arterial drainage first entered the realm of public

49

works with the Drainage Act of 1842. During the years of the potato famine and its immediate aftermath, public works activity was more intensive than at any time since and about 100,000 hectares were affected by arterial drainage between 1847 and 1852. Many of the schemes involved were hurriedly designed and subsequently poorly maintained but further public support for arterial works was provided by Acts of 1863 and 1925 and by the 1940s a total area of around 190,000 hectares had been drained.

A new and much more intensive programme was launched by the 1945 Arterial Drainage Act. This over-hauled existing arrangements for organising and financing work and established a fundamental new principle that all arterial drainage would be carried out by the Commissioners of the Office of Public Works on the basis of entire catchments only. The Office of Public Works (OPW) acquired sole responsibility for conducting surveys, carrying out the necessary construction and maintaining the arterial system, all entirely at public expense.

The OPW was quick to define its new tasks, drawing on surveys and local reports to estimate that a total of about 500,000 hectares needed arterial drainage to permit adequate flood relief, about a tenth of all farm land. A programme of works was drawn up covering 28 major catchments, excluding the Shannon, and a further 30 minor ones. These were ranked in order of priority, based on an appraisal of where needs were most urgent, modified by considerations of cost and technical feasibility. With few exceptions, the OPW has adhered rigidly to this list and to date has completed works in 10 major catchments and four minor ones, as well as undertaking about 20 smaller projects, mostly involving the construction of flood banks. Four further major schemes and one minor scheme are currently in progress and others are under consideration.

The latest phase of arterial drainage work has been heavily supported by the EC. As part of a programme to accelerate drainage operations in the less favoured areas of the west of Ireland, set out in Directive 78/623, aid from the FEOGA Guidance Section was made available for arterial drainage in three catchments, the Corrib/Mask/Robe, the Boyle and the Bonet. With certain financial limits, which were later extended, Community funds were made available to meet half the costs of work over an area of 30,000 hectares within the three catchments. Furthermore, works within the Corrib/Mask/Robe catchment, together with two other catchments where drainage works are nearly completed, the Boyne and the Maigue, have been aided by the European Regional Development Fund and partly financed by a huge loan at a subsidised interest rate from the European Investment Bank. In short, almost every major arterial drainage scheme under way in Ireland is now being subsidised by the Community through one or more channels.

Approximately 240,000 hectares were drained under the arterial drainage programme between 1950 and 1980, mostly in the northern and north-western parts of the country. The major catchments are shown in Figure 2 and some basic information about the works in individual catchments is set out in Table 3.1. As this Table suggests, the programme built up steadily to reach a zenith in the early 1960s and then went into a sharp decline, only recovering after Ireland joined the EC. This revival has been due in part to Community support for drainage works, especially in the west. Furthermore, the European Regional Development Fund and the Irish government have between them allocated IR £1 million for a feasibility study to determine the best drainage scheme for the Shannon catchment, at 100,000 hectares the largest in Ireland.

State aid for field drainage was not introduced until 1931 and little is known about the extent of private efforts in the previous 200 years. Some of the larger landowners installed rubble drains on their own property in the 19th century or even earlier, and a number of these still function. However, field drainage was highly localised until 1931 and even the availability of grants led to no more than 57,000 hectares being drained in the 20 years for which this first scheme operated. It was superseded by a much more ambitious programme of field drainage and land reclamation (removal of boulders and scrub etc) launched in 1949 under the title of the Land Project. By this time more specialised machinery and the skills to accompany it had become available, and the impending arterial drainage programme was about to open up improved river outfalls, without which progress was difficult in some parts of the country. At the time it was estimated that poor drainage was inhibiting productivity on about 2.1 million hectares, more than a third of all the farmland in Ireland.

The Land Project and its successors have made remarkable inroads on this target. Figures from various sources agree that around 2.9 million acres (1.2 million hectares or more than a fifth of Irish farmland) were subject to state supported reclamation or field drainage in the thirty years from 1949 and of this at least 80 per cent was drained. There have been considerable fluctuations between years, but an annual average of about 31,000 hectares has been maintained, a level not reached in France until about 1974. Field drainage has been one of the main planks of state investment in drainage, absorbing a third more public funds than the arterial drainage programme. Over the period in question, the state paid out around IR £350 million (in IR £1980) for land reclamation and field drainage, 58 per cent of a total expenditure of IR £600 million (4).

Whereas arterial drainage has taken place largely in the north and west, field drainage has been more concentrated in the south-east, where suitable river outfalls are more readily available, land values are higher and both soils and climate are more appropriate for arable farming. In the west, the costs of drainage have tended to be higher and it is often not worthwhile for farmers to undertake the necessary investment until arterial drainage has been completed. However, there has been a new emphasis on the west since Ireland joined the European Community.

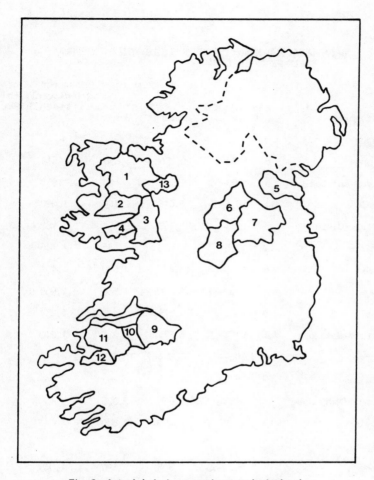

Fig. 2: Arterial drainage schemes in Ireland

1. Moy
2. Mask/Robe (tributaries to the Corrib)
3. Clare (tributary to the Corrib)
4. Corrib/Headford
5. Glyde and Dee
6. Inny
7. Boyne
8. Brosna
9. Maigue
10. Deel
11. Feale
12. Maine
13. Boyle—Bonet

Table 3.1: MAJOR AND MINOR CATCHMENTS IMPROVED BY ARTERIAL DRAINAGE IN IRELAND

Catchment	Map Ref.	Date of Works	Area Benefitting (ha) Farmland	Bog	Cost per ha of agricultural land benefitting (IR1980)
Major					
Brosna	8	1948–55	20,256	14,658	614
Glyde and Dee	5	1950–57	10,605	40	978
Feale	11	1951–59	8,616	2,125	1,090*
Corrib/Clare	3	1954–64	21,167	9,194	1,182
Maine	12	1959–63	4,665	55	1,346
Inny	6	1960–68	15,621	4,679	1,101
Moy	1	1960–71	19,400	4,536	1,965
Deel	10	1962–68	4,815	—	1,234
Corrib/Headford	4	1967–73	5,671	2,211	1,240
Boyne	7	1969–	37,544	10,733	
Maigue	9	1973–	12,375	—	
Corrib/Mask/Robe**	2	1979–	7,690	2,025	
Boyle**	13	1982	6,480	4,860	
Minor					
Nenagh		1955–60	2,605	97	1,045
Ballytoige/Kilmore		1959–61	932	—	734*
Broadmeadow and Ward		1961–64	2,981	—	630
Killimore/Cappagh		1962–68	5,123	—	1,274
Bonet**	13	1982			

Note The last column shows actual rather than design costs and refers only to farmland, except for the two schemes which are asterisked where the cost is for all land benefitting, including bog.
**Schemes receiving direct support from FEOGA under the Western Drainage Scheme.
Source: Based on information supplied by Patricia Kelly, Bruton and Convery (3) and Whilde (17).

In 1974 the Land Project was replaced by the Farm Modernisation Scheme, introduced in conformity with EC Directive 72/159. Under these arrangements, which divide farmers into several different categories for grant purposes, the public purse meets on average about half the cost of field drainage compared with around two-thirds of the cost under the Land Project. However, this has not inhibited activity, which has risen significantly since 1974. This buoyancy must be partly attributed to the initiation of a supplementary scheme applying only to the less-favoured areas of the west of Ireland. One of the earliest and most important of a series of EC structural measures aimed at specific regions, the Western Drainage Scheme came into operation in 1979 on the basis of Directive 78/628.

Under this Directive, which also included support for arterial drainage, referred to above, funds are available from FEOGA to aid field drainage over an extensive area of the west. Grants are also available to agricultural co-operatives in the area for the purchase of drainage machinery. For the purposes of the CAP, 3.5 million hectares, or rather more than half the total agricultural area of Ireland, is designated as a "Less Favoured Area". Broadly speaking, this corresponds to the north-western half of the country.

Initially the scheme aimed to assist field drainage up to a maximum of 100,000 hectares over a five year period, but this was raised to 150,000 hectares by Council Regulation 2195/81, which also extended the time limit to 1986. The scheme has proved extremely popular, largely because 70 per cent of the cost of drainage is met by the grant. In the first two years of operation, the area of fields drained rose by about 40 per cent in the counties where the scheme applies (5). By the end of 1981 more than 48,000 hectares of field drainage had already been completed and work had been approved but had not yet started on a further 60,000 hectares (6). The generous terms, the simultaneous development of arterial work and the new enthusiasm of the institutions involved have combined to build up a considerable momentum and it is possible that the scheme will be extended beyond 1986.

Table 3.2 shows the distribution of both field and arterial drainage by county for the years 1945/49 to 1978/80. The areas concerned are expressed in acres and the figures for field drainage rather over-estimate the amount of field drainage accomplished, perhaps by 25 per cent, as they include land reclamation as well. However, the table does give a good indication of regional patterns and make it clear that there is no simple relationship between the pace of field and arterial drainage. For example, the county with the largest proportion of farm land drained over the period was Carlow in the south-east, where no arterial work took place at all. On the other hand, in three of the major arterial schemes currently in hand, the Maigue, the Boyne and the Corrib/Mask/Robe, it is estimated that about three-quarters of the land requires follow-up field drainage if the full agricultural benefits are to be exploited.

Table 3.2: PROGRESS OF DRAINAGE PROGRAMMES BY COUNTY

	Arterial drainage 1945–80		Field drainage 1949–80	
	(Acres 000)	% of farm land	(Acres 000)	% of farm land
Carlow	–	–	68.5	36.7
Dublin	3.1	1.9	31.1	18.8
Kildare	14.7	4.1	128.4	35.6
Kilkenny	–	–	108.0	23.7
Laois	4.0	1.2	123.4	36.5
Longford*	11.4	5.4	36.9	17.4
Louth	11.7	6.7	32.6	18.6
Meath	68.6	12.4	146.6	26.6
Offaly	84.6	23.4	71.2	31.2
Westmeath	85.2	22.5	119.8	31.7
Wexford	4.9	1.0	173.7	34.2
Wicklow	–	–	87.2	29.7
LEINSTER	288.2	7.2	1127.4	28.5
Clare*	10.3	1.8	86.9	15.0
Cork*	2.0	0.1	272.3	20.1
Kerry*	38.1	7.1	171.0	31.9
Limerick	54.2	9.1	140.5	23.6
Tipperary	8.1	0.9	237.1	27.4
Waterford	1.0	0.3	93.3	28.7
MUNSTER	113.7	2.7	1001.1	23.5
Galway*	116.5	14.0	179.0	21.5
Leitrim*	2.2	0.8	35.6	12.9
Mayo*	64.7	10.6	149.7	24.4
Roscommon*	2.2	0.4	74.7	15.2
Sligo*	10.8	3.6	40.1	13.3
CONNAUGHT	196.4	7.8	479.1	19.1
Cavan*	7.1	1.8	101.3	25.5
Donegal*	8.4	1.9	107.4	23.9
Monaghan*	4.4	1.6	71.2	25.2
ULSTER	19.9	1.8	279.9	24.7
STATE	618.2	5.2	2887.5	24.3

* These are counties "designated" for assistance under the Western Drainage Scheme. Part of West Cork and West Limerick are also "designated".

Notes

i)   Field drainage includes land reclamation as well as field drainage proper
ii) Area improved under arterial programmes included both agricultural land and bog land
iii) Farm land includes areas under crop and pasture

Source: Quoted in Bruton and Convery (3)

In practice, the proportion of farmers who do make the necessary investment in field drainage is unknown, although it is an important consideration in assessing the economic return on an arterial project. The OPW do not undertake follow-up studies to investigate farmers' responses to their projects and so the figures which they give for areas improved under arterial works, which are shown in Tables 3.1 and 3.2, are in fact somewhat notional - reflecting the OPW's estimate of potential or expected benefit rather than the actual outcome. All figures for areas improved by arterial drainage therefore should be treated with caution, and should not be added to the totals given for field drainage. The latter are based on grant applications and should be an accurate estimate of work completed. The area of land drained without public aid is unknown, but is almost certainly small.

Much as in the other three countries considered in this report, the rationale behind the drainage programme in Ireland is a mixture of the agronomic, the economic and the social. Some of the most common problems which schemes are designed to tackle are tight, slow-draining and impervious soil layers, the seepage of water from outside an area into it and high ground water levels. These conditions are a restraint on agriculture, depressing productivity during the growing season and holding down output and farm incomes. Drainage is thus seen as a "public good", meriting state support as well as private investment.

The argument is taken to its logical extreme in the Arterial Drainage Act of 1945 under which the state meets the entire cost of capital works and maintenance too is paid for by the public purse, by means of a levy on the counties benefiting from the scheme. A similar but slightly more cautious approach had been foreshadowed in an earlier Drainage Commission report in which drainage was described as an "essential service", a matter of "national pride" and not subject purely to economic considerations. It was argued that arterial drainage was a prerequisite for private investment, that it would provide public benefits in the spheres of transport, public health, urban flood control, sewage outfalls and the spin-off effects of higher farm incomes. In the absence of a programme, it was suggested that drainage problems would be aggravated and remedial action would become increasingly expensive. In effect, economic niceties were largely over-ruled by the Commission and the subsequent Act went further still, doubling the size of their proposed programme and giving the OPW greater powers. When the OPW drew up its list of catchments to be included in the programme, "the emphasis was on handling the drainage problems subject to certain constraints rather than applying economic criteria in the selection and ordering of projects" (7).

The statutory basis for this approach is Article 45 of the Irish Constitution which lists the directive principles of social policy, which include the following statement: "the state shall in particular direct its policy towards....securing that there may be established on the land in economic security as many

56

families as in the circumstances shall be practicable". The question is, of course, whether the state can best meet this aim by providing drainage or by some other activity and it would appear pertinent to discover exactly what the economic costs and benefits of drainage are and how these compare with alternative investments in rural areas. The Drainage Commission report deliberately eschewed enquiry of this kind and even today there remains a heavy presumption in favour of arterial drainage. It has been a feature of public works programmes for nearly a century and a half and there is almost an element of heresy in questioning its value. Yet the lack of rigorous economic analysis invites precisely such criticism. The Department of Finance had a representative on the Commission and he dissented from the majority view concluding instead that the proposed programme, which was rather more modest than the one eventually adopted, would, prima facie, involve "a dissipation rather than a creation of national wealth" (8).

These doubts were somewhat confirmed by a Department of Finance Appraisal Team in an unpublished report completed in 1968. They confirmed that the primary objective of arterial drainage is "to increase the level of incomes of those landlords whose lands are diminished in productive capacity by flooding and/or waterlogging and are dependent on arterial drainage works for relief" (9). However, they were sceptical about the economic returns from the programme, arguing that the cost of drainage was greater than the increase in the market value of the land where the benefits arose and was often greater than the full value of the land after drainage had been completed. They suggested that the arterial drainage programme should be halted and that future works should be subject to a full cost-benefit analysis to demonstrate their viability.

This was accepted in 1970 with the establishment of a steering group to devise an appropriate procedure for economic appraisal, with members drawn from several Ministries including the Department of Finance. Subsequently new schemes have had to be justified by reference to a formal cost-benefit analysis, but the methodology employed in this analysis is subject to a considerable number of criticisms, many of which are set out in a recent report by Bruton and Convery, entitled "Land Drainage Policy in Ireland" (10). In addition to making methodological criticisms, such as the lack of Ex-Post analysis, Bruton and Convery drew a number of other conclusions, one of which is that "net income to farmers could be increased if resources were to be reallocated from drainage to other activities". For this reason they recommend that the pattern of subsidies should be changed so that drainage of both kinds is brought more into line with other agricultural inputs for which farmers have to meet a larger proportion of the total cost. This would probably involve a charge to landowners for arterial drainage.

Since Bruton and Convery's criticisms have yet to be rebutted, at the very least there remain serious unanswered questions about the economic justification for maintaining such a heavily subsidised programme. By the same measure there must be genuine doubt about whether the concentration of FEOGA aid on drainage activities, especially in the west of Ireland, is the most cost-effective means of raising farm incomes. With increasing constraints on the growth of milk and beef production, it is vital to make a realistic appraisal of the prospects for agriculture in the west and to tailor subsidies accordingly. There may be better means of alleviating poverty and stimulating new employment than supporting further drainage work. Tourism and wood production are possible examples.

The Organisation of Agricultural Drainage

Land drainage is a highly organised, professional and politically sensitive operation. The principal institutions involved vary according to the nature of the works, i.e. arterial or field drainage. As we have seen, normally the two operations are carried out independently, the former under the control of the OPW, the latter under the auspices of the Department of Agriculture. The basic roles of the main bodies have not changed since the introduction of EC aid, but the volume of work has increased. Environmental interests are represented by a number of different organisations and, although their involvement has increased recently, their powers in this sphere remain rather limited.

For arterial drainage, the ultimate decision-maker is the Minister for Finance. The OPW is a self-contained unit within the Department of Finance, responsible for a number of activities including the preparation, design, construction, execution, completion and financing of all arterial drainage schemes in Ireland. The Minister arbitrates on issues unresolved at lower levels and in principle could promote alterations even to an approved drainage design, but in practice this has never happened.

The OPW is obliged to maintain and repair the schemes which it initiates and this has become an increasingly large component of its activities, accounting for between a third and a quarter of its expenditure in the late 1970s. County Councils are responsible for the maintenance of older schemes and also reimburse the OPW for costs entailed in maintenance. Generally, the OPW has somewhat draconian powers, being exempted from the Fishery Acts, the Planning Acts and the Water Management Acts and being permitted to compulsorily purchase land, fisheries, water, navigation and other rights in the course of works. Compensation is mandatory but does not have to be settled in advance.

The procedure for designing and constructing schemes includes a number of consultative arrangments, but in most cases the OPW is empowered to ignore the views of other bodies if it so wishes. However, under the 1945 Act, the OPW is required to make provisions for the protection of fisheries in its schemes. Since the passage of the 1976 Wildlife Act it has been obliged also to consult officials from the Forest and Wildlife Service (part of the Department of Fisheries and Forestry) on the possible suitability of sites as nature reserves or refuges in catchments where drainage is planned. Consultation with the Department of Fisheries and Forestry (DFF) takes place at the design stage and although the OPW can overrule objections to its proposals it usually attempts to minimise damage to fisheries, for example by agreeing to a rehabilitation programme to commence after works have finished and the river has "settled down".

Design alterations to meet other environmental objections are less common, although the consultative procedure has been extended in recent years to take more account of environmental interests. Bodies consulted now include An Foras Forbatha - the National Institute for Physical Planning and Construction Research, which may give an opinion on the environmental implications of a scheme, for example on water supplies, on which the Institute has considerable expertise. In the case of the three arterial schemes currently being funded by FEOGA they were asked to express an opinion on the wildlife implications of the work. Lack of adequate data makes this kind of task difficult to fulfil, but An Foras Forbatha is also constrained by political considerations, since it is a small body with limited powers and derives most of its income from the Department of the Environment. The latter Department is consulted by the OPW on the effects of schemes on roads, bridges, water supply, etc., but to date it has shown little interest in the conservation aspects of schemes.

Consultation with the Forest and Wildlife Service is also valuable, but its effectiveness is equally limited. The Service is a small part of the DFF, constrained by lack of funds and enjoying much less power than the Fisheries Division. Although it advises the OPW on the suitability of sites within pre-drainage catchments for use as state nature reserves, very little money is available to acquire land for this purpose and it is a quite inadequate mechanism for protecting important wetlands. Whereas the DFF prepares a detailed analysis of the disruption caused to fisheries by OPW schemes and estimates rehabilitation costs and these are included in the cost-benefit analysis for the catchment, other environmental impacts are only noted qualitatively. However, it is probably true to say that the role of the Forest and Wildlife Service has been strengthened by the advent of EC funding. Of the three arterial schemes to which FEOGA contributes under the Western Drainage Scheme, a programme of protection for wildlife and wetlands has been drawn up and research efforts have been strengthened.

Other bodies now consulted by the OPW on certain schemes include Bord Failte, the Irish Tourist Board, and An Taisce, the National Trust for Ireland, the country's leading voluntary environmental organisation. The former has recently become involved in assessing the implications of schemes for tourism and the development of tourist facilities, especially in the area of the proposed works on the cross-border catchments of the Finn-Lackey and Monaghan Blackwater. However, information on which to base such an assessment is relatively scarce, the Bord have no specific policy on arterial drainage and it is not one of their priorities. To date, An Taisce have been involved only in discussion of the proposed cross-border schemes and they are only beginning to acquire the necessary expertise to make detailed comments and criticisms of OPW proposals.

The OPW are required to notify the public in the affected area when a scheme has been prepared and to make the design available for public inspection for a few weeks, following which objections can be submitted in writing. However, this process is rather narrowly conceived and rarely induces a great deal of response from the public, the great majority of whom are not well informed about the potential effects of schemes of this kind. Nor is the OPW obliged to take any notice of the objections which are submitted. A more satisfactory process of consultation might be through the conventional planning system, from which arterial works are exempted, as in the UK. This would almost certainly increase the effectiveness of bodies like An Taisce.

The OPW's drainage work is dominated by engineers and engineering considerations and the ecological expertise within the organisation is minimal. It makes some attempt to avoid damaging the environment, but only if this does not involve substantial design compromises. Areas of particular ecological significance may be omitted from a scheme, there are some examples of this in the Corrib/Mask/Robe catchment, and small changes in scheme design and special remedial work, such as tree planting, are becoming more common. However, there are a large number of factors working against effective environmental controls, including a lack of public understanding of the issue and limited political pressure for change. The Department of the Environment has not taken a lead on the issue, leaving smaller bodies in a weak position, particularly as they are poorly co-ordinated and the onus is on them to convince the OPW of the need to modify their schemes. With little money available for nature reserves, the environmental bodies must also secure the agreement of landowners to conservation.

For survey and construction work the OPW has a budget of around IR £9 million per annum and they have access to a fund of around IR £19 million from FEOGA for arterial work carried out under the Western Drainage Scheme between 1979 and 1986. To get access to this, the OPW must submit programmes of proposed works to the Department of Agriculture (DOA) which combines them with its own field drainage proposals and applies to FEOGA for advance payment. The DOA is the sole official agent for the administration of FEOGA grants in Ireland.

Field drainage is under the control of the DOA and its subsidiary agencies. Encouragement is given to farmers to apply for group projects rather than individual ones, although the arrangements are much more flexible than in France. The co-operative movement, which involves the majority of farmers in Ireland, is actively involved in promoting group schemes and providing advice and support, both locally and through its central body, ICOS, the Irish Co-operative Organisation Society. Registered co-operatives operating principally in the designated western counties were eligible for a 25 per cent grant towards the cost of drainage machinery during the first two years of the Western Drainage Scheme. The co-operatives may in turn lease the machinery to local contractors, who undertake the works.

The organisation most concerned with administering drainage work in the western counties is the Farm Development Service, a specialised agency with 38 offices and a brief to implement the Western Drainage Scheme. This body operates in parallel with the DOA's local offices, the County Committees of Agriculture, which cover all aspects of agriculture and have their own advisers. Grants for drainage are administered under a variety of schemes, all of which originate in EC measures and are described briefly in the next Section.

Farmers owning land which can be drained in one operation usually initiate field drainage proposals, either individually or in a small group. They do not usually form new legal entities in order to receive grants, as in France, but may call on the services of their local co-operative in preparing and developing a proposal. About 40 per cent of farmers applying for aid under the WDS in 1979 did so as part of a group. In the west applications are sent to the local office of the Farm Development Service (FDS). An officer then inspects the site concerned and must be satisfied that it is suitable for agriculture and that drainage will permit a reasonable increase in productivity. In this assessment the local advisor may also be involved and, less frequently, someone from An Foras Taluntais, the Agricultural Institute, which is a source of technical and scientific advice. The FDS officer then draws up specifications for the project and approves it for grant. Works are usually carried out by a contractor and may be subject to inspection.

There are no special arrangements for taking account of environmental factors in field drainage proposals. A new Western Drainage Scheme Advisory Committee was set up at the end of 1979 to help the Minister of Agriculture "in furthering the successful implementation of the recently announced Western Drainage Scheme". The Committee both promotes the scheme and provides advice and is the central co-ordinating body for the different organisations involved in field drainage. The Committee's membership extends to all the major farming organisations but no environmental agency is represented.

Finance for Drainage

As we have already seen, arterial and field drainage are separately financed, with both receiving support from FEOGA.

Arterial drainage is entirely financed from the public purse and neither landowners nor local authorities are required to contribute towards the cost of capital works. Maintenance work is paid for by County Councils, whether they do the work themselves or it is done by the OPW.

Over the first 30 years of its life, the arterial drainage programme absorbed, on average, about 1.5 per cent of Ireland's total public expenditure on capital works or about an eighth of state capital spending on agriculture, which amounts to a considerable sum. Expressing all outlays in 1980 Irish pounds, a total of around IR £5.5 million was spent on survey work, about IR £232 million on construction and about IR £39 million on maintenance between 1950/51 and 1981 (11). Current expenditure is around IR £200,000 a year on survey work, IR £8-9 million on construction and about IR £3 million on maintenance.

The pattern of expenditure over the last three decades is shown in Table 3.3.

Table 3.3:   ARTERIAL DRAINAGE PROGRAMME EXPENDITURE
              1950-1979   (IR £000)

	Survey and Con-struction costs	Average of annual % of public capital programme	Hectares drained (000)	Cost (IR£ 1980/hectare
1950-59	57,202	1.5	85.4	670
1960-69	104,005	1.8	83.1	1252
1970-79	59,495	0.6	63.5	937

The data include the 50 per cent EC contribution to arterial drainage in the west started in 1979. The deflator used is the implicit price index of "Other Buildings and Construction (including Land Rehabilitation)" derived from the National Income and Expenditure Accounts.

Source: Appropriation Accounts: Budget Booklet. Table derived from Bruton and Convery (3).

It can be seen that the costs per hectare drained rose dramatically in the 1960s when the programme reached a peak and then fell again in the 1970s, following the introduction of cost-benefit analysis. It is also interesting to note that annual expenditure on construction built up to over IR £14 million a year in 1964 and then declined steadily for a decade, going as low as IR £3.6 million in 1974. Since then it has revived to the level of the late 1960s and in some part this must be attributed to the availability of aid from the European Community.

The most prominent form of Community aid is the Western Drainage Scheme, which came into force in 1979. This only covers three catchments: the Corrib/Mask/Robe, the Boyle and the Bonet, all in the west. The first of these is a substantial scheme begun in 1979 with annual expenditure growing to £3.7 million by 1981; work on the latter two did not begin until late 1982. Half the cost of expenditure on capital works in the three catchments is reimbursed by FEOGA. Initially, this contribution was limited to a ceiling of 18.1 million EUA under Directive 78/628. However, this sum proved too small to meet the escalating costs of channel works and the Irish government requested an increased budget in order to meet the original target of work affecting 30,000 hectares. The response to this was favourable and the ceiling of FEOGA expenditure was raised by a further 30 million ECU in July 1981 when Regulation 2195/81 was adopted. Of this 30 million, perhaps half will be used to subsidise arterial drainage.

There is a further area which has been selected for special FEOGA aid. In 1979 a programme was launched to promote drainage in river catchments spanning the border between Ireland and northern Ireland. 15.1 million EUA are to be made available over a five year period to meet half the cost of suitable joint schemes, with the respective national governments paying the other half. Two catchments have been designated for this purpose, the Blackwater in County Monaghan and the Finn-Lackey in County Donegal, but progress to date has been somewhat slow.

A second, and much less important, source of EC grants for arterial drainage is the European Regional Development Fund, ERDF. The ERDF has made a number of relatively small grants for arterial drainage work, mostly affecting the three main catchments of the Corrib/Mask/Robe, the Maigue and the Boyne. These grants are paid direct to the exchequer and had reached a total of 4.67 million ECU by the end of 1981. ERDF is also the source of a grant of about IR £500,000 to meet half the cost of design and survey work for an arterial drainage scheme for the river Shannon catchment. As we have seen, this is potentially of great environmental significance.

This network of grants is supplemented by a substantial Community loan towards the costs of arterial drainage work borne by the Irish government. This covers the three schemes which were under way in 1979, the Boyne, the Maigue and the Corrib/Mask/Robe. All three have been the subject of small ERDF grants and the latter is part of the Western Drainage Scheme. The loan also covers field drainage work in these three catchments and is for a total of 28.2 million ECU, intended to cover half the total expenditure incurred by the government during the period 1979 to 1983. The source of the loan is the European Investment Bank (EIB) which is the Community's chief source of loan finance, advancing substantial sums at lower interest rates than the commercial banks. Twenty three million ECU had been advanced by the autumn of 1982 (12) and part of the loan was subject to a 3 per cent interest subsidy.

To summarise this rather complex web of subsidies; the OPW meets all the cost of arterial drainage in Ireland and in doing so draws on grants from the Community, mainly for work in the west, and loans from the EIB.

Schemes are undertaken in the order which was drawn up by the OPW's Chief Engineer in 1945 and it is likely that diminishing returns are setting in as progress is made down the list towards the lowest priority schemes. Some indication of this is given by the fact that completed schemes have given rise to a 69 per cent increase in the value of the agricultural land drained, schemes in progress are expected to add only 43 per cent to land values and projected schemes 52 per cent (13).

Turning to field drainage, costs are split between the Department of Agriculture and farmers in different proportions according to types of farm and location. A varying percentage of state expenditure is reimbursed by FEOGA. Between 1949 and 1974 field drainage was financed under the Land Project, described briefly in the second section of this Chapter, and since then it has been assisted under the Farm Modernisation Scheme. Estimates made during the course of the Land Project suggested that approximately 2.43 million hectares of agricultural land needed improvement in Ireland, five sixths of it by drainage. Since 1949 about 1.2 million hectares, about half of this target, have been improved with state aid, with field drainage extending to nearly 1 million hectares. Field improvement schemes have accounted for about 18 per cent of state capital expenditure on agriculture since 1949 or about 2 per cent of total public sector capital investment. Total expenditure had reached about IR £600 million (in 1980 prices) by 1980, £350 million, or about 58 per cent being met out of state funds.

Under the Land Project, farmers carried out field drainage works themselves, usually by employing a contractor, with the state meeting two-thirds of the "standard cost" (often more than the real cost), up to a specified maximum sum per acre. Initially there was an alternative option under which a state contractor undertook the work and the Department of Agriculture paid 60 per cent of the cost. This proved rather expensive, farmers only utilising the service for the most difficult works and the option was withdrawn in 1958. The other option was widely used and the cost ceiling per hectare rose considerably between 1949 and 1965, resulting in state grants per hectare in 1980 prices rising from IR £119 in 1951 to £392 in 1967.

After 1965 the ceiling remained unchanged despite inflation and in real terms annual state expenditure, which had reached a peak of IR £13/14 million in the late 1960s, tailed off to little more than IR £6.5 million by 1974. This downward trend was reversed with the introduction of a new scheme in 1975 and, with FEOGA aid, annual expenditure had reached a new peak of £16.5 million by 1980. Under the Western Drainage Scheme, which began in 1979-80, the cost of grants for field drainage rose to £329 per hectare.

In 1974 a number of different national schemes for making capital grants to agriculture were phased out and replaced by the Farm Modernisation Scheme devised in accordance with EC Directive 72/159. The Directive is designed to raise farm incomes to a level comparable to the average amount earned locally by those employed outside agriculture. Farmers earning less than this average are encouraged to draw up development plans showing how they will make new investments and build up their business over a period of years, six in the case of Ireland. At the end of this time they should reach a "comparable income" to their urban neighbours. If their development plans are approved they are offered relatively generous grants towards the cost of buildings, land improvements and other investments specified in the plan. FEOGA then reimburses the state for a quarter of the cost of these grants. There are some limitations on the kind of expenditure which can be grant aided, for example restrictions on pig and dairy farm investments, and there is a limit to the total amount of money that can be paid per labour unit, ie per full-time worker employed on a holding.

"Development farms" are a minority in all Member States. Most farms are either part time or too small to be modernised sufficiently to produce a "comparable income" or, in some cases, are too prosperous and have already achieved the income target. In Ireland only about 22 per cent of farmers applying for grants are designated as development farmers and in the less favoured areas in the west, which cover about half the agricultural area, the proportion is only about 11 per cent (14). For the majority without development plans, Directive 72/159 permits national grant schemes, provided that they are not more generous than the FEOGA scheme. In Ireland, those who have already achieved the "comparable income" are termed "commercial farmers" and those disqualified from development plans for other reasons, usually because they are part-time or have very small holdings are termed "other farmers". Both are eligible for drainage grants under the Farm Modernisation Scheme.

In the west of Ireland the great majority of farms have insufficient commercial potential to qualify for the EC scheme, and the provision of more generous grants for development farmers in the Less Favoured Areas (under Directive 75/268) has therefore failed to find much application either. Since farm incomes are exceptionally low in the west and the opportunities for alternative work scarce, it was decided that special Community measures would be justified for this region. One of these measures was the Western Drainage Scheme, which offered additional FEOGA funding for field drainage. Another was the Western Agricultural Development Programme. The latter was approved in 1980 by Regulation 1820/80 and covers most of the Less Favoured

Areas of western Ireland. It is a large scheme designed to run from 1980-1990, with a budget of 224 million ECUs or about IR £150 million for FEOGA contributions. It permits substantially higher rates of capital grant than apply in other parts of the country and covers a wide range of investments including land improvement, roads, buildings, forestry, food processing, water supplies and electrification.

The parallel operation of these different schemes means that farmers in the west are eligible for higher capital grants for drainage than those in the rest of Ireland, where the development status of a farm will determine the size of grant available. Four different categories of farm can be distinguished:

1. Farmers in the west, whether full or part time, are eligible for 70 per cent grants for drainage

2. "Development farmers" in the remainder of the country are eligible for 45 per cent grants

3. "Other" farmers, those not qualifying for development status, are also eligible for 45 per cent grants

4. "Commercial" farmers, with reasonable incomes, are eligible for 35 per cent grants.

The average rate of grant paid in 1981 was about 56 per cent, little different from the aggregate rate in 1968 under the old Land Project.

The largest Community involvement in field drainage is through the Western Drainage Scheme. Originally 100,000 hectares were covered by the scheme, with FEOGA contributing half the cost of the state grant with a ceiling on the amount payable per hectare. Under these arrangements the cost of drainage to farmers fell by about 40 per cent and this stimulated a rapid burst of activity. Within two and a half years almost two-thirds of the prescribed area had been drained and plans for the remainder had been finalised. In the summer of 1981, a further 50,000 hectares were added to the scheme under Regulation 2195/81 and the ceiling on the sum payable per hectare was raised. The cost of drainage is relatively high in the west and grants are correspondingly more costly. FEOGA has set aside approximately 15 million ECU to cover the extra 50,000 hectares over the period up to December 1986, but if the scheme's popularity continues, this sum will be exhausted at a considerably earlier date.

The other main source of Community funds for field drainage is through FEOGA reimbursement of a quarter of the cost of capital grants for development farmers, although this again is subject to certain limitations. As we have seen, development farmers are not a large proportion of the total in Ireland*, and

---

* The position may change in future as Directive 72/159, on which the Farm Modernisation Scheme is based, expired at the end of

prior to the introduction of the Western Drainage Scheme (WDS), FEOGA was meeting only about 5 per cent of the costs of field drainage grants under the Farm Modernisation Scheme. However by 1980, with the WDS in full operation, the EC was paying almost a fifth of all field drainage grants, more than IR £3 million. At the same time, FEOGA was offering agricultural co-operatives 25 per cent grants towards the cost of purchasing new drainage machinery and the Irish government was meeting its share of drainage costs in the west with the aid of the EIB loan already referred to.

There has been little rigorous economic analysis of field drainage since the work of the land project survey team in 1968. They looked at only a small sample, but their results suggested that drainage was economically attractive at the time with a simple pay-back of less than five years (15). However, they also revealed that returns on drainage were extremely variable, with 37 per cent of projects not covering their costs and 16 per cent not covering as much as half their costs. In the western counties the cost of drainage was almost a third higher than in the north-east and midlands but the improvement in income per hectare was about 45 per cent less. Indeed, the team estimated that about half the farmers in their sample could have found cheaper ways of increasing their incomes, by better management and improvement of existing practices. Bruton and Convery suggest that these results continue to have some relevance today and it seems likely that the returns on drainage investment are still extremely variable and probably least attractive in the west. A new survey of field drainage is long overdue, but it would be surprising if there were not more cost-effective ways of increasing incomes than drainage on many Irish farms.

Impact on Wetlands

The broad scale and sustained momentum of post-war drainage work in Ireland has undoubtedly resulted in important environmental changes, scarcely any of which have been adequately recorded. Many of the wetlands drained in recent years or now threatened by proposed schemes may have been affected by earlier work, some of it of a substantial nature, and although Ireland enjoys a reputation as a haven of bogs, tranquil lakes and superb scenery, its wetland heritage has already been severely impoverished. As elsewhere, there are many threats to surviving wetlands, but agricultural drainage is of particular importance.

Drainage in Ireland is usually for agricultural purposes. Naturally well-drained land is relatively scarce and the demand

---

1983 and is expected to be replaced with a new Community farm structure policy during 1984. This is likely to loosen the restrictions on development farmers and to make aid available to a much wider range of small farms.

for urban flood relief and land reclamation for industry is much less than in more densely populated parts of Europe. Nonetheless urban threats should not be discounted. Cork harbour, an important site for waders, is reported to be threatened in several places by industrial development, pollution, sewage and eutrophication (16). Rogerstown estuary near Dublin, a wintering ground for around 400 Brent geese and other birds, is in serious danger from the dumping of domestic refuse which has already caused the geese to desert the western half of the estuary. Further areas have been cordoned off for dumping and there are additional threats from eutrophication and the spread of "spartina" (17).

The Shannon estuary, an area of mudflats fringed by reed swamps, saltmarsh and wet meadows is an exceptionally important wetland, acknowledged to be the finest wader haunt in the Republic (18) but is threatened by large scale industrial development, land reclamation and pollution. Sewage discharge is recorded as a threat at a number of sites, for example at Akeragh Lough, a brackish lagoon on the Kerry coast, where one area has lost all its acquatic vegetation and the remainder is threatened by eutrophication. This and certain other important wetlands are shown in Figure 3.

The dramatic decline in Ireland's once expansive seas of bog can be attributed not only to agricultural improvements, but also to turf exploitation and to afforestation. Many of the great raised bogs of the Midlands have been excavated to provide peat for power stations, while the shallower blanket bogs in the west have been selected as one of the main areas in the country for planting conifers (19).

The protection offered to wildlife habitats in Ireland is meagre. Of 36 sites of international importance for waterfowl, about two thirds are completely unprotected and where there are sanctuaries and no shooting areas, they rarely extend to the whole of a site (20). As in most other countries, shooting can be an important threat to wildfowl on unprotected sites, not only because of the number of birds killed but also because of the disturbance to others. It is probably a major contributor to the falling population of some species, although the lack of kill statistics makes it difficult to assess the position at all accurately.

What is clear is that wildfowlers are becoming increasingly concerned about the decline in numbers and the threat to breeding and wintering grounds posed by drainage. An important survey of Irish wetlands was undertaken in 1981/2 under the sponsorship of FACE, the Federation of Hunting Associatons of the EC and NARGC, the National Association of Regional Game Councils of Ireland. Tony Whilde, the author of this report, identifies hunting pressure as "heavy" at four wetlands of international importance, and "high" or "moderate to high" at a further seven international sites (21). The number of gun licences issued to hunters doubled between 1965 and 1980, from approximately 35,000 to 70,000 (22).

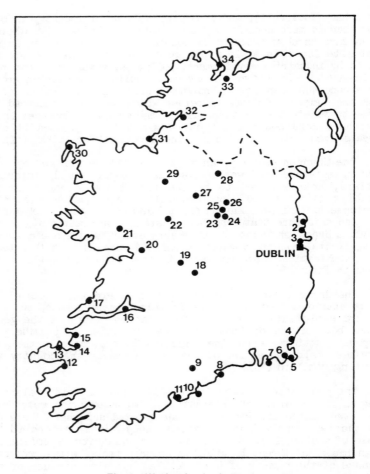

Fig.3: Wetlands in Ireland

1. Rogerstown Estuary	18. Little Brosna River
2. Malahide	19. River Shannon, Athlone to
3. North Bull	Portumna
4. Wexford Harbour and Slobs	20. Rahasane Turlough
5. Lady's Island Lake	21. Lough Corrib
6. Tacumshin Lake	22. River Suck
7. Bannow Bay	23. Lough Iron
8. Dungarvan Harbour	24. Lough Owel
9. River Blackwater Callows	25. Glen Lough
10. Ballymacoda	26. Lough Derravaragh
11. Cork Harbour	27. Castle Forbes Complex
12. Castlemaine Harbour	28. Lough Oughter
13. Lough Gill	29. Lough Gara
14. Tralee Bay	30. Inishkea Islands
15. Akeragh Lough	31. Cummeen Strand, Sligo Bay
16. Shannon Estuary	32. Birra Lough
17. Mutton Island	33. River Foyle
	34. Lough Swilly

The majority of Ireland's remaining wetlands are located either around the coast, most of which contains sites of some interest, or are freshwater habitats to be found mainly in the north west of the country, with a heavy concentration in the catchment of the Shannon and its tributaries. The north west is well endowed with rivers, streams, lakes, water meadows and peat bogs and these habitats are most at risk from drainage. Coastal wetlands are typically estuaries, mudflats, salt marshes, coastal lagoons and islands, amongst which coastal lakes and lagoons are most vulnerable to drainage, which may be conducted purely locally in order to reclaim land for farming. At Lady's Island Lake, near Wexford on the south coast, a site where 22 species of wader and 15 species of wildfowl occur annually, the water level is lowered each spring by making a drainage channel through the shingle which separates the lake from the sea. This enables a larger area of shoreline to be grazed by cattle during the summer, but if made permanent it would reduce the area of the lake and lead to important ecological changes (23).

Although it is quite clear that agricultural drainage has had a major impact on Irish wetlands, a satisfactory assessment of the position is precluded by the great paucity of pre-drainage and post-drainage scientific data. This deficiency is by no means unique to Ireland and efforts are now being made to correct it. For example the Forest and Wildlife Service is in the process of conducting botanical surveys of important wetlands and the EC has commissioned a study of the environmental impact of arterial drainage at one site as part of a project to develop a methodology for assessing the impact of agricultural developments in the Community. However, these initiatives are recent and on a modest scale; the effects of more than 30 years of intense drainage activity remain largely unrecorded.

The most immediately visible consequences of arterial schemes are changes in the landscape. Many meandering rivers have been canalised, resulting in straighter watercourses, confined by sharply graded banks and often denuded of trees, scrub and other vegetation. Spoil from dredging operations is frequently dumped in piles along the river banks and "even where this spoil is spread, a bare treeless and shrubless appearance gives an unfinished tarnish to post-drainage watercourses" (24). In the west of Ireland where tourism is one of the main planks of the economy, this form of drainage could result in financial as well as aesthetic and cultural losses.

Dredging, canalisation and the grading of river banks also have an effect on fisheries, causing disturbance during the course of works, usually followed by longer-term changes. The impact on fisheries varies greatly, depending on pre-drainage conditions and the nature of the scheme, but most fish benefit from bankside vegetation, the presence of holding pools and generally diverse conditions in the stream bed. In low cost schemes where there is no attempt to compensate for the loss of pools, meanders, riffles, stones and bankside vegetation, the impact on fisheries is likely to be negative. The rivers Boyne,

Blackwater, Little Brosna, Feale, Inny and Maigue have all been cited as good fisheries where arterial drainage has done irreparable harm (25).

In the main tributaries of the Boyne, one of the few schemes to be subjected to pre- and post-drainage studies, the re-establishment of salmon has proved slow and there has been a substantial population decline and increased reliance on stocking. Breeding was particularly affected and natural smolt in the Boyne system became largely dependent on a single tributary.

The replacement of salmonids by coarse fish is not always associated with arterial drainage, but changes in channel profile, vegetation, invertebrate life and water levels will nearly always affect fish productivity. The OPW has become increasingly concerned with the rehabilitation of fisheries in recent years, but is not always willing to shoulder the costs of meeting fish and wildlife requirements, even in those cases where the probable long-term effects of drainage have been established. Rehabilitation can also be threatened by channel maintenance work, which is a task of growing importance. As in the UK, unnecessary damage to vegetation and spawning beds is often attributed to poor planning and lack of appropriate training and supervision amongst the maintenance gangs.

The clearance of trees and other riverside vegetation and the grading of the banks also affects otters, which may not face a shortage of food, but are less able to find appropriate sites in which to make their holts. Otters are still relatively common in Ireland, but reductions in their distribution and numbers have been noted in a recent survey (26) and further expansion of the drainage programme can only worsen breeding conditions.

It is difficult to assess the impact of drainage on most species of wetland fauna and flora because of the lack of data. However, such work as there has been has concentrated mainly on birds and this gives some indication of the extent of ecological change. About 125 species breed regularly in Ireland and nearly a third of these are wetland birds, to some degree dependent for their survival on freshwater wetlands (27). Most of these have already been affected by drainage, some severely. The lowering of water levels in lakes and clearance of reed beds are particularly damaging. The rarer breeding ducks such as gadwall, wigeon, pintail, shoveler, pochard and scoter might lose some or all of their remaining habitats if the drainage programme continues and are thus in danger of becoming extinct as Irish breeding birds. The black-necked grebe has become extremely rare, possibly extinct as a breeding species in the Republic, as a result of turlough drainage.

Ireland's wetlands are particularly important as a passage and wintering area for migrant wildfowl, lying at the end of flyways stretching north to Arctic Canada, Greenland, Iceland and Scandinavia and east to Scotland and central Europe. Large numbers of migratory duck depend on Irish lakes, freshwater marshes, turloughs (shallow temporary lakes) and callows (flood meadows), all of which are subject to drainage. As the area of wetlands shrinks, the duck are forced onto a smaller number of sites and consequently come under increased pressure from hunting, disturbance and, eventually, food shortages. For example, whooper and Bewick's swans (Ireland has more than 20 per cent of the European population) have been particlarly affected by the drainage of callows and turloughs, where they previously grazed the short grasses. Forced to move on, they have added to pressures at other sites.

One of the best documented visitors is the Greenland white-fronted goose. Between 8,000 and 9,000 now appear every winter, comprising between half and three-quarters of the world population. However, in the 1950s, the annual count varied between about 10,500 and 14,500 and drainage is thought to have been an important factor contributing to the decline. There is some evidence for this from site surveys undertaken in the Corrib catchment area in the 1960s and 70s by Ruttledge and Ogilvie (28). Their observations show that a number of white fronted goose haunts were either impoverished or destroyed as a result of arterial and field drainage in the locality.

The Clare and Cregg sub-catchments were the object of an arterial scheme in 1954-64 and a second scheme covered the neighbouring Headford area in 1967-73. These schemes increased the discharge capacity of the Clare and Corrib rivers and the incidence of annual winter flooding was reduced in the catchment by lowering the water table. Between them the two schemes were intended to benefit almost 27,000 hectares of agricultural land, although the precise area of improvement was probably rather less in reality. As well as improving farm land, the arterial works were intended to permit the drainage of about 10,000 hectares of bog, a habitat for white-fronted geese, curlew, snipe, grouse and other birds. However, the geese were particularly affected by the disappearance or severe diminution of many former turloughs, with which the area was well endowed. Ruttledge and Ogilvie identified seven haunts which were either destroyed or severely damaged. The varied vegetation of these temporary lakes, a habitat unique to Ireland, was replaced by ordinary grasses, impoverishing the winter feeding grounds of migrants as well as local species. Drainage further affected bird life in the catchment by eliminating callows, reducing the water level in local lakes and canalising watercourses.

The Irish headquarters of the white-fronted geese is the Wexford Slobs, a mixture of estuarine, coastal and agricultural habitats, part of which is a sanctuary. Even here there is some risk from the development of agriculture, while haunts elsewhere in the country have been described as "severely threatened by drainage, turf exploitation, afforestation and disturbance" (29).

The lowering of lakes, destruction of callows and, less frequently, elimination of turloughs are common features of arterial drainage in the west. Some of the other catchments already drained may not have been as valuable for wildlife as the Corrib/Clare, but the general pattern of habitat change does not appear untypical. Indeed, examination of the current arterial drainage scheme in the neighbouring Corrib/Mask/Robe catchment reveals that the threat to wetland birds remains very extensive despite the increased awareness of wildlife habitat in the OPW and the environmental stipulation attached to EC funded schemes, such as this.

The Corrib/Mask/Robe scheme is intended to benefit 7,690 hectares of agricultural land and a further 2,000 hectares of peatland, together comprising about 11 per cent of the total catchment. It is designed to give farm land immunity from the three year flood, most channels will be broadened and deepened and the water table will fall by about 0.75 metres. The scheme, which was started in 1980, has been criticised by Tony Whilde, author of the private 1981-82 survey of Irish Wetlands already alluded to. In a previous survey undertaken in 1974 he identi- fied 53 different sites used by wildfowl in the catchment. These are a mixture of lakes, ponds, bogs, reed beds, pasture, rough grazing and streams, all but 10 of which will be affected by the scheme. He categorised 22 of these as vital to the needs of wildfowl in the catchment and a further 23 as important and likely to be damaged by the proposed scheme. In assessing these sites, the OPW regarded 13 as vital to the success of the scheme, 14 as in compromise situations and the remainder as either peri- pheral or not expected to be affected by the proposals.

Although compromise appears possible from this initial des- cription, it has not emerged in practice. The same sites appear crucial, both for wildfowl and for drainage. Half the "vital" sites for wildfowl will be seriously affected by the scheme and nine of the twelve highest priority sites. All of these nine sites occupy critical points in the catchment and to protect them would necessitate their removal from the scheme, greatly impairing its effectiveness.

In evaluating the scheme the OPW conceded that there would be "substantial damage to wildfowl habitats by elimination of wetlands", but nonetheless concluded that "the case in favour of preserving wildfowl habitats does not appear to be sufficiently strong to recommend the omission of all or even part of the proposed scheme". This judgement perhaps reflects the relative lack of political pressure for conservation and the absence of any sites of international importance in the catchment. The scheme is now proceeding as originally planned and most of the important wetlands wll disappear or be damaged. The OPW asses- sment recommended a number of measures to reduce the deleterious effects of drainage, for example the avoidance of excessive disturbance at breeding times, but these constitute good practice rather than any modification of the basic design (30).

Detailed assessments of this kind are not available for other EC supported arterial schemes, but Whilde has made some general comments applying particularly to wildfowl. The minor scheme on the Bonet river in counties Leitrim and Sligo is not expected to affect any ornithologically important wetlands. The much larger Boyle scheme, also in the north west, is not expected to have a major impact either, provided that the water level in the internationally important site at Lough Gara is not affected. However, the now completed scheme on the river Boyne in the east has severely impoverished fisheries, and led to serious damage to Raheenmore Bog.

For waterbirds, the picture is more serious on the proposed cross-border schemes, neither of which have yet been started. The Finn-Lackey scheme is expected to benefit more than 5,000 hectares in the south, partly by increasing the depth of all drains by a metre. This would cause water levels in 30 to 40 lakes to fall by a similar amount, reducing their area and affecting their ecology; the consequences of this have yet to be established. Similarly, there is concern about the impact of the more imminent Blackwater scheme, affecting about 2,370 hectares south of the border, including bogs, lakes and callows and including 13 sites of local importance for wildfowl (31).

Mention should also be made of one other catchment where drainage plans are being considered. This is the Dunkellin River catchment in the southern part of Galway, an area of slightly less than 40,000 hectares overlying carboniferous limestone. On the lower reaches of the river lies Rahasane Turlough, one of the last turloughs in the country and an internationally important wintering ground for teal, wigeon, shoveler, whooper and Bewick's swans and Greenland white-fronted geese. The water level in the turlough varies considerably. Much of it is dry in the summer months, when it is used for grazing, while in the winter it may reach a depth of three or four metres at times when the Dunkellin River overflows.

Plans for a drainage scheme are still under discussion, but to provide relief from winter flooding upstream it will probably be necessary to widen and deepen the river. Unless special measures are taken, this is likely to destroy the turlough and possibly threaten the Clarinbridge Oyster Fishery which lies in the river estuary. Studies of the effects of drainage were under way at the end of 1983 (32).

The much discussed possibility of draining the Shannon catchment is undoubtedly the largest and most significant of all the proposed arterial drainage schemes. Seasonal flooding in some reaches of the river considerably depresses the value of extensive areas of farmland and has given rise to demands for drainage stretching back for more than a century. An effective scheme for the Shannon would entail very substantial works, including the diversion of tributaries, the creation of greater storage capacity, main channel dredging and embankment construction, the improvement of tributaries and so on. The Shannon and its tributaries constitute the most important wetland in Ireland, containing five sites of international importance, two of national importance and at least 100 subsidiary sites with others yet to

74

be documented (33).

In the absence of effective compensatory measures, this network would be badly damaged by a major drainage programme and the extensive field drainage which would follow from it. In the past, work has been inhibited by the cost of a full scheme and the somewhat uncertain returns. The "Summer Relief Scheme", a variant proposed in more than one recent report, was expected to cost IR£45 million in 1976 and the price will have risen substantially since. The fate of the catchment is still to be decided, since the most recent of a series of inquiries, the IR£1 million Shannon Drainage Feasibility Study, has yet to be completed. ERDF, which is meeting half the cost of this study will expect some assessment of the environmental impact of any scheme proposed, but it is not yet clear how this will be done.

A full environmental impact study for the Shannon would include some analysis of the ecological functions of the wetlands to be altered. Information on the contribution of wetlands to waste assimilation, the attenuation of flooding, the provision of nutrients to coastal fisheries, etc., is relatively scarce in Ireland, although potentially valuable, especially where drainage is being considered. According to one authority, single purpose arterial schemes can cause difficulties for water supplies where the level of natural lakes is altered, reducing the capacity available for supplementing drought flows and thus the volume available for abstraction (34). The other implications of drainage for water supplies are considered less important and there does not seem to be great concern about reductions in the waste assimilation capacity of rivers after drainage (35).

One aspect of agricultural drainage which is generally considered a benefit in Ireland is the effect on neighbouring peatlands, which may be difficult to exploit without a lowering of the water table and provision of new drainage channels. Bogs must be drained before they are suitable for turf cutting, an activity of considerable economic importance, particularly in the Midlands and parts of the west. Eighty thousand hectares of bogland have been drained and used for peat extraction since 1946. Bord Na Mona, the national peat exploitation undertaking is expected to cut around 400 hectares a year for future exploitation (36). The Board receives substantial loans from the European Investment Bank. Peat currently provides about 15 per cent of Ireland's energy requirements and the industry is a significant source of rural employment.

Turf cutting by the Bord and by private individuals working on a small scale has undoubtedly been assisted by arterial drainage. Between them, the major schemes listed in Table 3.1 were expected to "benefit" just over 55,000 hectares of peatlands of different kinds. In the cost-benefit analysis which now proceeds the initiation of a major scheme the drainage of peatlands is counted as a secondary benefit. However, while drainage is clearly a benefit, both to the Bord Na Mona and to many individual peat cutters for whom the bogs are an important res-

ource, there is growing concern about the environmental consequences of continued turf exploitation. The bogs adjoining
wetlands are often used by geese and other wildfowl which are
usually driven away when the turf has been cut. Exploitation not
only affects habitats but can also lead to the pollution of lakes
and water courses by turf silt, for example, in Lough Ree and the
river Suck (37). Furthermore, Ireland's extensive heritage of
bog and fenland is now itself under serious threat.

In March 1983 the European Parliament passed a resolution
urging protective measures for certain Irish bogs. In a pre-
ceeding report drawn up on behalf of the Committee on the Environment, Public Health and Consumer Protection, it was pointed out
that types of bog once common throughout north-west Europe are
now rare outside Ireland. In particular, there remain more than
half a million hectares of different sorts of blanket bog, which
otherwise can be found only in western Scotland. However, only
about 5 per cent of Irish bogs have survived in their original
state and the report notes that "Reputable scientists and conservationists calculate that the unique ecosystems of the Irish bogs
will vanish completely in the next five years unless effective
preventive measures are taken very soon" (38).

Attached to the report is a list of 40 bogs of various
types, the conservation of which is deemed to be "absolutely
essential" by the National Peatlands Preservation Committee. At
least two of the raised bogs on this list are vulnerable to the
drainage of surrounding wetlands. Raheenmore raised bog in
County Offaly, considered of international scientific importance,
was handed over to the Forest and Wildlife Service as a nature
reserve in 1981. However, administrative caution delayed its
acceptance until 1983 by which time it had already been damaged
as a result of the Boyne arterial scheme and subsequent field
drainage. The bog is now drying out and its integrity cannot be
maintained unless it is isolated from the farm drainage channels
on its edges (39). Recent reports suggest that three further
bogs on the list proposed for conservation have subsequently been
damaged or destroyed. Carbury Bog is to be exploited for turf,
Clan Bog has been damaged by Bord na Mona and Bellacorrick Bog
damaged by the Forest and Wildlife Service (40). In this and
many other cases the conservation of bogs and other wetlands must
be considered together and there is a continuing need to investigate the combined effects of drainage and turf exploitation.

The European Parliament's resolution on the protection of
Irish bogs, which was designed to provide Community support for
the efforts of the newly formed National Peatlands Preservation
Committee, is the latest of a series of initiatives by the
Parliament. A number of MEPs were aware that the Community's
financial support for drainage in Ireland could have detrimental
consequences for the environment and that the impetus behind
conservation in Ireland was relatively weak. They asked questions in the European Parliament and responded to requests for
support from Irish conservation groups.

Partly as a result of this an "environmental clause" was inserted in Regulation 1820/80 for the stimulation of agricultural development in the less favoured areas of the west of Ireland. Article 2/D of this Regulation states that the programme should include "an assurance that the actions undertaken are compatible with the protection of the environment". In the following year, Regulation 2195/81, extending the original Western Drainage Programme, was held up in the European Parliament until it had been reviewed by the Environment Committee and a new clause added. This requires the drainage programme to be "such as to provide an assurance that the measures envisaged are compatible with the protection of the environment". None of these initiatives have received much support from Irish MEPs, most of whom ally themselves to what appear to be farming interests and are suspicious of intervention by foreign politicians.

It is too early to say whether the "environmental clauses" have been of much service for wetland conservation. They do seem to have added to pressure on the Irish government to make a more careful assessment of the impact of drainage and to consider more active conservation measures. The addition of an "environmental clause" to Regulation 2195/81, extending the Western Drainage Scheme, apparently resulted in a series of exchanges between the Commission and the Irish government. The Commission tried to make the requirements of the clause more specific by listing a number of points on which they would need to be satisfied before they could approve the drainage programme from an environmental point of view. These points included an environmental impact assessment of the programme, a description of the criteria to be used to identify projects likely to have a significant effect on the environment, and a description of the administrative procedure for applying these criteria and making impact assessments (41). The Commission also wished to be informed of arrangements for public participation and consultation with voluntary environmental bodies.

When the Irish authorities came to submit the drainage programme for funding, the environmental provisions were regarded as inadequate by the Commission, which asked for more specific information (42). They suggested that the effects of the programme should be assessed more thoroughly using the kind of procedure set out in Annex 3 of the draft EC Directive on environmental impact assessment (OJ No C169 9.7.1980). Particular attention was requested for the effects on areas of high scientific interest, including wetlands of national or international importance. They also asked for a better description of the procedures and guidelines which would be used for assessing environmental impacts and requested comments on the programme from both statutory and voluntary bodies. The request for the views of voluntary environmental organisations was later dropped, but the Irish authorities were required to reply to the other points. The precise nature of their response has not been reported (43).

This kind of pressure from the Community has led to

increased efforts to gather base-line data on Irish wetlands, to more regular contact between drainage engineers and officials from the Forest and Wildlife Service and to more active consideration of the effects of arterial schemes. The OPW has undertaken cost-benefit analysis on four catchments, the Maigue, the Corrib-Mask, the Boyle and the Bonet and it is only on those schemes, all receiving some kind of financial support from ·the EC, that any kind of environmental impact assessment has been attempted. These assessments have not been very detailed, for example, wildlife was given scant attention in the Maigue scheme, but the trend is towards more thorough investigations backed up by better data. When the EC-funded study of the environmental impacts of an arterial drainage scheme in County Mayo is completed and published it should provide a useful methodology for assessing future schemes - if the resources are available to utilise it.

Valuable as they are, the influence of these Community initiatives should not be exaggerated. The "environmental clauses" are couched in extremely vague terms and to operate as they were intended, they need to be reinforced by more specific requirements and an adequate system both for anticipating the impact of schemes in advance and for monitoring the results in practice. While such crucial issues remain a matter of negotiation between the Irish government and the Commission's Environmental Directorate much of the force of the clauses is likely to be lost.

Formally, conservation may appear to receive fuller consideration, but in practice it may remain a low priority, particularly for agricultural authorities working within well established engineering traditions. Past attempts to accommodate conservation requirements have frequently been unsatisfactory as in the Corrib/Mask/Robe catchment where the OPW did make some concessions but most of them consisted of excluding from the scheme wetlands where the economic returns on drainage were expected to be low anyway. The stipulation of precise procedures and criteria by the Commission would greatly strengthen the environmental clauses and allow their results to be monitored. The Commission appears to be pursuing this approach, but implementation will of course remain in the hands of the Irish authorities. It is uncertain how vigorously they will apply any agreed conservation measures and regrettable that their efforts are subject to rather scant public scrutiny. Indeed, without the growth of a more powerful conservation lobby in Ireland, the political strength of agricultural interests will continue to militate against any radical changes in drainage techniques.

This imbalance is equally apparent in both Irish and Community institutions. Those responsible for drainage and agriculture are conspicuously powerful and relatively unfamiliar with conservation. Environmental institutions, on the other hand, are smaller and less influential. Even the Commission's Environment Directorate has only a fraction of the staff, influence and budget of the Agricultural Directorate and is in a correspondingly weak position when negotiating with the Irish Government. It does not get strong support either from Irish MEPs or from public opinion.

Even when Community law does extend to the environment, it is not necessarily applied with great urgency or conviction. Suitable legislation to implement the EC Bird Directive has been adopted in Ireland, but by early 1983 its efficacy was in doubt since the government had not informed the Commission which sites would receive "special protection" in conformity with the Directive or which would be designated as wetlands of international importance. Article 2 of the Directive requires Member States to "take the requisite measures" to maintain the population of each wild bird species at a level described broadly in the Article. For certain species, particularly the Greenland white-fronted goose, the population appears to be below the specified level. However, no habitat protection measures have been taken in compliance with this Article, except for the negotiation of management agreements at a single site at Wexford Slobs. Under Article 3, Member States are required to take the requisite measures to preserve habitat of sufficient area and diversity for all wild birds. This has some relevance in Ireland, since several wetland species, such as gadwall and black-necked grebe are threatened by habitat reduction. Steps to protect wetland habitats have been largely absent, however, with some limited exceptions, such as the exclusion of a few sites from arterial drainage schemes.

This is not due to a lack of legal provisions. Under the 1976 Wildlife Act the government can create nature reserves, acquire land or manage state property for wildlife conservation purposes, recognise private reserves of an adequate standard, negotiate management agreements with private landowners and designate appropriate areas as refuges for selected species of fauna and flora. Furthermore, under the 1963 Local Government (Planning and Development) Act, orders can be made to conserve particular areas. This array of legal machinery has been little used for habitat protection, because of lack of political pressure, failure to provide adequate funds and an unwillingness to interfere with agricultural projects. It is symptomatic that agricultural activities are specifically exempted from several of the requirements imposed on other land users under the 1976 Act. Very few management agreements have been arranged and the status of nature reserves has been granted almost exclusively to deciduous woods.

Unless the Irish government displays much greater determination in conserving wetlands, the prospect of further arterial drainage work, particularly in the Shannon catchment, can only be interpreted as a major threat to the environment. It is not difficult to see why the author of the recent private survey of wetlands comments that "...if arterial drainage and land reclamation are allowed to continue at the pace witnessed since 1945 it will be possible to envisage the almost total demise, as waterbird wetlands, of many of Ireland's remaining freshwater wetlands within the foreseeable future" (44).

Conclusions and Impact of the Common Agricultural Policy

Agricultural drainage has been an important element of public works programmes in Ireland for 140 years. The prevalence of wet and periodically flooded soils gives drainage a special significance greatly reinforced by agriculture's central position in the Irish economy. Rural poverty remains widespread, particularly in the west and the small scale and limited resources of many Irish farms makes it difficult for families to earn a reasonable income. Relatively remote from the prosperous centre of the European market, Irish farmers are understandably determined to improve their land and increase their output by all the means at their disposal. In these circumstances drainage may seem a logical and highly desirable form of investment and the loss of bog, turloughs, and wildlife may seem a small price to pay.

Since drainage is seen as a national priority, it is perhaps not surprising that it is supported so generously by the state. For more than 30 years arterial drainage has been funded entirely by the exchequer and maintenance has also been the responsibility of the public purse. Farmers have had to bear some of the costs of field drainage but the terms have not been onerous. Indeed, they have been more attractive than for many other forms of capital grant. Drainage has been a highly favoured investment. On the basis of secure finance and strong institutions, drainage has progressed steadily and on an impressive scale. About a fifth of Ireland's farm land has been drained since 1949 and a sizeable number of catchments have been the subject of comprehensive arterial schemes.

There is little doubt that Ireland's membership of the EC has proved a stimulus to agricultural drainage and opened up a substantial new form of finance. State capital expenditure on new arterial schemes underwent a constant decline between the mid 1960s and mid 1970s and revived sharply within a few years of Ireland's accession. Expenditure on field drainage also recovered from a fall and by 1980 had reached a new peak. This turn about in public expenditure coincided with the boom in Irish agriculture brought on by membership of the Community. Higher prices, incomes and land values encouraged a rash of new investments, amongst which was new and improved drainage. At the new prices for milk, beef and barley the drainage of marshy, previously neglected fields became worth contemplating for the first time. This wave of private investment in agriculture has now passed, but state investment continues to be buttressed by a series of Community schemes, providing both direct grants and low cost finance. Initially, these schemes covered a small proportion of the cost of drainage works but Community grants rose sharply under the Western Drainage Scheme and are unlikely to fall until after it is completed.

Membership of the Community had a much more immediate impact on agriculture in Ireland than in most other countries because it brought both a sharp rise in prices and a major change in market conditions at the same time. Milk production from the Irish dairy herd grew 4.5 per cent a year between 1973 and 1980, much faster than anywhere else in the Community. However, after the boom ended at the end of the decade and farm incomes plummeted, the disadvantages of Community membership became more apparent. The growth of Irish agriculture is now constrained, not only by inflation, high interest rates and other domestic problems but also by European efforts to cut back milk production, tighten budgets and balance political interests.

On both geographical and economic grounds, Ireland has a strong case for special assistance under the CAP and it is not surprising that some of the aid has been earmarked specially for infrastructure projects, which are usually uncontroversial and may otherwise be difficult to finance. As recipients of EC support, drainage projects have the further advantages that they are a well-established form of public works and regional aid in Ireland, are well organised and administered by competent official bodies, are popular with farmers and are easily able to absorb large sums of money. By targeting a major portion of Community schemes at the west of Ireland, it is possible to reach some of the poorest farmers in an area where there is little alternative employment and the soils are proverbially wet. The logic of this argument must seem particularly attractive in Brussels, and it is quite clear that Community aid has shifted the balance of the Irish drainage programme to the west.

In this Chapter we have looked at some of the environmental aspects of the drainage programme and despite a serious shortage of data found evidence that damage to wetlands is widespread and the machinery for conservation severely under-utilised. Many of Ireland's finest freshwater wetlands are in the north west, where drainage efforts are being increasingly concentrated and with a diminishing area of habitat and growing threats to wetland species, the case for conservation can only get stronger. The government's response to date has been to introduce new legislation but to withhold the financial resources and political energy required to strengthen conservation and modify the drainage programme. The Commission has attempted to exert some countervailing pressure on behalf of the environment, but ultimately such issues must be resolved internally, in the light of a fresh look at Ireland's own interests.

It is almost unpatriotic to question the value of the OPW work but despite this a number of independent voices in Ireland have recently called for a reappraisal of the drainage programme on both environmental and economic grounds. As elsewhere, there is a need to base schemes on a more rigorous and far-reaching evaluation of costs and benefits, taking environmental impacts into account as much as possible. There is also a strong case for reviewing alternative forms of aid for farmers, such as grants for new buildings, silage making, forestry and low ground pressure vehicles. This is particularly relevant in the west where drainage costs are high and the benefits most doubtful. At present it is unclear whether there are more appropriate and cost-effective ways of assisting farmers in the west and the very question seems to be obscured by the momentum of the drainage programme. The programme should not be elevated above criticism simply because it has become an established method of directing aid towards farming families in an area of need.

A clearer analysis and more diverse forms of aid would not dissolve the conflicts between agricultural improvement and environmental protection, but it would provide local people with a better foundation for choosing their own balance. Although the beauty and richness of the natural environment is much appreciated, not least by foreign tourists, it has provided little in the way of income and economic security to the people of the west. In a sense their environment may be less valuable to them than it is to the people of Europe as a whole and if so there may be a role for Community assistance in reducing the discrepancy. Merely continuing to finance drainage is a much easier option for the EC but, by reinforcing the dominance of a single form of agricultural improvement, the Community may be helping to forestall the changes which are so evidently required.

References

1. An Foras Forbartha, 1981, Areas of Scientific Interest in Ireland, Dublin
2. Scott, D. A., 1980, A Preliminary Inventory of Wetlands of International Importance for Wildfowl in West Europe and North West Africa, IWRB, Slimbridge, Glos, UK
3. Bruton, R., and Convery, F. J., 1982, Land Drainage Policy in Ireland, Economic and Social Research Institute, Policy Research Series No 4, Dublin
4. Ibid
5. Ibid
6. Commission of the European Economic Communities, 1983, The Agricultural Situation in the Community: 1982 Report, Brussels
7. Bruton and Convery 1982, op. cit.
8. Ibid
9. Maigue Drainage Scheme Cost Benefit Analysis, 1975, The Stationery Office, Dublin
10. Bruton and Convery 1982, op. cit.
11. Ibid
12. Official Journal, 6th December 1982
13. Bruton and Convery 1982, op. cit.
14. Arkleton Trust, 1982, Schemes of Assistance to Farmers in Less Favoured Areas of the EEC, Langholm, Scotland
15. Survey Team 1968 Land Project Survey: Report, Mimeo, Department of Finance, Dublin
16. Scott, 1980, op. cit. and Whilde, A., personal communication
17. Whilde, A., 1982, Irish Wetlands Survey 1981-82, FACE/NARGC, Dublin
18. Forest and Wildlife Service, 1974, Report on Wetlands of

International and National Importance in the Republic of Ireland, Dublin

19. See Reynolds, J., 1984, "Vanishing Irish Bogs", World Wildlife News, Spring 1984
20. Scott, 1980, op. cit and Whilde, 1982, op. cit.
21. Whilde, 1982, op. cit.
22. Whilde, A., personal communication
23. Forest and Wildlife Service, 1974, op. cit.
24. Kelly, P., 1983, personal communication
25. Kelly, P., 1980, "Resources down the Drain", Taisce Journal, Spring 1980, Dublin
26. Merne, O. J., 1980, Impact of Drainage on Wildlife, paper for workshop on Impact of Drainage in Ireland, National Board for Science and Technology, November 1980, Dublin
27. Ibid
28. Ruttledge, R. F. and Ogilvie, M. A., 1979, "The Past and Current Status of the Greenland White-Fronted Goose in Ireland and Britain", Irish Birds, Vol 1, No 3, 293-363
29. Whilde, 1982, op. cit.
30. Ibid
31. Ibid
32. Whilde, A., personal communication
33. Whilde, 1982, op. cit.
34. McCumiskey, L. M., 1980, A Perspective on the Impacts of Arterial Drainage on Water Resources, paper for workshop on Impacts of Drainage in Ireland, National Board for Science and Technology, November 1980, Dublin
35. Ibid
36. European Parliament, 1983, Report drawn up on behalf of the Committee on the Environment, Public Health and Consumer Protection on the Protection of the Irish Bogs. Rapporteur: Mr M. Mertens, Working Document 1-1188/82
37. Whilde, 1982, op. cit.
38. European Parliament, 1983, op. cit.
39. Reynolds, 1984, op. cit.
40. Question asked in the European Parliament by Mr Hemmo Muntingh, Official Journal, 22.2.84
41. Kelly, P., 1982, Environmental Review in Agricultural Development Projects, European Environment Bureau, Brussels
42. Ibid
43. Ibid
44. Whilde, 1982, op. cit.

CHAPTER 4 : THE NETHERLANDS

Introduction

Quite unlike the other countries considered here, the nation's very survival depends on the successful management of water. Water plays a crucial part in almost all aspects of life in the Netherlands.

Once a marshy, thickly wooded delta formed by the rivers Rhine, Meuse, Ems and Scheldt, the Netherlands is now the most densely populated country in Europe. Nearly all the woodland has gone and most of the land area is devoted to intensive modern agriculture and horticulture. In order to utilise the rich soils and control the predations of the sea and the threat of river flooding the Dutch have constructed a sophisticated network of dykes, canals, dams, pumping stations and drainage works unequalled in the world. This catena of waterways allows a highly urbanised society to live securely in an otherwise precarious environment. About a quarter of the country lies below mean sea level and perhaps half of it would be subject to flooding by the sea or rivers if it were not for the dams, dykes, pumps and defences constructed over several centuries.

Most of the country is flat, interrupted only by small. hilly areas in the south and east. The lowest lying land stretches along the western side of the country, from Zeeland in the south up to Groningen in the north and includes substantial areas of polder, mainly reclaimed areas in which the water level is artificially controlled. The mild temperate climate is favourable to agriculture and the soils, which are remarkably varied, include rich alluvial clays and fertile peat soil highly suitable for horticulture. These natural advantages have been efficiently exploited by Dutch farmers who are highly skilled, and heavily capitalised. They make full use of modern technology and are supported by local co-operatives, well organised marketing arrangements and highly developed forms of state assistance. Production is not only intensive, but is concentrated on some of the most valuable produce, including flowers, vegetables, sugar beet and milk. This helps to explain why a country with only 3.5 per cent of the Community's agricultural land produces almost 12 per cent of the total output, when measured by value (1).

About a third of the agricultural area is devoted to arable farming with wheat, potatoes, sugar beet and fodder maize as the main crops. Although yields are some of the highest in Europe, the arable area has shrunk considerably over the last three decades, making way for horticulture and grassland. Flowers, bulbs and vegetables are perhaps the best known Dutch products but milk, meat and eggs are the most important economically and the country is notable for specialising in factory farming techniques and highly intensive dairying. Almost 60 per cent of the agricultural area is grassland, grazed predominantly by dairy cattle which also consume considerable quantities of concentrated foods and boast the highest milk yields in Europe. Farmers with dairy cattle can make a living from a relatively small area of grassland, often only about 20 hectares, but to do so they must aim for maximum yields and careful management of the water level.

Intensification has been achieved without the creation of large farms of the kind prevalent in East Anglia where conditions are somewhat similar. The average farm is smaller than in France or Ireland and nearly half the total number are less than 10 hectares. Nevertheless, amalgamation and mechanisation are taking place at a similar pace to elsewhere in Europe and farm employment fell by about a quarter during the 1970s. Farming now accounts for less than 5 per cent of total employment, but output has been rising rapidly and the agricultural sector is still of crucial importance to the economy, contributing nearly a quarter of total exports. Trade is the cornerstone of national prosperity and Dutch farmers are ideally placed at the hub of the north west European market. With the aid of a sophisticated marketing, trading and processing industry, their produce is distributed throughout the EEC and beyond its borders.

Although marshland has been reclaimed, peat dug out and water levels artificially reduced over large areas of the Netherlands, the country still contains a number of important wetlands; 49 wetlands of international importance for birds have been identified in a recent survey and some of these extend over a considerable area (2). Amongst these is the Waddensee, "undoubtedly the most important single wetland in western Europe" (3). The Waddensee is a stretch of shallow coastal water including a chain of islands extending from Texel in the Netherlands to Denmark, a network of ecosystems particularly valuable for not yet being extensively developed. It contains a variety of habitats including dunes, lagoons, mudflats, saltmarsh and wet grassland. In the summer the area may contain over 3 million birds and 50 species of ducks, geese, waders, gulls and terns depend on the area for at least part of the year (4).

A further concentration of coastal wetlands can be found in the delta area of Zeeland, including islands, mudflats and saltmarsh and a number of freshwater lakes created by sealing off the sea. In the centre of the country is the IJsselmeer, formerly a large salt water estuary, separated from the sea on the completion of the 30 kilometre barrier dam in 1932. Now a freshwater lake, the IJsselmeer itself is an important area for birds and on its boundaries are a number of other significant sites, such as reed beds still surviving on the shoreline of the reclaimed polders. Other wetlands include streams, lakes and river valleys and several areas of wet meadow and agricultural land where the water table is still high enough to support a range of interesting fauna and flora.

Agricultural Drainage

The hydrology of most parts of the Netherlands has been greatly affected by man. Water management activities are exceptionally extensive and are designed to meet a number of purposes including flood control, water supply, land drainage, waste disposal, and the provision of storage capacity. Flood control and land reclamation have been national preoccupations for many centuries and necessity has forced the construction of several large and sophisticated schemes. Land drainage has been an important part of these works along with the construction of dykes, weirs and canals. Indeed in the western part of the country, where much of the land is up to six metres below the level of the sea, and often below the level of rivers, canals and lakes, perpetual pumping is required to prevent gradual inundation. For this purpose, windmills were used from the early 15th century onwards, later to be supplemented by steam, diesel and electric pumps. Land drainage has thus been an integral part of national development and even today it can be difficult to isolate from other forms of land and water management. Careful control of the water level is vital throughout the lower parts of the country.

Amongst the four countries considered here, the Netherlands is somewhat untypical from the drainage point of view. This is not only because of the unusual historical development of the landscape and the special problems of water management, but because of the intensity of land use in a small, densely populated country. The need to accommodate growing demands for recreational facilities and nature conservation alongside established urban and agricultural requirements had led to increasingly sophisticated approaches to land use planning, involving some control over agricultural as well as urban development. Most drainage takes place as part of a land consolidation or integrated agricultural land development project rather than as an isolated activity.

Land is highly valued and expensive and agricultural concerns are primary in many integrated schemes. On the other hand, there is great interest in the environment and a relatively strong conservation lobby. Environmental bodies are now usually consulted before the commencement of major new projects and, although their arguments are not always accepted, they are able to inhibit the reclamation of important wetland sites, such as the Waddensee and the Markerwaard and to influence the design of most land development projects. Tree planting, the creation of fishing, riding, sailing or other recreational facilities and the establishment of conservation areas are now common features of development projects. Plans display meticulous attention to detail and are often based on lavish budgets.

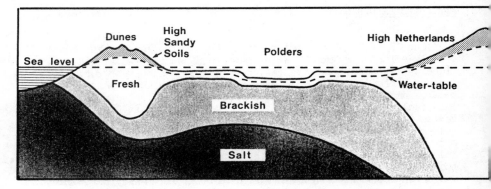

Fig.4: Cross-section of Netherlands water-table

　　　Figure 4 is a schematic cross-section of the topography and water table of the Netherlands stretching from the coastal sand dunes in the west to the higher sandy soils of the east. Although highly simplified, it helps to illustrate some of the basic hydrological conditions in the country. Dunes and artificial embankments along the coast provide protection against the sea. Inland low lying areas are continuously pumped out to achieve the desired water level which is usually higher in the summer than in the winter. Many polders are susceptible to the intrusion of salt water, partly originating from the sea or from the Rhine but also being forced upwards through the subsoil from the brackish groundwater underneath. The threat of salinity has been made worse by past drainage and reclamation efforts and by soil subsidence, especially in peat areas. In summer, water levels may have to be raised by admitting fresh water from the surrounding canals in order to control salinity and protect crops.

　　　Polders have been created in a number of different ways, starting in the 8th century AD when muddy flats of marine clay were reclaimed from the sea and tidal rivers with the aid of dykes and simple tide-operated sluices. Drainage occurred naturally at the ebb tide, and each new polder was separated from its predecessor by what had previously been a sea dyke. Once the reclaimed land settled, artificial drainage became necessary.

87

Somewhat later came a process of reclaiming peat soils, especially prevalent in north and south Holland and Utrecht. Drainage began by digging ditches along the edges of peat areas, which were often the most nutrient-rich, and working gradually towards the higher central parts, the oligotrophic dome of the blanket bogs. Natural drainage was gradually supplemented by the construction of dykes, allowing groundwater levels to be lowered and improving agricultural conditions, but leading to shrinkage and oxidation. Peat was cut for the growing cities of the Low Countries and after dredging became available around 1536 it was possible to exploit the peat deposits below the water level on a large scale (5). The large lakes which resulted in time became a threat to both settlements and agricultural land and polders were gradually extended across much of the south western portions of the country, reclaiming both natural and artificial lakes in the process. This period coincided with the large scale use of windmills which made it feasible to pump the water out of new polders and control the water level subsequently. Discharged water was often pumped into an encircling ring canal or into a local reservoir system (known as a "boezem"). These would be at a higher level than the polder, but often below sea level, so a further stage of pumping might be necessary in order to finally dispose of the water.

Largest of these polders is the Haarlemmermeer, near Amsterdam airport, an area of 18,000 hectares reclaimed in 1852. The ring canal is about 0.4 metres below the Amsterdam Data Point, to which drainage levels throughout the country are related, and the polder itself is 6 metres below the data point. Within the polder a number of areas where the peat was not cut over have been retained as recreational lakes and here the water level is 1.2 metres below the data point (6). One hundred million cubic metres of water a year have to be pumped out to maintain these levels.

The process of making new polders continued in the 20th century, mainly concentrated in the IJsselmeer. Here, large areas of agricultural land have been reclaimed by converting the estuary into a freshwater lake, shallow portions of which are then enclosed behind dykes on which are built pumping stations to extract the water. Drainage in the western part of the country is thus artificially controlled at a number of different levels, connected by a network of dykes, rivers, reservoirs and pumping stations. Levels vary between summer and winter and are determined by agricultural needs and the special requirements of recreation and conservation areas, modified by other considerations such as the costs of pumping in the winter and the threat of salinity in the summer months. Continued subsidence occurs in many areas, especially on peat soils, and the effects of lower groundwater in the dry months are counteracted by the extraction of river water, or irrigation, now used on a growing scale.

Natural drainage has played a much larger part in the development of the sandier soils in the east and south east regions. Here the land is higher, although by no means hilly. Only 2 per cent of the country is more than 50 metres above sea level. Arable crops were traditionally grown with little artificial drainage on land with a relatively low water table, while along streams and valley bottoms subject to flooding, the land was usually put down to grass. Drainage was by natural water courses, slightly modified, and farm ditches. High water levels were aimed for and deliberate flooding of valley meadows with silt-laden water was still practised in some places until the 1940s (7). Heathland, which covered a large part of the higher ground until earlier this century, was used for extensive sheep grazing and acted as an important reservoir releasing water slowly into surrounding grassland in the summer.

The development of modern agriculture has brought profound changes to drainage in both east and west. To make maximum use of fertilisers and increasingly heavy farm machinery, there has been a demand for lower water tables, on both arable and grassland. In the west this has meant more field drainage, deeper ditches, and faster water discharge. Ditches are often 80 cms beneath the soil surface and on clay land up to 150 cms lower. In the east lower water tables meant that the heathlands were no longer required as a reservoir and "they were subsequently extensively drained and turned into highly productive arable and grassland. Consequently high peak discharges became more frequent. As a result of this, extensive flooding occurred along the brooks which now became too small; consequently nearly all watercourses were straightened, widened and deepened. More or less natural and meandering rivulets and brooks are quite a rare phenomenon nowadays even in nature reserves" (8).

This highly abbreviated history indicates some of the ways in which drainage has developed, greatly modifying the natural environment in the process. Contemporary efforts are aimed mainly at improving flood defences, up-grading the already extensive main drainage system and further lowering water levels, by deepening ditches, installing new field drains, etc. Although the creation of new polders has not been abandoned, it is now less common and where new land is reclaimed it is likely to be used for urban or recreational purposes rather than for agriculture. Since 1961 land reclamation has been only from the sea or coastal lakes and the main focus of contemporary interest is the IJsselmeer, where four large polders have been created since the formation of the lake in 1932 when it was cut off from the sea by the Zuiderzee dyke. From the beginning it was intended to create a fifth polder in the south west corner of the lake, the Markerwaard, an area of about 40,000 hectares. This proposal has been under consideration for some years and has been vigorously opposed by environmentalists. The area is an internationally important wetland, especially valuable for fish and as a feeding ground for migrating birds. However, if it is eventually reclaimed it will probably be used partly for agriculture and partly for some form of urban development.

Some individual farmers install their own field drainage, but changes in water management more usually occur on a larger

scale, affecting a number of farms, the district round a village
or perhaps a whole polder. The agricultural area is sub-divided
into small parcels by interlacing water courses and these form
convenient units for drainage purposes.

Drainage work in the Netherlands most commonly takes place
as part of some kind of land or waterway development project.
This broad grouping includes some works which might be categorised as arterial drainage and others that are forms of
collective land improvement, usually involving field drainage.
The main types of works are:

- rural infrastructure improvement projects undertaken by
  local authorities, especially water boards. These have a
  variety of names, including "Polder District Works" and can
  be grouped together under the general title of "hydraulic
  and municipal works". These projects particularly affect
  arterial drainage, the improvement of dykes, rivers, bridges, pumping systems, locks, etc., and often include an
  element concerned with water supply or rural roads. Both
  rural and urban areas may benefit;

- private reallotment works. The redistribution of small
  parcels of land to create many more compact holdings, organised primarily by the farmers concerned with the aid of
  government subsidies. Many include an element of field
  enlargement and field drainage. Agreements for schemes
  covering about 3000 hectares were passed in 1981 (9);

- private land development works. Undertaken by private individuals or groups of farmers independently of local authority intervention, with or without subsidies;

- land consolidation schemes, a more comprehensive form of
  redevelopment and the main focus of this Chapter.

The most important form of agricultural land development in
the Netherlands is **ruilverkaveling**, most commonly translated as
"land consolidation". Consolidation schemes are similar to
remembrements in France, although they are often more comprehensive and more far-reaching in their effects. The object of land
consolidation is, in the words of an official Dutch publication,
"to provide optimal working conditions for farmers and market
gardeners" (10). In the past this meant the creation of larger
fields, the resiting of farmhouses, reallotment of land into
larger and more convenient parcels, improvements in field and
local arterial drainage, construction of new roads, etc.
Originally, many farm houses were built in villages which were
often sited on raised dykes for safety. Farm houses were frequently rather remote from the family's land which usually consisted of scattered plots which have become increasingly incon-
venient to work. In a consolidation scheme, the government buys
all the land in the area concerned, puts in new roads, drainage,
fencing, etc., and creates a smaller number of more compact
holdings, often equipped with new farm houses. The entire infra-

structure is altered, largely at public expense, and a new land-scape created. Environmental and recreational features are now usually incorporated into such schemes.

The area covered by a scheme varies considerably, but the average is 4,000 hectares. Most schemes involve considerable changes in water management, aimed at improving drainage, and providing adequate water supplies for the summer months, for example by irrigation and other measures to improve farming conditions. They may also include the creation of a new lake or wetland area and perhaps an improved domestic water supply. These works typically cover both arterial and field drainage operations, which are often undertaken at the same time.

Field drainage may also be undertaken by individual farmers quite independently of land improvement schemes, but most occurs in the polder areas, where conditions favour a collective approach. Land improvement schemes are generously subsidised whereas private field drainage no longer is, and the latter probably accounts for no more than a third of the total under-drainage installed in a year.

Land consolidation first began in 1924 and it has made particular progress in the west of the country, beginning mainly on clay soils and in arable areas, where farms tend to be larger. Schemes covering 811,400 hectares had been completed by the end of 1981 and others were still in progress over a very large area, around 550,000 hectares (11). The process of organising, plan-ning and undertaking schemes is a long and delicate one involving the total uprooting of some farmers and a general rearrangement of the landscape and community. The preparation phase may take eight or nine years and the average execution time is 13 years (12). This helps to explain why schemes covering a further 353,000 hectares were in the preparatory stage at the end of 1981 and beyond that applications had been submitted for an additional 573,000 hectares. Since the total agricultural area of the Netherlands is only a little over 2 million hectares, it can be seen that much of it either has been or is presently affected by a consolidation scheme. Indeed, some areas have been subject to more than one process of consolidation.

The foundation for the current programme is the Land Con-solidation Act of 1954, which clearly states that the object of **ruilverkaveling** is the improvement of agricultural structures. The leading official agency involved is the government Service for Land and Water Use, which is part of the Ministry of Agricul-ture. However a large number of other bodies participate in preparing schemes, and there is a strong emphasis on co-ordinated effort.

The change in emphasis towards a more integrated land deve-lopment approach has been enshrined in a series of recent policy changes bringing consolidation projects more firmly within the sphere of national planning policy. As part of this process, a national structural Outline Plan for Land Development was published in 1981. This plan has still not come into full force, but it does lay down certain principles for future land development projects.

The intention is that future land development projects, including consolidation schemes, will be largely confined to a specified area of about 700,000 hectares. In practice this is not likely to prove a major limitation on further developments as the area is a large one and most of the schemes currently being proposed lie within it. Furthermore, it is anticipated that some schemes outside this area will continue to be permitted, up to a ceiling of 2,000 hectares a year.

At the same time as the Outline Plan for Land Development appeared in 1981, two other Outline Plans were published covering Nature and Landscape Conservation and Outdoor Recreation respectively. All three are intended to be complementary and to "exert an equal influence on rural areas" (13). Although land consolidation is seen primarily as a tool for agricultural improvement, it is expected also to contribute to wider planning goals. These include the preservation of green belts around cities, the provision of better facilities for open air recreation, the enhancement of nature conservation and forest and landscape management, etc. Central agricultural goals are the reduction or removal of regional farm income disparities and the improvement of working conditions.

Drainage and other hydraulic works are likely to continue being a prominent feature of consolidation schemes. For example, the Plan indicates a total area of 529,000 hectares where there is thought to be considerable scope for increasing yields and the bearing capacity of soils (14). Most of these zones are either on peat in the west or clay in the north and the lowering of water tables is seen as a major method of utilising the soil's potential more fully. The new policy has in effect sanctioned a very considerable future drainage programme.

Recent policy has been to take in hand every year new consolidation projects embracing a total area of about 40,000 hectares and the Plan anticipates that this will continue. However, land development projects have been subject to increasingly tight budgetary pressure for some years and the new government which came to power in October 1982 has decided to reduce expenditure in this area. In consequence, fewer projects were begun in 1983 and the total area concerned fell to 36,000 hectares.

Although the Outline Plan has yet to be finalised, and precise levels of expenditure set, the general direction of land development policy has already emerged. The emphasis on integrated development is being strengthened. Many future schemes will tackle areas with very small parcels of land or other conditions which have deterred land consolidation efforts in the past. In these "difficult" areas, many of which are environmentally sensitive, development requires rather stronger powers than are available under the existing Land Consolidation Act and a new

Bill has been published by the government which is expected to become law in 1984. The new Act will give local planners greater control over development, including powers of compulsory purchase. This will allow them to impose significant changes in local land use and accordingly give greater priority to conservation if they wish. In principle this will be a powerful mechanism for integrated planning. However, it may also have the effect of bringing development and lower water tables to several hitherto undisturbed landscapes.

Within land consolidation schemes there are a number of different categories of investment, separated out for financial purposes. Three of these categories may involve drainage.

The first of these is "water management works", which are concerned with water supply and arterial drainage and may involve the construction of new waterways, the deepening of existing channels, new weirs, pumps, embankments, etc. These works are usually carried out by the local water boards, elected local authorities which control the water level in the drainage system and are responsible for the discharge and extraction of water from the smaller rivers and channels. These boards are the authorities concerned with all but the largest arterial drainage projects and are also responsible for the maintenance of water courses.

A second element in most schemes is the "restructuring of land parcels". The creation of larger fields often involves filling in the old ditches separating existing fields, levelling the land and installing a new system of field drainage. Small ponds and lakes may also be filled in and field drainage within the area improved to allow a general lowering of the water level. Up to 90 per cent of the area of open water may disappear in the course of this process, mainly because of the elimination of ditches. In some cases field drainage is designed to improve yields of grass or field crops, but often the water table is already sufficiently low to suit most crops during the growing season. In these circumstances the benefits of further drainage are mostly exploited in the spring and autumn, when a lower water table allows the use of farm machinery earlier in the year, leads to higher soil temperatures, a better response to early nitrogen applications, and possible improvements in soil structure and microbiological activity. Increased mechanisation has led farmers to attach much greater importance to the bearing capacity of their soils. The standards aimed at vary according to local conditions, but widely applied criteria at a discharge rate of 7 mm per day are that water tables should not rise above 0.3 metres below the surface for grassland, 0.5 metres for arable land and 0.7 metres for orchards and outdoor horticulture (15). To achieve this, water levels in the drainage ditches have to be substantially lower.

A third element in consolidation schemes is "reallotment works", the redistribution of land amongst different farms. Field drainage often occurs in the course of these works, although less frequently than in the reparcelling of land.

Investment of the three kinds which may involve drainage generally accounts for more than half the total cost of a consolidation scheme. Other major items of expenditure are the provision of public roads, the resettlement of farmhouses and improvements in landscape and recreation facilities. Each of these categories is subsidised by the government, but to different degrees, as explained later in this chapter.

The joint effect of land consolidation schemes and other drainage works has been a substantial lowering of water tables over much of the agricultural area. On peat soils, for example, particularly in the north it is common for schemes to reduce the water level from 40 cms to 70-100 cms below the soil surface (16). However, designs vary considerably and on peat soils in South Holland there are several projects where a much more modest sinking of the water table is planned. Lower water levels are relatively expensive to achieve and are not always popular with farmers. On peat soils excessive drainage can lead to oxidation and high levels of acidity. The shrinkage which follows drainage can result in an uneven field surface, and instability in the banks of ditches. As the water levels fall in the ditches, farmers are obliged to meet the additional costs of fencing in animals and installing water pumps and the wooden foundations of old farmhouses may become rotten. In peat areas where holdings are small and old farm houses are common, as in parts of South Holland province, farmers and conservationists may find common ground in their opposition to government drainage proposals, particularly where their cost is high and the benefits are uncertain. In at least one case they have joined forces to make an independent assessment of the impact and purported agricultural advantages of lowering the water level (17).

Despite these reservations, the pursuit of lower water tables remains a central feature of many land improvement schemes and a keystone of the highly intensive forms of farming practised in the Netherlands. Drainage techniques have been developed for all soil types, including the heavy river clays which until recently had presented engineers with considerable difficulties because of their vulnerability to poaching in wet conditions and tendency to shrink and develop large cracks in the driest periods. The installation of plastic pipe drainage a metre or more below the field surface is now widely practised on these soils even though it may cause cracking and reduced yields in the summer, sometimes countered by irrigation to maintain grass growth. The process of field drainage has been taken much further in the Netherlands than in most other parts of the Community and the state has actively supported high levels of investment and continued technical advance. All arable land and most pasture has been subjected to drainage, often more completely than in similar areas in East Anglia, for example.

The impact of a modern consolidation schemes can be seen from "Bommelerwaard West", a block of around 4,200 hectares along the Waal river, one of the major branches of the Rhine. Most of the land was in agricultural use when the scheme started in the late 1960s, about half used for horticulture and fruit growing and the remainder heavy clay down to pasture. The number of farms was greatly reduced as a result of the scheme and horticulture was partly regrouped into three "centres", each with 30 holdings and a substantial area of glass. Forty-four kilometres of new road were built, dykes reinforced, slums cleared, new houses provided, the village extended, and a substantial number of trees and shrubs planted. A riding school was built and a water course widened and supplemented with new ponds in order to create 16 hectares of fishing grounds. Arterial works were a major feature of the scheme. Ninety-four kilometres of main drainage canals were excavated or improved, 32 weirs and three boosters constructed, all involving the movement of 350,000 cubic metres of earth. The reparcelling works entailed the levelling, draining and resowing of 1,000 hectares of pasture, while on the horticultural land more than half the existing ditches were filled in and replaced by 125 kilometres of new or improved ones (18).

Field drainage is achieved by a mixture of open ditches and subsurface tiles and pipes. Ditches are used on peat or other deep pervious soils or where a shallow groundwater is required. Traditionally it was common for the land to be divided into long extremely narrow strips, separated by ditches or hedges. However, larger fields and modern methods of cultivation require a greater spacing between ditches and this is only compatible with a low water table on the most freely draining soils. On heavier soils, and especially marine clays, under-drainage is required, particularly when field size is being increased. For this reason, under-drainage is most common in polders adjacent to the sea and the west of the country is likely to continue to be the most intense area of activity in future.

The existing area of subsurface drainage is thought to be about 500,000 hectares or 22 per cent of the agricultural area (19). About half this area does not meet modern standards and is expected to be upgraded in future, added to which there are plans to continue installing new drainage. The combined target for new and improved schemes is around 500,000 hectares. In sharp contrast to France, the rate of new drain construction has been remarkably steady over the last two decades, consistently around 25,000 hectares a year. The most dramatic change has been a technical one. Clay tiles, which were used exclusively until 1960, have now been almost wholly replaced by corrugated plastic pipes. Smooth plastic pipes, which enjoyed a brief vogue in the 1960s, are now no longer used either. Installation of these pipes is undertaken by 40 private contractors, who between them own 80 machines on average capable of laying between three and five kilometres a day (20). Average costs were slightly over US $1 per metre at the beginning of the 1980s, suggesting a cost per hectare of around $800, not untypical of other countries at the time.

Prior to the recession beginning in 1973 land development projects were generously funded, but over the last decade costs have been more tightly controlled and government expenditure has fallen sharply in real terms. In the early 1970s the average government contribution was around 8,000 Dutch guilders (Hfl) per hectare (in 1981 prices), falling to around 6,500 guilders in the middle part of the decade and an average of Hfl 4,500-5,500 in 1981 (21). In 1970 land development absorbed around 1.2 per cent of the total government budget, but this had declined to 0.22 per cent by 1980. Expenditure on private field drainage and improvement projects was first cut back and then eliminated during the same period, and central subsidies for local water authority works were trimmed drastically also from Hfl 75 million in 1970 to Hfl 20 million in 1981 (both expressed in 1981 prices).

The all-encompassing nature of land development projects inevitably makes them expensive and they are not necessarily the most cost-effective form of land improvement. One British visitor to the Netherlands in the late 1970s remarked that "although precise costs of land consolidation and flood protection were not available it was obvious that they are very high and that the return on this capital injection is lower in the short term than would normally be acceptable (in the UK)" (22).

In 1982 a new method of assessing consolidation schemes was introduced. It includes a form of cost-benefit analysis applying solely to the agricultural components of the scheme and a largely qualitative environmental impact study.

The agricultural investment appraisal excludes ancillary costs arising from new roads, housing or environmental works and is based on assumptions about future farm productivity and output.

In common with proceedings in other countries, EEC market prices are used to value the additional output, although an effort has been made to take account of Dutch contributions to Community surpluses and deflate the expected benefits accordingly. Most schemes are expected to increase yields by allowing further intensification. They must show a projected internal rate of return of 10 per cent or more if they are to be approved. If the internal rate of return is between 5 and 10 per cent, which it often is, then the anticipated non-agricultural effects must be taken into account. In principle, such schemes should qualify for public funding only if the wider benefits are thought to justify the low financial returns. In practice, schemes are rarely rejected, even though most of them fail to produce any net benefits for the environment.

The strictly financial appraisal is accompanied by a wider assessment of the impact of the scheme on the local community, on recreation and on the environment. This is couched in much broader terms, but does include a quantitive assessment of the anticipated effects on the densities of meadow bird species in the area (23). This assessment is an integral part of the planning process and is applied to the major alternatives being considered. However, it does not bind the Preparatory Committee responsible for planning to adopt any particular alternative and they are free to explore any number of options and arrive at their own choice. Since the majority of Committee members are farmers, they may not be swayed by environmental arguments, however pressing, and there is no guarantee that the plan eventually adopted will be desirable from an environmental viewpoint. However, the procedure does serve to open up the issue and may help to stimulate public concern and also strengthen the position of the Committee member representing environmental interests.

The Organisation of Agricultural Drainage

The disposition of powers over agricultural drainage in the Netherlands reflects its historical importance and at the local level is notably more democratic than in the other countries considered here. There are three main tiers in the administrative structure, beginning at the top with the Ministry of Agriculture and the Ministry of Transport and Public Works. In the middle tier are the water boards or **waterschappen** and at the bottom are the farmers. Land consolidation schemes are the responsibility of the Ministry of Agriculture but both the farmers themselves and a wide range of other organisations are involved in planning.

The Ministry of Transport and Public Works is in charge of large rivers, canals, estuaries and roads. It initiates, manages and maintains large capital projects, such as the famous "Delta Plan" which is designed to close off several important estuaries from the sea and also maintains the existing system. These practical functions are fulfilled by its operational arm, the **Rijkswaterstaat,** which has a network of local offices. Large individual projects, such as the reclamation of the Lake · IJssel polders, are often managed by special agencies created for the purpose, but the Ministry retains overall control. In general it takes the lead among the group of different Ministries involved with water issues and has responsibility for national rather than regional interests.

The Ministry of Agriculture has a relatively wide remit over rural land use and since October 1982 has taken over responsibility for the government's Department of Nature Conservation and Outdoor Recreation. This gives it fairly comprehensive powers over land development, including drainage. Aside from an overall administrative department, the Ministry contains two Directorate-Generals, one for Agriculture and Food and another for Land Development, Land and Forest Management. The latter Directorate is concerned not only with structural changes in agriculture, planning and land use and forestry, but also with fishing, hunting and shooting, nature reserves and the management of wildlife.

The section of the Ministry most concerned with drainage is the government Service for Land and Water Use. The Service has technical, design and economic expertise in the field and is the source of grants. It is also closely involved in the planning process for rural areas and with land development in particular. In each of the 11 provinces its local staff are supervised by a chief Land Utilization Officer, who also officiates over forestry, fishery and wildlife staff (24). This officer is part of the extensive co-ordination arrangements at national and provincial levels designed to tie together the efforts of the different Ministries involved in planning and avoid unnecessary sectoral conflicts.

The **waterschappen** or water boards are perhaps the most individual of the bodies concerned with drainage. Their names and histories are varied and they are the oldest surviving form of governmental institution in the country. They first appeared as "Polder Districts", local boards elected to manage individual polders. The need to maintain the integrity of the dykes was a matter of pressing mutual interest for landowners and the tradition of a specialised, democratic management body is a long established one.

The boards are still predominantly local bodies, covering an area of 10-40,000 hectares each, but their numbers have fallen drastically over the last 20 years, from around 2,500 to about 200 today. They are now under the control of the Provincial Councils, the elected bodies which represent regional interests and oversee the municipalities. The Provincial Council can establish, dissolve and alter the responsibilities of water boards and effectively delegates to them the management of local water levels, flood defences, water courses, sewerage and some roads and bridges. The precise functions of the boards vary and a few are now concerned with water quality, but none have competence over the supply of drinking water or the management of groundwaters. The Chairman, traditionally called a "dike-reeve" or "water-reeve", is often appointed by the Crown. However, the governing body is elected under local rules; there is usually a fixed division of seats between sectional interests and voting rights are apportioned in accordance with property ownership.

The water boards are broadly responsible for arterial drainage works, including the maintenance of water courses, dykes and pumping stations and the regulation of water levels. Vegetation is generally cut back mechanically, often twice a year, and the use of aquatic herbicides is closely controlled. Major maintenance works, such as dredging and channel improvement, occur every five to fifteen years (25). The boards also maintain the larger reservoirs. During dry periods, they may need to augment water levels in order to protect agricultural crops and control salinisation from groundwater. At one point near Gouda the local water boards release 210 million cubic metres of water a year to sustain fresh water levels (26). For the most part they are self-financing, having the power to levy local property taxes, but they receive grants from central government towards the cost of major improvement works.

On the bottom rung of the ladder are the farmers, who are responsible for field drainage construction and maintenance, including the smaller ditches, draining 50 hectares or less. They maintain the ditches themselves, but the laying and cleaning out of underground drainage is in the hands of contractors. A few of the larger farmers own their own pumps and operate local drainage systems of their own. However, these are unusual and most farmers rely on the water board's services. Similarly, most improvements are undertaken as part of a local land development or reallocation scheme and, although individual drainage works are fairly common, they are not appropriate in areas where farms are small and improved drainage can only be achieved by lowering water levels in the communal ditches. Relatively few private land development works have qualified for government aid in recent years and grants have often been smaller than for collective projects, such as consolidation schemes. However, the government's record on this point is somewhat erratic, with relatively large sums being allocated to support individual farm projects in the late 1970s, followed by the complete withdrawal of grants in 1980.

The making of land consolidation schemes draws in organisations from each tier in the hierarchy as well as the local people concerned. Schemes can be proposed by landowners, farming organisations, local authorities or water boards and must be approved by the Central Land Consolidation Committee (CCC) before they advance any further.

The CCC is ultimately responsible for all the subsequent phases of preparation and is the central pivot of the system. A wide variety of interests have a place on the Central Committee, including representatives of several government departments, amongst them the Ministries of Agriculture, Planning and Environment, Transport and Public Works and Finance. The secretariat is provided by the Government Service for Land and Water Use. Also represented are farmers' organisations, water boards and even conservation organisations. The Stichtung Natuur en Milieu, a leading voluntary conservation group, has had a seat on the Committee since 1968 and another body, Natuurmonumenten, which is itself a major landowner, has also been represented since 1983 (27). Although representation on the Committee is broad based, the power of veto is reserved for the civil servant members and, where they disagree, the dispute has to be resolved between the Ministries concerned at a higher level. The members drawn from non-governmental organisations formally appear in an advisory capacity only.

In evaluating proposals, the CCC will undertake a preliminary survey and seek expert advice. If, after discussion, a scheme is adopted, the next stage is to appoint a local preparatory committee of 5-9 people, a majority of whom are local farmers, although there are also local authority members and at least one representative from an environmental organisation. The secretaryship is again in the hands of the Land and Water Service, which tends to co-ordinate the Committee's work, liaise with the CCC headquarters in Utrecht and help to marshal a bevy of officials who attend meetings and provide technical expertise. The Committee compiles a series of detailed plans, often five or six, considers alternatives, undertakes the assessment reports and organises the participation of local people. The Preparatory Committee's final draft plan is sent to the CCC which then amends and approves it and make it up into a "concept report" which is sent to the Provincial Council for their assent. If it surmounts these hurdles, the completed plan is put to local farmers who have the final say.

Only landowners and tenants have a vote at this crucial stage and a scheme is approved if either the majority of those affected vote for it or there are votes in favour from people owning more than half the total area. Where a piece of land is farmed by a tenant, the vote is shared with the landlord. Sometimes schemes go through on the vote of landowners, with local tenants opposing it, and clearly the system gives the larger farmers a great deal of power. The turn-out for voting is often low and in the last five or six years, all but one scheme has gone through. Once approved, a scheme is mandatory.

The execution of land consolidation schemes is a lengthy process and, once again, the CCC has a major role to play, as does a local Executive Committee appointed by the Provincial Council and consisting largely of farmers from the area concerned. The CCC is empowered to approve any changes in plan proposed by the Executive Committee.

As we have seen, the intensive planning and consultation process which precedes rural land development now includes some environmental assessment and also consultation with environmental interests. This stems from the growth in environmental concern in the 1960s and 1970s and the introduction of new legislation in recent years. Prior to this, the law provided that up to 5 per cent of the area affected by a consolidation scheme could be acquired for public use and often this was allocated for conservation or outdoor recreation. Furthermore, consolidation schemes usually incorporated substantial tree planting programmes aimed at enhancing the rather featureless and geometric agricultural landscapes which are typically the outcome of the infrastructure improvements. These rather limited environmental provisions provided little protection for wetlands and were the subject of considerable criticism. Partly in response, the government produced a series of reports introducing a new approach to agriculture and the environment in 1975.

The new policy, which was regarded as a considerable breakthrough at the time, foresaw a broad sub-division of the agricultural area into three main categories. In the first category, about 100,000 hectares, or 4 per cent of the total, is land in which nature conservation is the main priority. It consists partly of existing nature reserves and partly of further sites

expected to be taken into public management in future with little
or no commercial agricultural activity. In the second category,
much the largest, is land zoned for predominantly agricultural
activity, where further intensification is expected to take place
and environmental restrictions are limited. In the third category, also expected to extend to around 100,000 hectares, are
"management areas", land where conservation and agricultural
activities are both priorities and are to be pursued in parallel.
In this somewhat experimental category, management is to remain
in the hands of farmers who are to be compensated for the environmental restrictions imposed on them. The type of land in this
category includes areas zoned in local plans for their conservation interest as well as areas designated nationally as important
landscapes. In order to make the new policy more concrete, the
government published a "Priority Inventory" of rural areas containing both farmland and unspoilt countryside in 1977 and indi-
cated the sites for which nature reserves or management agreements were needed urgently.

Underlying this three-tier approach is a belief that modern
agriculture and conservation are increasingly incompatible and
that reliance on the local planning system is not sufficient in
areas of environmental importance.

Under the 1962 Physical Planning Act, each municipality is
required to draw up a local development plan which covers the
countryside as well as buildings. Conservation objectives are
incorporated into these plans by designating certain areas as
"farmland with natural values" in which major landscape alterations, such as hedgerow removal or a change in the water regime,
usually will not be permitted (28). Farmers can apply for permission to remove the designated landscape features, but this is
likely to be withheld. However, the planning authorities have no
powers to regulate day to day farming operations, such as the
choice of crop, and in practice the system has been found "inadequate in preventing a decay in the landscape and natural significance of a region" (29). This is partly because many municipalities have not yet completed their plans and not all of them are
binding.

In effect, the system offers a somewhat passive form of
protection, capable of slowing down, but not preventing, change.
To remedy this, the authorities have sought a more precise and
positive form of management and conceded the principle that
farmers must be compensated for the further restrictions which
this imposes on them. "Management areas" are thus an attempt to
achieve the desired compromise by voluntary means, albeit on a
small scale.

The procedure for establishing a management agreement
involves several different stages and is somewhat too involved to
justify a full explanation here. However, three of the key steps
are the designation of a management area, the subsequent preparation of a management plan for the area by a Provincial Land
Management Committee and the eventual negotiation of voluntary

agreements with individual farmers. Management agreements last for six years and typically restrict the farmer's choice of crop patterns and the application of fertilisers and agrochemicals, stipulate permitted times for mowing and grazing, etc. They generally prevent the intensification of farming and may require some reduction in livestock densities. Compensation is based on the principle that a farmer with such an agreement should be able to earn the same as one without such an obligation. Negotiations are conducted by the Land Management Office, which is part of the Ministry of Agriculture. The Office has an annual budget for management agreements of only HFl 2 million a year.

In practice, the introduction of these management agreements has proceeded slowly and farmers have often been reluctant to enter into them. By the end of 1983, management agreements covering an area of only about 876 hectares had been concluded, although management plans had been drawn up for about 7,200 hectares (30). Furthermore, the agreements signed to date are almost wholly confined to part of the rather small area of the country designated as "less favoured" under EEC 75/268. These sites are small and scattered. In 1981 there were 56 covering a little over 11,000 hectares but they have recently been added to and now cover nearly 19,000 hectares. All are designated under Article 3.5 of the Directive. According to the wording in the Directive, they have been categorised as "less favoured", which is not a term which most people would apply to the Netherlands because "on the one hand, of the existence of unfavourable natural production conditions due to poor drainage conditions and to the poor soil quality, and, on the other hand of handicaps resulting from restrictions prescribed for the preservation of the countryside..." (Official Journal L128/229). In other words, they are less favoured partly because they have been earmarked for conservation.

Farmers with land in a registered "Less Favoured Area" (LFA) have the option of signing a five year agreement with the Ministry under which they are paid an annual compensation sum, depending on the number of livestock they keep. They have to supply details of their holdings, cannot exceed a certain livestock density and are obliged not to destroy those natural features, such as hedgerows and ditches, which have caused them to be classified as "less favoured". The agreements are voluntary and only a minority of farmers enter into them, possibly those who do not intend to develop their holdings anyway. Some have accepted management agreements as well, and possibly it has been easier to persuade farmers to take this further step if they have already accepted an LFA agreement (31). The merits of concentrating management agreements in LFAs is debatable and the Ministry's Conservation Inspectorate is critical of the current confusion of objectives. What is clear, however, is that management agreements are being used on a very limited scale and without a change of policy they are unlikely to constitute a significant means of protecting wetlands from agricultural development.

The establishment of nature reserves, which dates back several decades, has been much less problematic and the successive Ministries responsible had purchased around 42,000 hectares of new sites by the early 1980s. Three different Ministries between them now own about 80,000 hectares of nature reserves and are adding more, while private bodies own a slightly larger area (32). Government grants are available to private conservation organisations to meet half of the cost of acquiring a new reserve and the balance can often be raised from local authorities. The main types of nature reserve are heathland, woodland and coastal dunes and beaches, but there are also some areas of peat moor and marsh (33). Relative to many other European countries, these reserves are quite extensive, but they cover only a small fraction of the total area of wetland habitat and, even within these limits, do not provide complete protection against the effects of drainage.

Aside from Nature Reserves, there are a number of other types of area designated for conservation or recreation purposes where controls are less restrictive. Amongst these are the National Parks, areas of at least 1,000 hectares where valued habitat and landscape require protection under a management plan which also allows for recreation and public access. These Parks are relatively new – only three had been established by early 1982, but a further 20 are planned. Some will cover wetland areas and all will involve restrictions on farming. It is rather too early to assess the effectiveness of these Parks, which will depend on how many are designated and in which location, and whether satisfactory management plans are developed and implemented. However, success will depend a good deal on the use of the planning system and the establishment of management agreements.

Appropriate land-use planning is perhaps the keystone of Dutch conservation policy, and both the creation of designated conservation areas and the use of management agreements are only tools for achieving specific goals within this framework. One indication of how planning policy will develop in future is the Outline Plan for Nature and Landscape Conservation. This was published in 1981, the same year as the Outline Plan for Land Development which was discussed in the previous section. Both are detailed elaborations of the 1977 Planning Memorandum setting broad policy for rural areas and both are intended to apply with equal force in the countryside. The Outline Plan applies to almost everything considered worthy of protection, from historic buildings and old cart tracks to large-scale landscapes and the sea. This heritage has been divided into 12 manageable categories, for each of which appropriate policies are to be devised, although few of these have been defined yet. Several of these categories cover wetlands in one form or another. For example:

1.   "Nature Areas in the traditional sense; sand drifts, dunes, peat moors and bogs, marshlands, fens, former river courses...as well as large geographical units made up almost entirely of nature areas, often of great diversity, where it

is desirable to conduct conservation policies from the viewpoint of the whole

3. Large stretches of water, eg the Waddensee, the Eastern and
   Western Scheldt and Lake IJssel

4. Rivers

5. Brooks and lowland streams

6. Stretches of countryside under cultivation which are interesting from an ecological, evolutionary, historical and
   ethical point of view

10. Historic and/or scenic views of particular attraction, eg
    river views

11. Large, compound geographical units of at least 10,000 hec-
    tares, comprising nature areas, waters and woods as well as
    cultivated land, farms and villages and containing a wealth
    of natural beauty and historic interest, together forming a
    unified and harmonious whole".

The Outline Plan is still subject to discussion and refine-
ment, but it shows the areas which are likely to be designated as
nature reserves, national parks, etc., and also identifies areas
of particular ecological interest. There are maps showing important sites for geese and meadow birds, for example. Perhaps most
significant for drainage is the proposal to designate a substantial number of "large landscape areas" or **Grote Land-schapseen-
heden** (GLEs). These are areas consisting mostly of agricultural
land where integrated management plans are proposed to guide both
conservation and agricultural development.

In practice, there is considerable overlap between the proposed GLEs and the areas identified for future consolidation or
development projects in the parallel Outline Plan for Land Development. Environmentalists fear that where potential conflicts
arise, agricultural priorities will overrule conservation plans
and the GLE designation will prove ineffective. No special legal
measures have been introduced to back up the creation of GLEs and
little money is available to make them a reality. In many areas
no management plans have been drawn up. By contrast, the impending Land Development Act introduces new powers to ease the way
for new consolidation schemes. In two GLEs marked on the map,
Krimpenerwaard and Nord-Roden, preparations have already started
for a land development project and the main focus seems to be on
drawing up management agreements to protect only small areas.
This is particularly unfortunate in view of the difficulties
encountered in reconciling agricultural and environmental
interests in the wider countryside, and underlines the trend
towards concentrating new management initiatives and financial
support in areas where land development is taking place.

The complexities of land use planning in the Netherlands and the spate of new initiatives and designations in recent years makes it difficult to judge the extent to which progress has been made in reconciling agricultural and environmental interests. The system has several impressive features, such as the detailed maps and plans for categorising rural areas, and the vigorous acquisition of nature reserves. It is also advanced in emphasising the need for integration and in attempting to overcome the limitations of small, isolated nature reserves by planning to increase the size of designated areas and manage large-scale landscapes. However, in practice it seems to have been difficult to settle effective management agreements with farmers over a very large area and neither the money nor legal powers appear to be available to make conservation a real consideration in predominantly farming areas. Even in land development schemes, where conservation does have to be taken into account, agricultural interests have the final say and are able to ignore the environmental assessment if they wish.

Environmental interests, which originally welcomed the new approach in 1975, have been disappointed with the outcome. They are critical of the limited area set aside for nature reserves and management agreements and fear that many sites are too small and difficult to protect from the effects of pollution, drainage and other external phenomena. There is concern that the cost of management agremeents will rise and thus limit the areas which it is possible to protect while those that do survive will be vulnerable to increasing recreational pressures. Already financial constraints have eaten into the target of designating 200,000 hectares either for nature reserves or management agreements and the limit may now be 100,000 hectares (34).

In effect, it can be argued, the commitment to integration has not been followed through, agriculture and conservation are becoming increasingly incompatible and there is intense competition for space between them (35). If this is so, nature reserves are perhaps the only reliable form of protection for wetlands, a situation not dissimilar from the other countries considered here.

Finance for Drainage

As we have seen, the majority of drainage in the Netherlands takes place as part of a land development project or a local authority infrastructure improvement scheme. Both these activities are heavily subsidised by central government and a small amount of the total outlay is recovered from FEOGA, the EEC agricultural fund.

There is no uniform rate of subsidy for all schemes and the amount of drainage work involved in land consolidation also varies considerably. The current position is illustrated in Table 4.1 which is drawn from a recent survey of land consolida-

Table 4.1: AVERAGE BUDGET BREAKDOWN OF SOME RECENT LAND CONSOL-
IDATION SCHEMES, 1981

Category of Expenditure	% of total investment	Government subsidy (as a % of total cost)
Public roads inc. bicycle routes	26	17
Water management works*	22	14
Reallotment works+	17	10
Land parcel restructur- ing+ & new approaches to farmhouses	18	9
Resettlement of farm- houses	7	2
Landscape & outdoor recreation facilities	10	9
TOTAL	100	61

*   Mainly arterial drainage.
+   Contains a large element of field drainage

Source: Quoted in Hermans, 1983 (12)

---

tion schemes in progress in 1981. Costs are broken down into six
different categories, the second of which, "water management
works" consists largely of arterial drainage works.   Field
drainage is not itemised separately, and is more difficult to
identify. Generally, it accounts for quite a large proportion of
expenditure under the fourth category, "parcel restructuring and
new approaches" and a smaller percentage of the third category,
"reallotment works".   On average, land drainage costs probably
amount to between 35 and 50 per cent of the total cost of consolidation projects (36).

     The government generally bears about two-thirds of the cost
of consolidation schemes, but there is some variation and the
Table shows that for the schemes included in the 1981 survey the
average was 61 per cent.   Subsidies for the drainage element of
schemes are broadly in line with the overall average, although
they are somewhat less for parcel restructuring than for water
works.   The share of the total cost not met by the government
usually has to be found by the landowners benefiting from the
scheme, although they may be able to take advantage of low cost
loans.   In some cases the water board\or municipality with an
interest in the scheme may also make a contribution to the cost.

Arterial drainage is an important element of a second category of public works, known as "Hydraulic and Municipal Works" or, more briefly, as A2 works. These are undertaken by the water boards or other local authorities and constitute infrastructure improvement such as dyke repairs, new bridges and drainage. The central government contributes to the cost of these schemes, paying fixed rates of grant for new works. The second part of Table 4.2 shows the share of water management schemes in "Hydraulic and Municipal Works" over a 20 year period during which it has fluctuated considerably around an average of just under 50 per cent. The left hand side of the Table shows that water management works have absorbed about 20 per cent of the total land consolidation budget over the same period. Thus, water management works are funded under two major budget headings. Total spending on such work is around Hfl 80-90 million per annum at present, or around double contemporary expenditure on arterial drainage in Ireland. Public expenditure on field drainage is probably rather less.

Table 4.2: "WATER MANAGEMENT WORKS"+ AS A PROPORTION OF TOTAL ANNNUAL EXPENDITURE ON LAND CONSOLIDATION (A1) AND "HYDRAULIC AND MUNICIPAL WORKS"(A2)

Year	% A1	Year	% A2
1963 and 64	9,8	1960-64	31,3
1965-69	18,6	1965-68*	57,8
1970-74	21,1	1974	58,7
1975-79	20,6	1975-79	46,0
1980	17,1	1980	57,0
1981	20,9	1981	41,9

* For 1969-73 no subdivision of expenditure is available
+ Mainly arterial drainage

Source: Hermans, 1983 (12)

Table 4.3 shows total expenditure on the three main categories of land improvement over the period 1954-82 and the proportion contributed by FEOGA. The first two categories are land consolidation and "Hydraulic and Municipal works", while the third is private works of various kinds, including field drainage. In each case, total capital expenditure is given, including grants, for schemes which received public funding. As we have already noted, the availability of grants for private works has been sporadic and has recently been withdrawn. Expenditure on eligible private projects has fluctuated widely as a result.

Contributions from FEOGA to the cost of land development have also fluctuated considerably, reaching a peak in the 1970s.

Table 4.3: INVESTMENTS IN THREE CATEGORIES OF LAND DEVELOPMENT WORK AND THE FEOGA CONTRIBUTION (Hfl millions)

	LAND CONSOLIDATION PROJECTS			HYDRAULIC AND MUNICIPAL WORKS			Private Works*
	Total Investments	FEOGA subsidies	% FEOGA	Total Investments	FEOGA subsidies	% FEOGA	Total investment
1950-54	160	–	–	91			74
1955-59	476	–	–	141			26
1960-64	452	–	–	264			7
1965-69	910	<1	<1	419	<1	<1	0
1970	236	5.7	2,4	89.4	2.3	2,6	
1971	255	2.4	0,9	70.0	1.4	2,0	
1972	268	12.8	4,8	70.0	1.3	1,8	21
1973	220	16.4	7,5	68.2	0.6	0,9	
1974	199.6	11.5	5,8	87.1	3.3	5,2	
1975	224.1	20.4	9,1	60.1	1.8	3,0	
1976	260.5	13.9	5,3	68.2	0.5	0,8	
1977	242.5	31.7	13,1	87.1	6.7	7,7	546
1978	260.6	10.1	3,9	89.9	7.4	8,2	
1979	245.9	8.1	3,3	83.7	7.8	9,3	
1980	259.7	10.1	3,9	83.0	6.3	7,6	44.2
1981	262.2	6.1	2,3	73.2	4.3	5,9	25.0

* No FEOGA contribution

Source: Quoted in Hermans 1983 (12)

The chief recipient of Community aid has been land consolidation, although FEOGA has never met a very large share of the costs involved. Directive 72/159 on the modernisation of farming, one of the principal structure Directives, has been the chief conduit for Community funds. This Directive is intended to help farmers to raise their incomes to the local average by giving them special incentives to invest in land improvement, buildings, and other forms of modernisation over a period of up to six years. Drainage is one of the improvements most often assisted. The great majority of land consolidation schemes have qualified for aid under this Directive without difficulty, although it is known that the preparation of some has been delayed because they did not meet the required criteria. Indeed, two recent schemes have failed to qualify and have been refused FEOGA support, but this is still the exception* (37).

FEOGA subsidies for A2 works stretch back over a longer period, but have been on a smaller scale and have recently ceased altogether. Funds for such projects used to be available from FEOGA under the now lapsed Regulation 17/64 which provided for grants towards the cost of investments intended to improve agricultural structures.

Finally, it should be added that the Dutch government also receives FEOGA funds under the Less Favoured Areas Directive 75/268, but not for aiding drainage. Those areas designated as "less favoured" under Article 3(5) of the Directive include several with a high water table as explained in the previous section. Some farmers receive annual compensation payments and have committed themselves not to remove certain landscape features. Part of the cost of this compensation is recovered from FEOGA, although it amounts only to rather small sums.

It is unlikely that the overall level of drainage activity in the Netherlands has been affected greatly by the availability of Community subsidies although it may well have been a factor for a number of individual schemes. Perhaps more remarkable is the fact that the Community is still helping to finance infrastructure improvements, including drainage, in a country where massive resources have already been devoted to such investments, and both productivity and land values are extremely high. There may be strong arguments for land reform and reallocation designed to raise the income of smaller farmers, but it is questionable whether the Community should be aiding the concomitant intensification of land use.

Impact on Wetlands

The Netherlands contains a large number of important wetlands of different types, despite its small size and the dense

---

* The schemes were Oosterwolde, 4,716 hectares, 1979 and Terschelling, 1,375 hectares, 1983

pattern of human activities. It contains breeding grounds for a substantial number of species and wintering areas for many others. Sites include the Waddensee shallows and an array of islands, salt marsh, dunes and large fresh water lakes along the coast. Several of the lakes are former saline estuaries now separated from the sea, including the IJsselmeer and others in the delta area of Zeeland and Zuid-Holland. Although subject to considerable management, the large rivers, such as the Rhine, IJssel and Maas still contain stretches of international importance (38). Inland there are extensive areas of wet meadow and grassland supporting considerable wader populations, freshwater lakes of ornithological and limnological interest, a few remaining peat bogs, areas of fen and marsh, brackish ditches, etc.

Centuries of drainage, dyke building, peat exploitation and other forms of human activity have helped to transform the delta region from a vast wetland into a country with little or no true wilderness. Most of the wetland sites which survive are in the western part of the country, which is in some senses an artificial zone sustained by intensive water management, and the division between "natural" and "man made" habitats can be difficult to make. An example of the latter is the mud flats and marshland which appears in the early stages of reclaiming new polders from the IJsselmeer. This provides a transitory habitat for large numbers of birds including waders, ducks, cormorants, heron and avocets. As the land dries out, most of this habitat disappears again, although some of the pasture in the southern polders provides an important wintering ground for geese and a few areas of marsh remain as nature reserves. Even where relatively "natural" freshwater wetlands have survived, it may be necessary to artificially protect them from the effects of drainage and falling water levels in the surrounding area.

Drainage and other accompanying changes in the water regime are undoubtedly one of the major threats to the country's remaining freshwater habitats. Of particular concern is the continued lowering of water tables in land development projects, which are expected to continue at a rate of around 40,000 hectares a year and to be extended into areas which have previously been difficult to develop. Not only will there be a further lowering of groundwater levels in the lowlands, which in turn increases the demand for irrigation and deeper drainage channels upstream, but it will also be accompanied by an intensification in agricultural practice and increased use of fertilisers, resulting in greater nutrient loads, reduced species diversity, etc. The additional use of irrigation can increase the leaching of nutrients from the soil and in some cases lead to further groundwater extraction. Drainage, water supply and agricultural improvement are thus closely interconnected.

Although of central importance, changes in the water regime are not the only source of pressure on Dutch wetlands. In general terms, shooting pressures are probably less heavy than in neighbouring countries, but not insignificant, especially for geese.

However, the increasing demands of recreation and tourism are difficult to accommodate within the limited area available and in some cases wetlands are affected by heavy use and the development of new recreational facilities. Near the large cities, sites are particularly vulnerable to hunting and shooting, camping, caravanning, boating and the growth of holiday homes. One example is Wormer en Jisperweld, an area of fen, shallow waterways and small islands 15 kilometres from Amsterdam, which is of great botanical interest and an ideal breeding habitat for lapwing, redshank, snipe and other species.

Urban development of various kinds is a threat to both coastal and inland sites. For example, industrial development in the north east near the mouth of the river Eems threatens the Dollard, an unusual gulf containing brackish water, a soft sediment particularly attractive to birds, and unique fields of sea asters skirting the salt marshes. Water pollution from industrial, domestic and agricultural sources is a problem of particular concern in the Netherlands, not least because of the heavy pollutant load in the Rhine, received from countries upstream. Water pollution is recorded as a threat to many of the Dutch sites listed in the "Directory of Western Paleartic Wetlands" while the entry for the Waddensee reveals something of the full gamut of potential dangers. The threats to the site are listed as "mass recreation and other tourist activities; military training grounds; gas and oil exploitation; industrial and port developments; pollution by waste water; and construction, reclamation and dyke building" (39).

Detailed data on the environmental effects of agricultural drainage and land development in the Netherlands is not readily available but there is enough to construct a broad picture. As we have already seen, land consolidation schemes generally involve a major rearrangement of field boundaries, drainage systems, rural roads and sometimes buildings as well. The landscape is scaled up from a rectilinear mosaic to an arrangement of larger blocks, with the old field boundaries being removed in the process.

"In the western parts of the Netherlands, these boundaries have often been constituted by ditches, many of which have been filled up, with the remaining ones being straightened and standardised; in the eastern parts one more often finds hedgerows and wooded banks, many of which have been removed, with only poor compensation by some new standardised plantations.

"While ditches, hedgerows and wooded banks are being eliminated or standardised, the rich fauna and flora accompanying them wholly or partly disappears. One example is the common shrew, sorex araneus, the regression of which in turn has accelerated the decline of the barn owl, tyto alba. Thus, both nature and landscape undergo serious impoverishment, scale enlargement and levelling" (40). A revealing term used by these and other Dutch authors to describe the effects of consolidation is "standard landscape".

111

Field drainage tends to go hand in hand with other forms of agricultural improvement. It is now concentrated mainly on pasture, since most arable land has been drained already, and is often associated with greater use of fertilisers, an increase in the number of cattle per hectare and earlier mowing. The combination of lower groundwater tables and agricultural intensification can have marked ecological effects. The heavier use of fertilisers often leads to increased leaching of nutrients and subsequently to eutrophication. About 80 per cent of the Dutch flora is regarded as vulnerable to eutrophication (41). On peat soils, there is the additional hazard of oxidation, leading to shrinkage and subsidence. In the worst cases this can result in a highly uneven surface of limited use for agriculture, but more commonly there is a slow subsidence and ditchwater levels are kept reasonably high to control oxidation.

As might be expected, the effects of drainage and intensification on bird life have received the closest attention. The wet grassland in the west is particularly valuable as a breeding ground for waders, as well as an important habitat for wintering waterfowl. Several studies have shown that drainage has reduced wader populations substantially. Table 4.4 shows the change in the density (per 100 hectares) of seven species as a result of lowering the winter water table by 10–15 mm in Zuidzijde polder, part of a site near the Rhine called Alblasserwaard. Many polders in the Alblasserwaard have been drained and subsequently improved and managed more intensively. However, this site is particularly interesting as little improvement took place after drainage and the decline in species density can be attributed mainly to the lower water levels.

Table 4.4: SPECIES DENSITY OF SEVEN SPECIES BEFORE AND AFTER DRAINAGE

	Density*	
Species	1969	1979
Black-tailed Godwit	10.7	6.7
Lapwing	6.3	4.3
Shoveler	3.7	2.0
Garganey	3.7	0.7
Redshank	2.3	0.7
Oystercatcher	1.7	1.7
Snipe	0.7	0.7

* Number of birds observed per 100 hectares

Source: A. de Gelder (42)

Another report shows that drainage and subsequent agricultural intensification causes a pronounced fall in breeding populations. In two grassland areas previously considered as excellent breeding areas for waders, the number of breeding pairs of five species, including redshank, ruff, and black-tailed godwit, is reported to have fallen by between 70 and 100 per cent following improvement (43). This group of breeding birds included snipe, gallinago gallinago, a species which has been the subject of a special study. Relatively few breed in the Netherlands, and in recent years there has been a steady decline in both visitors and breeding birds. The main cause of this is changes in the management of Dutch grassland, which has forced the birds to find different moulting areas. New moulting grounds have been found in Britain and to a lesser degree in north western France, where shooting pressure is considerable (44). However, if neighbouring countries follow the Dutch path and further intensify the exploitation of their grassland the pressure on snipe will mount considerably. Indeed, if intensification continues in the Netherlands, some experts fear that 11 species, including stork, corncrake and shoveler, will vanish outside nature reserves (45).

Lower water tables have also reduced the variety of plant and invertebrate life. In common with other countries, the Netherlands has experienced a general impoverishment in the variety and distribution of flora. One estimate suggests that the average number of species per square kilometre fell from 120 in 1900 to 70 in 1970 (46). By no means can all this decline be attributed to agriculture, let alone drainage, but it is notable that plants depending on moist conditions have been particularly affected. It has been suggested that of 96 plant associations characteristic of wet or moist conditions, about 80 per cent are threatened to some degree by reduced water tables, eutrophication, changes in water chemistry, altered patterns or fluctuation in the water level, etc (47).

As we have seen, the reclamation of new polders from the IJsselmeer has more or less been halted, although the fate of the Markermeer, potentially the fifth large polder, has yet to be settled. In future, it is the wildlife of the wet grasslands and old ditches in the west which will be most threatened by drainage; in the sandier "brook lands" much of the damage has already been done and few natural streams or rivulets remain. Among the wet meadows threatened are several of international importance, such as Krimpenerwaard and Ablasserwaard in Zuid-Holland, both marked on Figure 5. Both of these sites are on a list of important bird areas in the Netherlands, drawn up as a result of the Bird Directive, and both are internationally important for their breeding populations of black terns, chlidonias nigra. Both are also threatened by drainage, indeed a land consolidation project has almost been completed at Ablasserwaard (48).

Krimpenerwaard is an area of around 12,500 hectares near the Rhine, made up of nine different polders mostly managed as grassland for dairy cattle. It is an important breeding site for

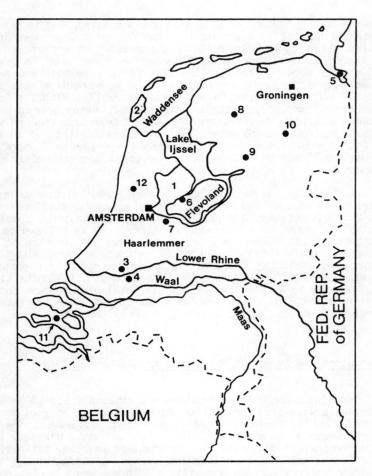

Fig. 5: Wetlands in the Netherlands

1.	Markermeer	7.	Nardermeer
2.	Texel	8.	Friesland Levels
3.	Krimpenerwaard	9.	De Wieden and De Weerribben
4.	Alblasserwaard	10.	Dwingelose en Kiralose Heide
5.	Dollard	11.	Oosterschelde
6.	Oostvaardersplassen	12.	Wormer en Jisperveld

shoveler and garganey, as well as for black terns, and is also a
wintering habitat of some significance for several species including gadwall, wigeon and Bewick's swans. It appears as an
"Extended Landscape Area" and also as an important site for geese
and meadow birds in the Outline Plan for Nature and Landscape
Conservation. On the other hand, it also appears as a site for
future land development in the parallel Outline Plan for Land
Development and preparations for a consolidation scheme have
already started. No management plan has been drawn up and the
site is basically unprotected (49). Some small sites may be set
aside for nature reserves or management agreements, but water
tables are likely to be lowered in the great majority of Krimpenerwaard.

Wetlands in the Netherlands are more protected than in some
other parts of the Community, but the coverage is still patchy.
The Dutch government has so far failed to designate special
protection areas for vulnerable species, as it is obliged to do
under the Birds Directive, and there is as yet no sign of it
doing so. An independent list of 62 wetlands of ornithological
importance, including 56 qualifying as internationally important
sites, suggests that six have no protection at all. Protection
only extends to a third or less of the total area in just under
half the sites (50). Six sites have been listed under the Ramsar
Convention, but all of these were previously protected.

Conclusions and Impact of the Common Agricultural Policy

For centuries the imperatives behind land drainage in the
Netherlands were flood control and the reclamation of good agricultural land. These have not disappeared, but as methods of
water management have become more refined and sophisticated, the
goals have shifted towards improving farm incomes, maximising
agricultural productivity, lowering costs and strengthening the
country's position in the competitive European market. Drainage
is typically part of a matrix of interrelated and costly land
improvement works, the viability of which depends crucially on
the market for Dutch produce.

There is little doubt that the Common Agricultural Policy is
a cornerstone of Dutch agricultural prosperity. The combination
of secure prices, free trade within the Community and protection
from agricultural imports has been particularly favourable for
farmers enjoying the advantages of excellent land, successful co-
operatives and strong trading and commercial links abroad.

The CAP has allowed the Dutch access to many new markets,
not only for traditional exports such as flowers and vegetables,
but also for intensively produced milk, poultry and eggs. Dutch
producers have been able to compete successfully with more traditional types of farming elsewhere in the EC, pointing the way for
further intensification. Indeed, the Community's price regime,

buttressed by the "green money" system, has provided a secure base for expansion, especially in the livestock sector, and made it worthwhile to invest in increasingly intensive and specialised forms of production. In particular, it has encouraged a rise in milk production from about 6.8 million tonnes a year in 1960 to 12.1 million tonnes in 1981 (51). Most of this output is exported elsewhere in the Community or disposed of on the world market with the aid of FEOGA subsidies and it is doubtful whether this level of expansion would have been sustained in the absence of the CAP.

The increase in milk production has been achieved by careful management, the large scale use of imported feedstuffs and an inexorable process of intensification. Grassland in 1950 carried an average of 1.1 dairy cows per hectare, but by 1980 this had been pushed up to around 1.8 cows. The use of nitrogen fertilisers quadrupled over the period and the yield of dry matter produced per hectare rose by more than 60 per cent (52). Drainage and land improvement works have been an integral part of this process of intensification and are likely to remain so. It is particularly significant that the Dutch authorities continue to attach considerable importance to drainage and the careful control of water levels as a means of further increasing yields. This is despite the low water tables which have already been established in many part of the country. The price regime and the grants available have made it worthwhile to continue lowering water levels and at the same time invest in irrigation equipment to make good the water deficit at crucial times in the summer. The environmental costs of this form of development are likely to be high, especially if the practice spreads to other parts of the Community.

We have seen that the progress of drainage and land development in the Netherlands has depended heavily on public subsidies. The European Community has made only modest direct contributions to the cost of such works, but this should not obscure the significance of the CAP in setting price levels and creating the economic conditions for agricultural expansion and intensification. Under the price support system, it is production which is subsidised and those who produce the most attract the largest share. This has benefited the Netherlands, not only because of the country's high output, but also because so many farmers are involved in dairying, perhaps the most heavily subsidised of all European agricultural products.

Several freshwater wetlands in the Netherlands are vulnerable to damage from agricultural development and it is wet meadows which are perhaps under greatest threat. The brief review undertaken here suggests that current plans to extend the land development programme are of particular concern. Although there are a number of mechanisms for rural planning, for conserving important sites and for trying to adopt a more integrated approach to development, agriculture is still the priority in most circumstances and only small areas tend to be set aside for conservation. The government has not designated special protection areas as it is required to do under the EC Birds Directive and, despite an evident concern with conservation, there is a clear reluctance to impose on farmers the kind of restrictions required to prevent further damage.

References

1. Commission of the European Economic Communities, 1983, The Agricultural Situation in the Community, 1982 Report, Brussels
2. Scott, D.A., 1980, A Preliminary Inventory of Wetlands of International Importance for Wildfowl in West Europe and Northwest Africa, IWRB, Slimbridge, Glos, UK
3. Carp, E., 1980, Directory of Wetlands of International Importance in the Western Paleartic, IUCN, Gland, Switzerland
4. Scott, 1980, op. cit.
5. Baaijens, G. J. and de Molenaar, J. G., 1983, "Water, water management and nature conservation" in Committee for Hydrological Research TNO, Economic instruments for rational utilization of water resources, Proceedings and information 29b, The Hague
6. Millington, P.R., et al, 1980, Agriculture, Conservation and Drainage of areas in Holland, Report of a study tour in 1979. Limited circulation, Ministry of Agriculture, Fisheries and Food, UK
7. Baaijens, and de Molenaar, 1980, op. cit.
8. Ibid
9. Hermans, B.P.G.M., personal communication
10. Netherlands Ministry of Agriculture and Fisheries, 1982, Aspects of Dutch Agriculture and Fisheries, The Hague, Netherlands
11. Ministerie van Landbouw en Visserij, 1982, Landinrictingsdienst, 1982, Utrecht, Netherlands
12. Hermans, B. P. G. M., 1983, Land Drainage and Wetlands in the Netherlands, Special report commissioned for this study, Stichting Natuur en Milieu, Utrecht, Netherlands
13. Ministerie van Landbouw en Visserij, 1981, "Government Service for Land and Water Use, Annual Report, 1981, The Hague, Netherlands
14. Hermans, 1983, op. cit.
15. Kempen, H. and Jansen, J., 1982, Drainage in the Netherlands, paper for a seminar at the Ecole Polytechnique, Paris
16. Hermans, 1983, op. cit.
17. Ibid
18. This account is based on the Appendix in Millington et al 1980, op. cit.
19. Kempen and Jansen, 1982, op. cit.
20. Ibid
21. Ministerie van Landbouw en Visserij, 1981, op. cit.
22. Millington et al, 1980, op. cit.
23. Hermans, 1983, op. cit.

24. Netherlands Ministry of Agriculture and Fisheries, 1982, op. cit.
25. Kempen and Jansen, 1982, op. cit.
26. Unie van Waterschappen, 1982, The Dutch Water Boards, place of publication unstated
27. Hermans, 1983, personal communication
28. Grijns, A., 1983, Management Agreements in the Netherlands, paper presented to a seminar on Landscape Conservation in Agriculturally Less Favoured Areas at Wye College, UK, July 1983, report in press
29. Ibid
30. Bennett, G., 1984, The Application of the Less Favoured Areas Directive in the Netherlands, Countryside Commission, Cheltenham, UK
31. Ibid
32. Netherlands Ministry of Cultural Affairs, Recreation and Social Welfare, 1981, Conservation in the Netherlands, a fact sheet from the International Relations Directorate, Rijswijk, the Netherlands
33. Ibid
34. Grijns, 1983, opp. cit.
35. See Hermans, 1983, op. cit. and van der Weijden, W. J., ter Keurs, W. J., and van der Zande, A.N., 1978 "Nature Conservation and Agricultural Policy in the Netherlands", Ecologist Quarterly, winter 1978, pp. 317-335
36. Hermans, B. P. G. M., personal communication
37. Hermans, 1983, op. cit.
38. Carp, 1980, op. cit.
39. Ibid
40. van der Wijden et al, 1978, op. cit.
41. Baaijens, and de Molenaar, 1983, op. cit.
42. de Gelder, A., 1980, quoted in Weidevogels in de verdrukking Nederlandse verenijing tot bescherining van vogels. Zeist, 1980
43. Baaijens, and de Molenaar, 1983, op. cit.
44. Netherlands National Report to the International Meeting on Wetlands and Waterfowl, Debrecen, Hungary, 1981. Reported in IWRB Bulletin No 47, December 1981, p. 47
45. Baaijens, and de Molenaar, 1983, op. cit.
46. van der Weijden et al, 1978, op. cit.
47. Baaijens, and de Molenaar, 1983, op. cit.
48. Hermans, 1983, op. cit.
49. Ibid
50. Osiech, E. R., 1982, Belangrijke waterriJke vogelgebieden in Nederland, Limosa 55, pp 43-55, 1982, Netherlands
51. Dutch Agriculture in Facts and Figures, 1982, official pamphlet produced by the Dutch Ministry of Agriculture
52. Grijns, 1983, op. cit.

CHAPTER 5: THE UNITED KINGDOM

Introduction

Any inventory of wetlands of international importance invariably includes a lengthy catalogue of British sites. This is because of the long indented coastline and its family of accompanying islands, the rich variety of freshwater wetlands and the mild temperate winters which attract visiting waterfowl. What remains of inland sites, however, is only a remnant of once extensive areas of bog, fen and marsh, since British drainage endeavours have been some of the most vigorous in Europe.

The British climate is somewhat similar to Ireland's, but a little drier, with average annual rainfall varying from around 600 mm in East Anglia to around 1,400 mm in Scotland. The western and northern parts of the country are wetter than the south and east and this, together with differences in soil and topography, helps to account for a regional divide in the pattern of farming. Arable farming, especially of wheat and barley, is most common on the eastern side of the country and, to a slightly lesser extent, in the Midlands, while the western half is mainly under grass and the emphasis is on milk and beef production.

The total agricultural area is about 19 million hectares, but about a third of this is relatively unproductive rough grazing, found mainly in the uplands of Scotland, Wales and the Pennines. The remainder is more intensively managed, especially in the east, and is divided fairly evenly between arable and pasture. Farms are large by standards elsewhere in the Community with full time holdings averaging about 118 hectares each. Only 120,000 farms account for about 90 per cent of production (1). Those in the west tend to be smaller and less affluent than the highly mechanised arable units on the east coast, while in the hills very large areas are required to make a living from grazing sheep or a modest herd of beef cattle.

Producing mainly milk, meat and cereals, Britain is now about 75 per cent self-sufficient in temperate foods, but is still a major net importer. Agriculture does not have the same economic importance as it does in the three other countries described here, but the British government has been equally committed to increasing output. It is not always realised that the UK has expanded its exports of agricultural products greatly over the last decade.

Much of lowland Britain is densely populated, but less than 3 per cent of the workforce are employed in agriculture and most urban inhabitants have little or no contact with farming life. Despite this, farmers still retain great political influence and are a powerful presence in most rural institutions. In the hills, in Northern Ireland and in some of the less accessible rural areas, agriculture is still the mainstay of the economy and the pivot of local society. In the south and around the larger towns, this is no longer the case; many villages have absorbed a wave of predominantly middle class urban migrants, commuters and the retired and have become satellites of urban society. One consequence of this has been a growing commitment to conservation from people living in the countryside, but not dependent on farming for their incomes.

The majority of important wetlands in Britain can be found on or near the coast and many are in Scotland. They include several river estuaries and stretches of salt marsh, parts of the relatively undeveloped Scottish coast and its neighbouring islands, and a number of coastal grazing marshes in areas such as East Anglia, Lancashire, North Kent and the Severn Estuary. Although much reduced in size, there remain patches of fen and mire and a varied collection of bogs and areas of peatland in different parts of the country. In the lowland valleys, especially in the east, there are a few unimproved rivers, flood plains, such as the Ouse and Nene Washes, and scattered pieces of wet pasture which are valuable for wintering wildfowl. Some sites depend on regular grazing and mowing to maintain the character of their flora and a few, such as Abberton Reservoir in Essex, are man-made.

Agricultural Drainage

The history of land drainage stretches back at least as far as Roman times, during which there were pioneering attempts to reclaim areas of fen and marsh for agricultural purposes. The dawn of the modern era can be placed in the 17th century when the first experiments in under-drainage took place. This was at the height of the "Enclosures", the movement whereby the majority of peasants were displaced from the land and the commons and large medieval open fields were divided gradually into private farms and estates. The new pattern of privately owned fields often reflected drainage conditions and ditches were dug along the boundaries. At about the same time the Dutch engineer Cornelius Vermuyden was constructing one of the first big arterial drainage system in the East Anglian fens, then perhaps the largest wetland in Britain.

The main difficulty encountered in the fens was a rapid shrinkage of the drained peat and a consequent struggle to keep it above the surface of the water. At the end of the 17th century, windmills became available to pump out the water to the sea, maintaining it at a level below that of the retreating surface of the peat. In the 19th century, a series of new channels were cut and steam brought much geater power and reliability to the pumps, allowing a larger volume of water to be evacuated and new areas reclaimed. In the 20th century the steam engines have been replaced by diesel or electric pumps and the fenlands have declined to almost nothing from an original expanse of around 3,500 square kilometres (2). The agricultural land resulting from these efforts is some of the best in the country and it is generally true that many areas of Grade 1 farm land were once some kind of wetland.

Field drainage work has been more concentrated in time than larger scale reclamation projects, with two notable periods of activity beginning in the 1840s and 1940s respectively. Under the medieval open field system, the "ridge and furrow" method of ploughing long thin strips of land was in common use. This facilitated the surface run-off of water into neighbouring ditches and served as a form of field drainage for many centuries. It took several generations of experiment with new methods and the growing impetus provided by other agricultural improvements before under-drainage became a widely accepted alternative. At first, a variety of techniques were tried involving the digging of parallel trenches into which were placed a layer of stones, brushwood or other materials, before being refilled with soil. Baked clay roofing tiles first came to be used in places without convenient supplies of stone and the clay design was later refined into a "U" shape and ultimately a cylindrical pipe around 1810. "Tile drains" is still the most common word for clay pipe drainage today (3).

A key advance for under-drainage came in 1845 when Thomas Scragg invented a satisfactory new extruding process for manufacturing pipes, which reduced their price to around a third of the former level. At about the same time the first government schemes for lending landowners money for drainage purposes were introduced, with the work supervised by the Enclosure Commission. Both developments helped to make the years between 1840 and the onset of the agricultural depression in the 1880s a period of intense drainage activity, with 100,000 hectares or more likely to have been drained annually in the peak years. In the 1850s, the production of clay drainage pipes was estimated to be about 420 million a year compared with about 90 million a year in the late 1960s, when they were still the main material used (4).

Agriculture went into decline at the end of the 19th century in the face of growing imports of cheap food. The way had been opened for large scale imports with the repeal of the Corn Laws in 1846 but it was several decades before supplies from North and South America, Australia and elsewhere took a large slice of the market. Land prices fell and subsequently drainage work tailed off rapidly. There was then little activity until the outbreak of the Second World War in 1939. It has been estimated that about 4,700,000 hectares of agricultural land in England and Wales had been drained by 1939, but nearly all of this had occurred in the Victorian era (5). Nineteenth century drainage affected most parts of the country and ranged from the reclamation of marsh and swamp to the installation of under-drainage in parts of the uplands where further work has never been considered worthwhile. Progress was more rapid than in many other parts of Europe, not only because of agricultural conditions but also because so much of the country was divided into large rural estates with a single landowner.

During the Second World War the revival of field drainage was once again a priority as part of an effort to increase food production. Work was encouraged by the introduction of 50 per cent government grants and the Ministry built up a fleet of its own draglines and trenchers. After the war ended, there was a continued commitment to increasing British food output and cutting reliance on imports. A new system of support for farming was introduced with the 1947 Agriculture Act, which established the deficiency payments regime. This system allowed in food imports at world prices but gave farmers higher guaranteed prices, reviewed every spring.

This ushered in an era of stability and rapid technical advance. Drainage and other forms of agricultural improvement were encouraged with capital grants, and farmers had a security which made investment of this kind worthwhile. The Ministry's own service was phased out in the 1950s and replaced with private contractors, and the annual area of field under-drainage began to rise sharply. From a level of 10-15,000 hectares a year in England and Wales in the 1940s it rose to around 40,000 hectares by 1960 and then doubled during the next decade, to settle at a level of rather over 100,000 hectares a year in the mid 1970s. On Britain's entry into the European Community in 1973 arable farmers in particular enjoyed a period of new prosperity, with both cereal and land prices rising rapidly.

Field drainage in the UK is the responsibility of individual landowners, who usually employ contractors to undertake the work. Under-drainage is the most common method of removing excess moisture, but in some areas only ditches or other surface channels are used. Ditching is particularly common in some of the flat deltaic stretches of land near the coast and in some hillier country, including Scotland and Northern Ireland, where hill drainage for forestry is also common. On rough grazing in the uplands a common form of drainage is "moorland gripping", the cutting of a series of relatively shallow open channels across a slope with a specially designed plough. This is a comparatively cheap and short-lived operation designed to remove surface water, improve grass and heather production and reduce the habitat available for liver fluke, an important livestock parasite. It is estimated that around 5,000 hectares a year are currently subject to hill drainage in Scotland for agricultural purposes (6).

Larger scale or arterial drainage works are carried out by a number of different authorities and the arrangements in Scotland and Northern Ireland are different from those in England and Wales where Water Authorities are the principal bodies concerned. There are nine Water Authorities in England and one in Wales, each controlling all aspects of water management in their catchment area. These Water Authorities are required by the 1976 Land Drainage Act to "exercise a general supervision over all matters relating to land drainage in their area". This means that they are concerned with agricultural drainage, river management, flood control and maintenance work. There are thus close links between land drainage and flood control at an administrative as well as an engineering level. Many of the Water Authorities' largest schemes are designed to provide tidal reaches and stretches of coast with protection from the sea, often with important implications for river management and drainage inland.

In England and Wales, minor works, such as improvements to ditches and streams, are mainly executed by Internal Drainage Boards, local bodies which are effectively groupings of local landowners. There are about 250 Internal Drainage Boards (IDBs) but they cover only about 1.2 million hectares, being concentrated in lowland areas where drainage problems are most pronounced, especially in the flat alluvial areas neighbouring the east coast. Where there is no IDB, powers over land drainage, flood protection and maintenance rest either with the Water Authority, the local District Council or the riparian (river bank) owner. Water Authorities only have powers over "main rivers", which in practice is an extensive network of about 34,000 kilometres of water courses of various size and includes many small channels in areas where there is no IDB.

In Scotland there are no Water Authorities or IDBs, but river flooding is a comparatively small problem and little arterial drainage work takes place. Where arterial drainage schemes are necessary, the responsibility lies with the riparian owners, who are eligible for capital grants from the Department of Agriculture and Fisheries for Scotland (7).

In Northern Ireland, there are no Water Authorities or IDBs either but a substantial amount of arterial drainage work is carried out by the drainage division of the Department of Agriculture, which has its own labour force and equipment. The Department is responsible for improvement and maintenance works on about 6,000 kilometres of water courses which have been designated by a special statutory body - the Drainage Council. Elsewhere, riparian owners are responsible for any minor works which may be required (8).

The organisation of drainage in different parts of the UK is described more fully in the next section. However, this sketch gives some indication of the variety of conditions and the main bodies concerned and perhaps helps to explain why England and Wales are often treated separately from Scotland and Northern Ireland in discussion of drainage.

With a long history of arterial drainage in Britain, most large areas of wetland have been drained already and improvement works have been effected on most of the rivers subject to flooding. Nonetheless a substantial amount of new work is taking place, mainly concentrated in low lying river valleys, and alluvial plains on the eastern side of the country. In 1980/81 the Ministry of Agriculture (MAFF) approved a total of 131 individual drainage improvement schemes put forward by Water Authorities and over 100 in the following year (9,10). The total capital value of these schemes in 1980/81 was £31.8 million and an average grant of 55 per cent was paid by MAFF towards this cost.

These schemes can be divided into three main categories. The largest is sea defence work, which accounts for about 40 per cent of total expenditure, followed by urban flood protection, with about 33 per cent of the total and purely agricultural drainage improvements accounting for 27 per cent (11). In practice, urban flood relief schemes may include an element of agricultural improvement and sea defence works may also be designed to benefit farm drainage. For example, the Anglian Water Authority wishes to build a barrier across the River Yare at Great Yarmouth to control tidal incursions, but the improved protection from flooding would be expected to lead to a substantial programme of agricultural drainage in the environmentally significant marshland neighbouring the rivers feeding into the Yare.

Many of the agricultural drainage schemes consist of channel improvement works, whereby rivers are straightened, deepened, and perhaps widened and re-profiled. Frequently, the object is to reduce seasonal flooding and to lower water tables in the vicinity. Embankment schemes are common in flat lowland areas and in towns and, where water levels have been lowered significantly, pumping stations are often built to discharge water into main channels, which may be at a higher level. Other types of project include the reclamation of coastal marsh and the construction of "highland carriers" transporting water from higher land upstream (in a separate channel) across low lying areas.

Although it is very little concerned with drainage, much the largest flood protection scheme in Britain is the Thames Tidal Flood Protection Scheme. This involves the construction of several river barriers and well over 100 kilometres of flood bank and is expected to cost somewhere in the region of £900 million by the time it is completetd.

The Internal Drainage Boards carry out a much smaller volume of minor arterial works, although many of them are in environmentally sensitive areas. In 1980/81 MAFF approved 144 individual drainage schemes, nearly all of which were for the benefit of agriculture. The total cost of IDB improvement schemes was £5.5 million before grant (12). All schemes qualify for a flat rate grant of 50 per cent, except for sea defence work

which is eligible for 75 per cent grants but is rarely undertaken by IDBs. Works are aimed at improving the outfalls for
field drainage, upgrading local ditch networks and improving the
discharge of drainage water into main rivers or water courses.
Channel works are sometimes accompanied by the installation of
new or higher capacity pumps and such schemes are often amongst
the more controversial from an environmental point of view.

The third category of arterial drainage works undertaken in
England and Wales is that undertaken by local authorities. This
work is concerned with flood prevention and is urban in character, but may also contain agricultural elements. Projects
attract grants from MAFF which currently pays out about £4
million per annum (13).

The identification of drainage priorities and selection of
individual schemes is in the hands of the various authorities
concerned and, with very few exceptions, is not determined at the
national level. The order in which schemes have been drawn up
and implemented has been somewhat ad hoc and undoubtedly reflects
local political pressures as well as an overall view of costs and
benefits. Often Water Authorities have felt obliged to respond
to the demands of influential farmers or the strength of local
feeling in the aftermath of a flood.

In an attempt to put arterial schemes on a more systematic
and rational basis, Water Authorities in England and Wales were
required under Section 24(5) of the Water Act 1973 to make
"surveys of their areas in relation to their drainage (including
flood protection) functions". After some years of labour, all 10
Water Authorities have now produced such surveys, although their
precise format, composition and level of detail varies
considerably; some are slender, others run into several bulky
volumes. The surveys have identified thousands of sites, where
there is some threat of flooding or scope for improving
agricultural drainage. For most of these sites, there is a note
of the type of remedial works envisaged and a very rough indication of the likely costs and benefits of making the proposed
investment. The surveys include a number of useful maps showing
where future drainage works may take place and often marking
areas designated by the Nature Conservancy Council as Sites of
Special Scientific Interest (SSSIs), some of which are wetlands.

The Severn-Trent Water Authority, the largest in Britain,
covered both main and non-main rivers in its survey, found 1,600
problems of some kind and has so far identified over 300
potentially cost-effective arterial schemes, likely to cost £92
million in 1982 prices (14). If adopted, this programme would
keep river engineers occupied well into the 21st century and it
is notable that most Water Authorities foresee the need for a
great deal more drainage work.

Most of the possible future projects identified in these
surveys are small relative to the schemes undertaken in the past,
and many of the problems they are addressing are of a

comparatively minor kind. In order to qualify for a government grant a scheme has to satisfy the Ministry of Agriculture's conditions, one of which is that it should achieve a cost-benefit ratio of one or more, using a 5 per cent discount rate. In other words, they are expected to produce a rate of return of at least 5 per cent.

The procedures used by the Ministry for assessing costs and benefits have been subject to considerable criticism in recent years and it seems likely that they will be tightened in the foreseeable future. Given this and the increasing limitations on the market for agricultural produce in Europe, it is likely that some of the schemes initially identified as worthwhile will not in practice be pursued, even if they are regarded as acceptable from an environmental point of view.

Water Authorities produce annual plans for both capital and maintenance work, but they are also required to prepare five year rolling programmes of work, which they do in consultation with the MAFF Regional Engineer. The survey results are intended to be kept up to date and in principle should be an important element in drawing up medium and long term plans. IDBs have a more ad hoc planning system and only the larger ones have their own engineering staff.

In Northern Ireland arterial drainage is on a similar scale to that of a Water Authority in England. Since 1947 works have been carried out on 166 main water courses, affecting 1,882 kilometres. In addition to this, improvements have been made to 3,790 kilometres of minor water courses and a considerable number of urban drains. Improvement works have yet to be carried out on rivers in a total of 10 catchments, but it is unclear what proportion of the possible schemes will pass the cost/benefit test (15).

One significant scheme which is going ahead is the drainage of the River Blackwater catchment, which contains a number of interesting wetland habitats and lies on both sides of the border between Northern Ireland and the Irish Republic. This is one of the projects being put forward for a grant from FEOGA under EC Directive 79/197 which is specifically for the promotion of drainage in catchments straddling the border. FEOGA will reimburse half the cost of eligible schemes, up to a limit of 15 million European Units of Account, which will be divided more or less equally between the two sides. The Blackwater scheme has been planned in co-operation with the Office of Public Works in the Irish Republic, and at present both governments are considering the possibility of a second cross border scheme in the Finn/Lackey catchment, although the economics of this appear rather less attractive.

The rather complex organisation of arterial drainage work and the joint pursuit of agricultural, urban and sea defence projects sometimes obscures the overall trends and priorities for purely agricultural work. There does appear to be a tendency

towards smaller schemes and also a greater willingness to take
account of environmental considerations in designing schemes.
However, standards of flood protection are also rising, putting
up costs and sometimes heightening the environmental impact.
With so much river improvement work already completed it might be
expected that substantial further investment would be subject to
diminishing returns, but this will only really become clear if
rigorous cost-benefit appraisals are applied to future projects
and these assessments are made publicly available.

Water Authorities do not appear to envisage any major
reduction in their arterial programmes although the comment is
sometimes made that they are in danger of running out of work
(16). Traditionally they have been active in positively
promoting agricultural drainage schemes and it seems likely that
they will continue to do so even where farmers are slow to follow
up with field drainage.

As we have seen, the annual rate of field drainage expanded
greatly between the 1940s and 1970s with the active support of
the Ministry of Agriculture. Farmers acquiring one of the leaf-
lets available on most aspects of drainage from the Ministry's
advisory service, ADAS, can get a succinct summary of official
thinking from the opening remarks:

"On more than half of the agricultural land in England and
Wales field drainage is a fundamental necessity for
efficient farming. A National Survey by the Ministry has
shown that agricultural production on approximately 3 million hectares of agricultural land is limited by the absence
of efficient drainage systems, while almost another three
million hectares depend upon the maintenance of existing
systems" (17).

A slightly more precise breakdown of the 11 million hectares
of agricultural land in England and Wales has been made (18):

"Post 1940 grant aided work   1.34 million hectares
Old drains still working, mainly from
  19th century   1.74   "   "
Naturally drained soils, chalk, etc.   4.25   "   "
Land needing improvement and likely
  to be economic to drain   2.63   "   "
Areas likely to be uneconomic to drain"   1.05   "   "

The author of this classification, who was Assistant Chief
Engineer of the Ministry's Land Drainage Service at the time,
suggests that old 19th century drains are decaying at the rate of
around 50,000 hectares a year. On this assumption, 100,000
hectares of new drainage per annum represents a net gain of newly
drained land of only half this amount. However, it must be
remembered that a sizeable proportion of Victorian drainage was
in the uplands where relatively little now occurs and the failure
of old drains appears to be the direct cause of new under-
drainage in only about 4 per cent of cases (19). The main

reasons for under-drainage are either a high water table or an impermeable subsoil, especially on the clay soils in the eastern parts of the country where most under-drainage is concentrated.

Almost all field drainage work in the UK is grant aided and traditionally grant application approval forms have been the main source of statistics about the area drained, the techniques used, the soil type, changes in land use, etc. However, since a cost-cutting exercise in 1980, farmers in most parts of the country have not been obliged to seek prior approval from the Ministry for investments such as drainage which normally qualify for grant. In the past, Ministry officials inspected proposals in advance and proposed changes in design and expenditure where they felt it appropriate, but now farmers make their own decisions and claim the grant afterwards.

As a result, few statistics are available at the national level and it has become difficult to estimate the precise amount of drainage undertaken annually. In England and Wales the annual area of field drainage may have fallen somewhat since 1980 but is probably in the range of 75-100,000 hectares a year.

Table 5.1 gives some indication of recent trends and it is interesting to note that full statistics are still available for Northern Ireland, where the system of prior approval has been retained. One of the main reasons for this is that it allows conservation interests to be taken into account before the work starts, if necessary (20). Prior approval is still required in National Parks and SSSIs in England and Wales on conservation grounds, but the government has made it clear that the system is not likely to be reinstated in the wider countryside.

Farmers are eligible for grants for ditching work as well as for under-drainage and this is often a prerequisite for an effective lowering of the water table. In Scotland, for example, ditching work potentially benefits about 4,500 hectares a year, affecting some land immediately and allowing subsequent under-drainage over a larger area (21). In Northern Ireland, ditching work, which is taken to include the replacement of open channels with pipes, is a particularly important form of drainage, affecting 8-18,000 hectares a year and absorbing a significant proportion of the total grants paid directly to farmers (22).

The rates of grant available for drainage have changed several times over the last 30 years, with a rate of 50 per cent being fairly typical. Since entry into the EC, higher rates have been available in the less favoured areas, most recently at 70 per cent. For much of the period drainage work has been eligible for a higher rate of grant than most other forms of farm investment, although recent downward revisions have somewhat eroded this privileged position. Under current arrangements, described in more detail in a later section, the Ministry contributes between 30 and 70 per cent of the cost of works, with no ceiling on expenditure.

Table 5.1: RECENT RATES OF FIELD DRAINAGE IN THE UK

	England & Wales	Scotland	N. Ireland
1949-76*	1,429,300(18%)	255,067(14.6%)	122,259(15%)
1977	91,373	-	5,853
1978	94,531	-	7,749
1979	107,847	12,369	8,651
1980	N/A	16,048	10,284
1981	N/A	12,694	10,387
1982	N/A	16,356	10,957

* The percentage figures are the proportion of the agricultural area drained in this period

Sources: All figures for 1949-76 from Green, 1979 (91)

Figures for England and Wales 1977-79 are from ADAS data for grant applications submitted for approval (not work actually done), drawn from Armstrong, 1978 (19) and Armstrong, 1981 (23). Such data was not collected after 1980

Figures for Scotland 1979-82 are from the Department of Agriculture and Fisheries for Scotland

Figures for Northern Ireland 1977-82 are from the Department of Agriculture, Northern Ireland and refer to "Pure Tile" under-drainage, specifically excluding the area improved by ditching work

---

It is clear that the rate of grant has influenced farmers' decisions. An announcement that the basic rate would be reduced from 60 per cent to a lower and variable rate led to a rush of applications in 1974. A reduction in the standard rate from 50 to 37.5 per cent in 1980 caused applications to fall (23). Other incentives, however, have been equally powerful. Mechanisation has reduced the cost of drainage, which was halved in real terms between 1954 and 1976 (24). At the same time, the introduction of new technologies and general adoption of high input – high yield systems has made drainage more important and worthwhile for many farmers, especially during the boom in agricultural land prices in the mid-1970s. Indeed, it is now not only financially rewarding but "increasingly necessary to reap the returns required given the high price of agricultural land" (25).

Generalisations are difficult because farming conditions vary so much and the precise effects of drainage on ordinary farms are rarely monitored, but drainage appears to produce the biggest returns where it allows arable land to be upgraded or pasture to be converted to arable. According to one authority, a farmer can recoup a drainage investment in as little as one year growing potatoes or similar crops and typically in under five years for cereals (26). The returns on grassland are less clear and probably vary from poor in some of the more marginal areas, for example in parts of Northern Ireland, to good on better lands, for example in wet lowland meadows in England.

Most under-drainage in the UK is installed on clayey soils of some kind, which generally become impermeable at a shallow depth (say 30 cms). Consequently, pipe drains often have to be supplemented by other artifically created channels and fissures to allow the water to move horizontally down to the drains, which are often 70-120 cms below the surface. The main techniques for doing this are mole drainage and subsoiling, both of which involve using an implement to shatter the soil and create temporary channels at a depth of around 50 cms (27). Such operations have to be carried out regularly, say at five year intervals, and are often a crucial part of drainage work on heavy land. There are many examples of the failure to mole drain negating the potential benefits of an expensive new under-drainage project.

Field drainage techniques have undergone certain changes in the last 20 years with several new systems and machines being tried and the current trend is towards more closely spaced drains and the greater use of plastic pipes in place of the traditional clay tiles. However, work has consistently been concentrated on the drier eastern side of the country, particularly in Lincolnshire, the Vale of York, the boulder clay area of East Anglia and the clay lowlands of the Midlands (28). This distribution reflects the intensity of farming and the predominance of high yielding and high value arable land in these areas. The economics of draining grassland in the west have tended to be less appealing, partly because the farms are smaller, hillier and less profitable.

About half of all field drainage in England and Wales takes place on arable land and only about a third on pasture or rough grazing, with the remaining share being accounted for by mixed farming.

The drainage work can be divided into three broad categories:

(a) The most common form of work in Britain is that designed to upgrade drainage on land which is already in agricultural use, where it is not intended to introduce a major change in the type of farming. On nearly 60 per cent of the land drained every year there is no subsequent change of use (29). Most of this is arable and most of it has been drained before.

(b) The second largest category is work designed to permit a change in land use, usually the conversion of pasture to some form of cultivation, either to a mixed farming regime or to an entirely arable system. In the 1970s about 15 per cent of all the land drained in England and Wales was permanent pasture which was subsequently converted in this way (30). Some of this may have been truly wet pasture of value to birds and other areas will have been of landscape interest.

(c) The third category is "new" work, the drainage of land which has either never been drained before or where a previous system is decayed or ineffective, leaving the water table at a high level. This category contains most of the "wetland" sites destroyed by drainage and so is of particular interest. Unfortunately the statistics which are available do not distinguish "new" drainage from other work and there is some doubt about how much takes place. However, it is worth noting that 63 per cent of extensively grazed pasture becomes arable or mixed farming land after it has been drained. Furthermore, about a third of rough grazing, much of it likely to be of wildlife interest, is also converted (31). The fact that this relatively low grade land can be up-graded so substantially by drainage suggests that it was probably wet before the pipes were laid.

The most widely quoted estimate of the amount of damp grassland drained annually is 8,000 hectares, a figure derived from the kind of land use estimates quoted above rather than from survey work or from data about pre-drainage water tables (32). Many Ministry of Agriculture officials regard this as an unrealistically high figure, but even if the losses are only 4–5,000 hectares a year, which is not unlikely, this still represents a very rapid erosion of the remaining resource. Many of the largest areas of loss arise from arterial drainage projects, which allow water tables to be effectively lowered for the first time, and this is often the most damaging aspect of a river improvement scheme from a wildlife point of view.

Government support for agricultural drainage since 1940 has been based consistently on capital grants and the provision of technical advice and research. The initiative for new schemes has been left with farmers and drainage authorities with the agricultural ministries assessing schemes, proferring advice and paying the grants without which little drainage takes place. Drainage is regarded as an important means of raising agricultural productivity and thus meeting wider policy goals, such as increased output and higher farm incomes. Frequently it is argued that the UK must increase its self-sufficiency in food, whether for strategic, economic or even moral reasons. Since agricultural land is a shrinking commodity, drainage clearly has an appeal as a means of upgrading a crucial national resource.

Some indication of the widespread support for drainage in the government and agricultural community can be gauged from a recent report by a House of Lords' Select Committee on the EC's agricultural structures policy. The Committee rather boldly proposed that most capital grants for agricultural investment should be ended, but made an exception of drainage on the grounds that "well-drained farm land kept in good heart is a national asset. Drainage equipment and skills, once lost, might not be easily recovered. Continued provision of capital aid could help encourage drainage in the national interest on farms where it might not otherwise be undertaken" (33).

In more formal terms, a senior Ministry official has stated that "government policy is to assist drainage improvements where:

(a) the works are soundly engineered
(b) economically designed
(c) cost effective, and
(d) have no unacceptable environmental consequences" (34).

Traditionally engineers have played a major role in drainage administration as well as in project design and the Ministry has always given considerable priority to supporting good technical solutions. Indeed, the reliance on capital grants tends to encourage engineering schemes, even where other solutions may be available, especially for urban flooding. For example, compulsory flood insurance and the purchase and demolition of flood prone property are not eligible for government grants. Consequently, large sums may be expended on protecting a small number of properties, where another approach might be more economic (35).

Field drainage schemes are eligible for flat rate grants, payable automatically provided that the works meet certain conditions. For arterial projects, there is no open ended commitment of this kind from the government and the Water Authorities, which are the bodies chiefly concerned, are subject to annual budgetary quotas and variable rates of grant. Thus, the Ministry of Agriculture can exercise considerable control over land drainage by changing the rates of grant payable for different kinds of work and altering budgetary allocations, as well as by its assessments of individual arterial schemes. However, the precise rationale for the particular set of grants available at any one time is rather difficult to decipher. The general objective of cutting public expenditure seems to have been an important consideration in the recent round of grant reductions.

Official references to the environmental consequences of drainage schemes are a relatively recent phenomenon and reflect changes in the law as well as a sharp increase in criticism of land drainage works by environmental groups in the last decade. Most large schemes are now subject to a form of consultation with environmental interests and some are contested strongly. It is also notable that environmental groups have been the strongest critics of the cost-benefit appraisals employed to assess arterial projects and this aspect of drainage policy has become highly controversial.

At present, the crucial cost-benefit appraisals for Water Authority and IDB schemes are treated as confidential, on the grounds that they contain sensitive information about farmers' private plans and business affairs.   The Ministry of Agriculture and   the   Treasury   are   the only external   bodies   to whom   the appraisals are made available,   and neither local authorities nor the   Nature   Conservancy Council is allowed to see them.   This degree   of secrecy seems quite excessive and has been   criticised heavily by environmental groups such as the Council for the Protection of Rural England and the Royal Society for the Protection of Birds (36).

In 1978,   the Minister of Agriculture took the exceptional step   of setting up a public inquiry into a river embankment   and pump-drainage   scheme proposed by the Southern Water Authority at Amberley Wildbrooks in Sussex.   The project, which would   have destroyed an important site, was opposed by several environmental bodies   and eventually turned down because it was not   considered cost-effective.   This decision, the first rejection of a major scheme   under   the current legislation, caused the cost-benefit appraisal methods to be changed, but even in their present form they   appear   systematically to overestimate the real rate of return for most projects.   In particular, the real social benefits   of greater agricultural production tend to be exaggerated because   they are based on the prices which farmers are   expected to   receive for their produce,   even though these are heavily subsidised.   If more rigorous methods were used, it is likely that   many   schemes would show a return of less than 5 per cent, which is the minimum acceptable to the Treasury (37).

The   procedure for assessing whether or not new arterial drainage schemes are economically worthwhile lies at the heart of land   drainage   policy.   Over the last 20 years appraisals have "improved from being mere intuitive judgements to becoming quite sophisticated economic analyses" (38).   However, most independent observers agree that a considerable number of deficiencies remain and   the Ministry is now showing increasing signs of listening to these criticisms and preparing adjustments.   Nonetheless, it has been   clear   for   some time that many schemes are not as cost-effective   as they have been presented to be and   the underlying rationale for maintaining the current level of work has been more political than economic.

The Organisation of Agricultural Drainage

Some   of   the administrative arrangements for land   drainage were   described in the previous section and it is perhaps unnecessary   to emphasise that the Ministry of Agriculture and   its counterparts in Scotland and Northern Ireland have a pivotal role in drainage affairs.   The Ministry advises on the potential both for   field drainage and larger schemes through its local   network of   ADAS field staff.   The MAFF Regional Engineer is consulted over   the   preparation of Water Authorities' five year rolling programmes   of work, as well as the design details of individual schemes.   The Ministry sets the rate of grant for both field and

133

arterial drainage projects, and determines total subsidy levels
for the latter. It requires Water Authorities to prepare cost-
benefit assessments for proposed drainage and flood alleviation
schemes and to submit these for scrutiny. If the grant is
denied, a scheme is unlikely to go ahead. In Scotland and
Northern Ireland, where there are no Water Authorities, the
agricultural ministries have even greater powers.

In England and Wales there are 10 Regional Water
Authorities, which were formed as a result of a general
reorganisation of water affairs in 1973. These statutory bodies
have wide responsibilities for water management, covering supply,
conservation, pollution control, land drainage, sewerage and even
water-based recreation and amenity. They are more akin to
nationalised industries than to local government bodies and since
the latest round of reorganisation in 1983 they have been managed
by small boards of between nine and fifteen members, appointed by
government ministers rather than elected. Centralised appoint-
ments have taken the place of the previous system whereby more
than half the members of the board were nominated by local government. Under the old system, between two and four members were
appointed by the Ministry of Agriculture, to represent drainage,
farming and fishery interests, but this quota has been reduced to
a maximum of two. The other members of the board are now
appointed by the Secretary of State for the Environment.

Although land drainage is only a small part of the Water
Authorities' total responsibilities, it receives special
treatment, being financed and organised separately from all other
activities. This privileged position has been defended fiercely
by the Ministry of Agriculture and farming interests during the
successive reorganisations of water affairs and has survived with
remarkably few changes. However, both the treasured independence
and the Ministry of Agriculture's influential role within what is
otherwise the Department of Environment's sphere of interest may
be threatened by an inter-departmental review of drainage affairs
set up in late 1982. This was expected to produce a discussion
paper within a short period, but nothing had appeared by spring
1984.

Under current arrangements, each Water Authority is obliged
to set up a Regional Land Drainage Committee to which it must
delegate all its land drainage functions. The Chairman and some
other members of this Committee are appointed by the Ministry of
Agriculture and only two members are appointed by the Water
Authority. The majority are representatives of County Councils
in the area, which provide a substantial share of the land
drainage budget.

In contrast to other water services, which are financed by
a direct charge levied on consumers, the Land Drainage Committee
obtain their funds by imposing a levy on the County Councils
within their jurisdiction. This becomes an element in the
general rate demand and in the early 1980s ranged from about
0.23p in the £ in Northumbria to 1.89p in Somerset (39). The

Ministry of Agriculture provides grants for improvement works, but not for maintenance.

In most, but not all, Water Authorities, the Regional Land Drainage Committees have delegated many of their powers to yet another layer in the administration, the Local Land Drainage Committees. There are currently 24 of these in England and Wales, drawing their membership from both the main Regional Committees and from the County Councils (40). These Committees tend to make most of the decisions about individual schemes as opposed to general policy, and may be responsible for quite large areas. Like the Regional Committees, they tend to be dominated by farmers and landowners, the group which traditionally County Councils have turned to when making their nominations. There is no formal representation of conservation intests.

The landowning interest has an even stronger hold on the smallest and most idiosyncratic form of drainage authority, Internal Drainage Boards (IDBs). These Boards originally grew up in areas where drainage was particularly important for agriculture and they still cover many of the low lying districts most subject to flooding. Some Boards have long and complex histories going back to medieval times and they developed in a somewhat haphazard pattern, varying greatly in size, powers and vigour. They still vary in size, from around 45,000 hectares down to about 100, but in 1930 they were all brought under a single piece of legislation, the Land Drainage Act. This preserved much of their autonomy, which has remained largely unscathed to the present day, since for most purposes they are responsible directly to the Minister of Agriculture rather than to the local Water Authority. In principle, the Minister has to approve many of the Boards' routine activities, even the expenses paid to the Chairmen (41), but in practice they are not subject to a great deal of outside interference.

The Boards levy drainage rates on all owners and occupiers of property within their district, whether rural or urban. However, it is only the agricultural ratepayers which elect the members, with the largest landowners having the most votes. Only local landowners and occupiers or their nominees can stand for election, the candidates for which must meet certain property requirements, and there are no places reserved for conservationists or any other outside interest. Sometimes there are no elections at all and the Board members simply co-opt new recruits as required. Some Boards are large enough to employ their own engineers and professional staff but many rely on outside contractors. The clerk is usually a solicitor and indeed some specialise in this line of work, one man is reported to be clerk to 32 IDBs (42).

The Boards are concerned mostly with the maintenace of main drains, pumping stations and minor water courses and with improvements where considered necessary. Often these channels discharge into the Water Authority's main rivers and works may be planned for mutual benefit. The Boards work in close association with local farmers and their outlook is very much agricultural. Some are dominated by only a few landowners, but they all have statutory powers to drain and enter land without permission. After decades of relative obscurity they have been the subject of some scrutiny and debate in recent years (43). Environmentalists particularly have criticised them as being antiquated and self-serving institutions able to obtain 50 per cent public grants for improvement schemes to benefit their own members with little reference to wider public interests such as conservation (44). The IDBs are somewhat of an anomaly in the contemporary hierarchy of drainage administration and their future is increasingly uncertain. There is a growing trend towards amalgamation and a few have been taken over entirely by Water Authorities. Those that remain can expect some erosion of their special status as a result of the current inter-departmental review.

Arterial drainage schemes are not subject to local authority planning controls and public inquiries are extremely rare. Until recently there were little or no formal procedures for taking account of landscape or wildlife interests when planning new arterial schemes. Most drainage engineers had scant knowledge or experience of conservation and their plans were dominated by technical considerations. Consequently, many schemes were designed unsympathetically, with rivers being straightened and dredged to an even depth, banks being graded to a uniform 45° slope, and trees and other vegetation removed and replaced with freshly sown grass.

Over the last 20 years a new body of environmental legislation has grown up, strongly reinforced by the efforts of the voluntary conservation bodies, the strength of which grew markedly in the 1970s. At first the environmental responsibilities placed on drainage authorities were rather general in character, for example under the Water Resources Act 1963 and the Countryside Act 1968. In the 1973 Act, the obligation on Water Authorities was to "have regard to the desirability of preserving natural beauty.." (and conserving fauna and flora). Only with the passage of the Wildlife and Countryside Act in 1981 was this strengthened to a requirement that, where it is consistent with the primary purpose of their work, they should "further the conservation and enhancement of natural beauty and the conservation of flora, fauna and geological or physiograhical features of special interest". Both Water Authorities and IDBs are covered by this requirement, the application of which is explained in Guidance Notes issued by the Department of the Environment, MAFF and the Welsh Office. Somewhat anomalously, Scotland has been exempted from this change.

Fisheries benefit from the general level of protection extended to all fauna, but are also covered by special legislation, particularly the Salmon and Freshwater Fisheries Act 1975 under which Water Authorities have a duty to "maintain, improve and develop the salmon fisheries, trout fisheries, freshwater fisheries and eel fisheries" in their area. The Act also requires them to set up advisory committees for consultation on fishery questions. More generally, there is a clause in the 1976 Land Drainage Act which requires of all authorities that in the exercise of their powers "due regard shall be had to the interests of fisheries (including sea fisheries)". Fisheries are also protected by ordinary property rights under which compensation is payable for damages. Most Water Authorities are aware of the value of the main salmon and trout rivers, but many coarse fisheries have suffered from improvement schemes in the lowlands.

Those wetlands which are sites of special scientific interest, SSSIs, now receive a limited amount of protection under the 1981 Wildlife and Countryside Act. This obliges drainage authorities to consult the Nature Conservancy Council (NCC) over schemes likely to affect SSSIs, which most of them had begun to do in the late 1970s anyway. However, there is still no general presumption against drainage improvement works within SSSIs. Much depends on the attitude of Water Authority staff, which varies considerably, and the informal consultation system which has built up between the Regional Water Authorities and some of the principal conservation bodies.

The consultation system involves the Royal Society for Nature Conservation, the Royal Society for the Protection of Birds and the Nature Conservancy Council in regular meetings with the land drainage committees of all the water authorities apart from the Thames. Typically, there is an annual meeting with the regional committee, where the rolling programme and Section 24(5) surveys may be discussed, for example. This is backed up by annual or sometimes more frequent meetings with the local drainage committee where prospective improvement works and major maintenance schemes can be reviewed. Sometimes this is followed by site meetings for sensitive schemes.

These meetings have given Water Authorities access to much specialised knowledge and a clearer understanding of conservation requirements and have led to compromises which have avoided public conflict over several schemes. This does not mean that schemes which have been vetted in this way are always acceptable environmentally. The wildlife conservation bodies are not especially concerned with the landscape and recreation aspects of improvement works, even though these may be of particular importance for local people. In 1983, for example, the Council for the Protection of Rural England objected to drainage proposals for the river Soar in Leicestershire mainly on the grounds of the beauty of the valley and the defectiveness of the economic appraisal. Most of the wildlife interests, on the other hand, had withdrawn their opposition following detailed compromises by the Severn-Trent Water Authority. Nonetheless, the consultations are undoubtedly valuable and are welcomed by several authorities as well as by conservationists.

With the passage of the new Water Act in 1983 the future of this consultation system appeared jeopardised, since each Water Authority was required to set up a "Regional Recreation and

Conservation Committee" as a forum for the views of amenity, conservation, fishery, recreation and sporting interests. These committees are only beginning to come into operation in 1984 and there were fears that the specific concerns of conservationists would disappear in a hotch-potch of different interests. In the event, however, it seems that all Water Authorities have agreed to retain the informal consultation arrangements at the divisional level and most at the regional level (45), and there is also likely to be some environmental representation on the statutory committees.

The environmental acceptability of arterial drainage schemes depends greatly on their design, the willingness of engineers to leave certain features untouched, to compromise on others and to carry out the works in a sensitive manner, for example confining heavy machinery to one bank. Such compromises have become increasingly common over the last decade and most conservation bodies agree that there has been a marked improvement in the way in which new schemes are tackled. Many local drainage committees have formally adopted the "Conservation and Land Drainage Guidelines", which suggest practical methods of reconciling drainage objectives with conservation, fisheries, recreation and other interests (46). Where followed, these guidelines have helped to forge successful compromises and it is ironic that the body which drew them up, the Water Space Amenity Commission, has recently been abolished.

Compromise is not always possible, especially where a scheme is opposed per se by environmental groups. This is most likely to happen where it is intended to make a significant reduction in the level of the water table, to the detriment of neighbouring wetlands, particularly marsh and wet meadows. In these cases an element of field drainage is likely to be involved.

Field drainage is administered entirely by MAFF through the Land and Water Service, itself a sub-division of the Agricultural Development and Advisory Service (ADAS). The Ministry has offices throughout the country, located at both the regional and the more local divisional levels. The ADAS advisory staff are in direct contact with farmers, offering them advice on drainage and responding to their enquiries, but no longer scrutinising plans before work begins. Until 1980 the ADAS staff maintained tight control over drainage design and the quality of workmanship and materials. Now, prior approval is required for drainage and other grant-aided improvements only in National Parks, in Northern Ireland and within national nature reserves and SSSIs; in the great majority of the country farmers and contractors can begin work when they like and submit their claim for grants afterwards.

Under the present arrangements, farmers can get drainage advice from a variety of sources, including contractors and consultants. It is too early to make a full assessment of the effects of this change. However, several contractors are experimenting with techniques which would not have met Ministry approval under the old regime and there are fears that "cowboy" companies may lower standards. There are about 250 drainage contractors in the UK, but the 30 per cent of firms which belong to the National Association of Agricultural Contractors do most of the work and they have recently published a specification of appropriate standards in an attempt at self-regulation (47).

Although their power to influence drainage design has diminished, ADAS officers have acquired a new statutory responsibility to advise farmers on all aspects of conservation under the Wildlife and Countryside Act. Their role is intended to be a positive one, promoting an awareness of conservation and seeking compromise between agricultural and environmental considerations. In doing so, they can draw on the services of the NCC and the Countryside Commission and some officers have developed a close relationship with the Farming and Wildlife Advisory Group, a voluntary body, consisting mainly of farmers with an interest in conservation. However, ADAS staff are traditionally concerned with promoting agricultural efficiency and this is still their main task. Many people doubt whether they are adequately equipped or well placed for a new role as environmental watchdogs.

Technically, all farmers have a general obligation to consider the effect of their work on the environment under Section 11 of the 1968 Countryside Act. When applying for a grant for a capital project such as field drainage, farmers must sign a declaration that, in the work which they have completed already, they have taken into account the conservation and amenity value of the countryside. Few farmers are known to have used this opportunity to express their misgivings.

It is rare for the Ministry to refuse a farmer's grant application and checks are made on only a small proportion of schemes. However, grants may be withheld if a scheme is regarded as technically unsound, unreasonably expensive or unacceptable from a conservation viewpoint. In principle, an ADAS officer could recommend that a grant should be withheld if a farmer ignores their advice and destroys a wetland site by drainage. In practice this occurs extremely rarely and, in one recent case, the Minister of Agriculture himself took the final decision not to pay a grant on a scheme in West Sedgemoor, which is now an SSSI.

In places where the prior approval system does still operate, there may be environmental objections to a farmer's drainage proposals from the NCC or the National Park Authorities (or the Department of Agriculture, Northern Ireland). No figures are available for the proportion of drainage schemes rejected on these grounds, but it appears that objections are raised on about 10 per cent of all prior approval cases and about 1 per cent cannot be resolved by mutual agreement (48). Such cases go to the Minister of Agriculture for a final decision, with a submission from ADAS on the farming case and from the NCC, or National Park Authority on the conservation arguments. In

England, the Secretary of State for the Environment is consulted. The farmer must be offered a management agreement if this objection is upheld; the implications of this are discussed in the last section.

Finance for Drainage

Land drainage in the UK is financed by ratepayers and farmers, with the aid of grants from the Ministry of Agriculture and some contributions from the European Community. In very broad terms, the cost of new arterial drainage works is divided fairly evenly between local authorities and the Ministry of Agriculture, while farmers installing field drainage can qualify for grants in the range of 30-70 per cent. The government reclaims a proportion of the cost of some field drainage grants from FEOGA, the EEC agricultural fund, and also gets contributions from this source for some specific schemes. Since there are several different capital grant schemes for farmers, a variety of drainage authorities and somewhat different arrangements in Scotland and Northern Ireland than elsewhere, the precise pattern of finance is rather complex, but it is perhaps useful to keep the overall view in mind.

The largest spenders on arterial drainage are the Water Authorities in England and Wales, with total outgoings of about £70 million in 1981/82. In that year they spent approximately £40 million on over 100 drainage improvement works of which about 27 per cent were classified as purely agricultural (49). As we have seen, the Authorities finance drainage work by raising a levy, known as a "precept" on County Councils in their area and obtain an average grant of about 55 per cent from MAFF for new projects. This average disguises quite a large range, from 12 per cent in Northumbria to 80 per cent in Lincolnshire. The precise rate for each Authority is worked out by a complicated formula taking account of MAFF's perception of local needs and resources. An extra 15 per cent is payable on sea defence works, except for the Thames Flood Protection Scheme which is a special case involving very substantial sums of money (50).

Although farmers benefit from these arterial drainage improvements, they escape any significant contribution to the cost, since agricultural land is exempt from County Council rates. Furthermore, farmers can claim sizeable sums in compensation for any land they lose in the course of river widening projects which may be designed to increase the profitability of their own farms (51).

Internal Drainage Boards finance their work by a levy on all property owners within their boundaries, using a rather peculiar system of calculating rateable values by reference to a form of income tax assessment last made in 1935. In districts containing an urban population, agricultural landowners may pay only a small proportion of these rates. In 1980/81 IDBs spent a total of about £18 million, mostly on maintenance work, but received grants totalling £2.78 million from MAFF, which pays half the cost of improvement works (52). Since it is only improvement works which are grant aided, there has been some controversy about whether IDBs are obliged to replace old pumps with more powerful machines able to lower water tables more than their predecessors in order .to qualify for grants. In principle, grants should be available at the end of a pump's life for a new machine of similar capacity. However, in practice the additional cost of installing a larger pump is likely to be small and this option is more often chosen by IDBs.

Local authorities are also eligible for grant aid from MAFF for drainage work, although most of this is of an urban character. The precise rate varies with the scheme and authority involved, but the usual range is 20 to 50 per cent with an average of about 45 per cent. Approximately £4 million is paid annually (53).

By 1983/84, the MAFF land drainage grant allocation for Water Authorities, local authorities and IDBs had risen to £35 million, but was expected to be underspent (54). In a climate of reduced public expenditure, it is now planned to lower these grants by five percentage points and to reduce MAFF's expenditure in this area considerably (55).

In Scotland, there is relatively little expenditure on arterial drainage and in most cases the cost of new works is borne by the landowners concerned, who are eligible for a 50 per cent grant in the lowlands and 70 per cent in the "less favoured areas", which include most of the Scottish hill country. In Northern Ireland, the Department of Agriculture has the sole responsibility for draining main rivers and water courses and employs its own staff for the purpose. Total expenditure was £8.9 million in 1982/83, of which 38 per cent was accounted for by rural maintenance work and 18 per cent by rural new works (56). Some contribution to these costs is made by local ratepayers under rather complex arrangements unique to Northern Ireland, and the European Regional Development Fund has provided some grant aid for urban schemes.

The major contribution from the Community is for cross-border arterial schemes, of which the first is the drainage of the Blackwater catchment, due to begin in the spring of 1984. In this case, FEOGA will finance up to half the cost of eligible works. In the past, it was also possible to obtain FEOGA grants for certain individual arterial drainage projects in any part of the UK under the now superseded Regulation 17/64. Most of the schemes for which Community aid was requested were in East Anglia and the East Midlands and about £2 million has been obtained for arterial work in the Fens. Almost half ot his has been spent on a single large scheme near March in Cambridgeshire where the peatland is shrinking rapidly as a result of earlier drainage and a powerful new pump has been installed, together with extensive new channel works (57).

Farmers installing field drainage usually do so individually rather than in a group. The Agricultural Ministries paid out about £60 million in grants for field drainage in 1982, most of it under one of two basic schemes. Both are designed in conformity with the EC farm structures policy and one, the Agriculture and Horticulture Development Scheme (AHDS), is the principal means whereby Directive 72/159 on the modernisation of farms has been implemented in the UK. It is equivalent to the scheme for "development farms" in Ireland, described in rather more detail in Chapter 3.

The scheme is aimed principally at small farmers proposing a planned series of investments to modernise their holdings over a period of up to six years. The procedure for qualifying is relatively complex and no more than 8,000 farmers made applications in the peak year, which was 1981. However, the rate of grant available is more generous than under the less restrictive scheme, being 50 per cent generally and 70 per cent in the less favoured areas. This is a higher rate of grant than that offered for any other form of agricultural investment, despite the environmental sensitivity of drainage.

Those farmers who enter the development scheme frequently include some field drainage in their farm plan and this item accounts for about 20-25 per cent of the total grants paid. Grants for field drainage totalled £17.7 million in 1981 and £26 million in 1982, a quarter of which is recoverable from the Community's agricultural fund (58).

Slightly more is spent on field drainage under the other main scheme, the Agriculture and Horticulture Grant Scheme (AHGS), which is available to farmers of any size at any time, without having to have a development plan. There are some restrictions, for example on pig farms, but many forms of investment are eligible for grant and the rates for field drainage are amongst the highest. In the early 1970s most farmers were able to obtain 60 per cent grants for field drainage, but this has declined over the last decade and now stands at 30 per cent, having been reduced from 37.5 per cent in 1983 as one of a series of economy measures which also affected arterial drainage. Rates for less favoured areas have traditionally been higher, but were also trimmed from 70 to 60 per cent in 1983. In 1981 total grant payments for drainage under the AHGS were £24.2 million rising to around £31 million in 1982 (59).

Farmers investing in field drainage have a number of sources to which they can turn for loans to meet their share of costs. Amongst these is the Agricultural Mortgage Corporation which lends money relatively cheaply and looks kindly on drainage plans. According to one spokesman, "We realise how important drainage is and will quite happily lend money for drainage purposes" (60).

One of the areas of most concentrated expenditure on field drainage in the UK is Northern Ireland. In 1982 capital grants under the two schemes described above totalled £6.3 million for piped under-drainage, £2.2 million for the cleaning or piping of open drains and £423,000 for hedge removal and piping open drains alongside. In addition to this there is substantial further aid to drainage under the special "Agricultural Development Plan" which applies solely to the less favoured areas of the Province and is intended to balance the special Community aid schemes for agriculture in the Republic. The scheme is intended to run for 10 years, assisting farmers who do not qualify for development plans, and covers fencing, pasture improvement, farm roads and other investments as well as drainage. Drainage qualifies for a 70 per cent grant and the Department paid out £3.9 million under this heading in 1982/83 (61). The whole Agricultural Development Programme is expected to cost £80 million over its 10 year life of which £28 million will be refunded by the Community's agriculture fund.

Another regional project receiving EEC support is the Integrated Development Programme for the Western Isles of Scotland. This is intended as a pilot project for socio-economic development in relatively poor regions, involving investment in agriculture and fisheries at the same time as building up tourist facilities, rural crafts, training and education. It is intended to last five years, with an agricultural budget of £20 million, of which 40 per cent is recoverable from FEOGA.

The scheme has been highly controversial because the area covered by the programme contains 35 SSSIs and a substantial area of "machair", unique strips of sandy grassland along the coast. The machair supports some of the highest densities of breeding waders in Western Europe and is vulnerable to development by drainage, ploughing, reseeding and more intensive stocking rates, the kind of developments which the Programme is designed to promote. The availability of more generous grants has certainly stimulated local drainage efforts in the first year of operation. Initially, these have been small scale, but it is expected that larger projects with a potentially serious impact on the environment will be submitted in the next few years and the NCC is already negotiating voluntary management agreements to safeguard important wetlands on one island, North Uist (62).

Impact on Wetlands

It is beyond dispute that drainage has had a profound effect on Britain's freshwater wetlands. One recent report commented that "...the compound effect of land drainage improvement works over the years has been to dramatically reduce the area of wetland habitat. Most of our river valleys are now impoverished of wetland wildlife" (63).

Some of the more important British wetlands are shown in Figure 6. Many of the remaining areas of fen, marsh, mire and bog are remnants of once greater expanses, drained over centuries of agricultural improvement. With the quickened pace of drainage activities over the last three decades reserves of wetland habitat have been considerably diminished and there are likely to be further substantial losses. These will include not only scientifically valuable sites, but also hundreds of distinctive if not necessarily scientifically distinguished ponds, streams and patches of marsh.

Wetlands are often vulnerable habitats and are threatened from many different quarters. Besides drainage, some of the principal causes of damage are industrial reclamation, pollution from agricultural and urban sources, afforestation, waste dumping, shooting, peat exploitation, recreational development and reservoir construction. Chemical enrichment, mainly by nitrogen and phosphorous, is a particularly important threat to lowland sites. Often it can be traced to fertiliser or slurry run-off from neighbouring fields or from the discharge of sewage into water courses. Enrichment has been a severe problem in the Norfolk Broads area, where many sites have been damaged by an accumulation of phosphorous. Another example is Rostherne National Nature Reserve in Cheshire, which receives treated effluent from three local sewage plants and is being affected by a build-up of phosphates. At this Ramsar site there are also threats from silage effluent and concern about aerial pesticide spraying (64).

In the lowlands and along the estuarine mudflats, urban as well as agricultural developments are liable to encroach on valuable sites. For example, at Seal Sands in the Tees Estuary, the Port Authority is proposing to reclaim an area of about 175 hectares of mudflats and marsh used by large numbers of wintering waders, even though less than a tenth of the original site remains undeveloped (65). At Hayle Estuary in Cornwall, the threats are as various as dredging, the development of a marina and a proposed commercial shellfish farm (66). Several sites are used for waste tipping, including part of Crymlyn Bog near Swansea, the largest lowland fen in Wales. Peat extraction is on a much smaller scale than in Ireland but is still important in some areas such as the Somerset levels. In a recent court case, an elderly naturalist was awarded the medieval right of turbary, the freedom to cut peat, from a moor near Doncaster known as the Waste of Thorne in an effort to prevent a large fertiliser company from exploiting the site (67).

In the uplands, large areas of acid peat bog have been afforested, even though there are some doubts about the capacity of many sites to sustain commercial levels of production in the long term. Investigations into the history of 120 raised bogs in lowland Scotland have revealed that about half their total area has been afforested in the last hundred years or so (68). On the thinner areas of blanket bog in the uplands, over-grazing, afforestation and, in some areas, air pollution are amongst the main causes of damage.

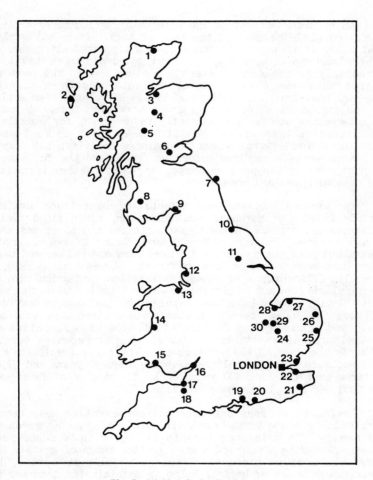

Fig. 6: Wetlands in Britain

1. Strathy River Bogs
2. Hebridean machair, South Uist
3. Moray Firth
4. Insh Marshes
5. Rannock Moor
6. Lock Leven
7. Lindisfarne
8. Silver Flowe
9. Solway Firth
10. Teesmouth Flats and Marshes
11. Derwent Ings
12. Ribble Estuary
13. Dee Estuary
14. Borth Bog
15. Crymlyn Bog
16. Severn Estuary
17. Bridgewater Bay
18. Somerset Levels
19. Chichester Harbour
20. Amberley Wild Brooks
21. Romney Marsh
22. North Kent Marshes
23. Foulness and Maplin Sands
24. Wicken Fen
25. Minsmere
26. The Norfolk Broads, includes Halvergate Marshes
27. North Norfolk Coast
28. The Wash
29. Ouse Washes
30. Woodwalton Fen

An accurate account of the effects of agricultural drainage is not possible because of the lack of data. It is quite plain that substantial areas of wetland have disappeared altogether and others have been greatly modified by drainage activities, especially in the mid-nineteenth century and in the post-war period. However, there is an almost total dearth of rigorous pre- and post-drainage studies and little effort has been applied to monitoring the effects of drainage work over time. A number of interesting studies are currently in progress, for example an investigation into the history of Romney Marsh in Kent where there have been several waves of drainage activity, but a great deal more work is required before we understand the full impact of past work or the precise consequences of further inroads on the remaining wetland ecosystems.

The wetland habitats most affected by agricultural drainage include freshwater marshes, fen, saltmarsh, river flood plains, unimproved rivers and streams, farm ditches and ponds and areas of wet meadow. The Nature Conservancy Council have estimated that about half the country's lowland fens and valley and basin mires have been destroyed or significantly damaged since 1949, as a result of "drainage operations, reclamation for agriculture and chemical enrichment of drainage water " (69). Over the same period, many rivers have been "spoiled by drainage operations" and more than 60 per cent of lowland raised mires have also been destroyed or damaged, a decline attributed to reclamation for agriculture, afforestation, peat winning or repeated burning (70). In the Wash, 2,100 hectares of saltmarsh and mudflats have been reclaimed for agriculture over the last 30 years and 32,000 hectares over the last 400 years (71). The number of farm ponds has declined steeply in many counties (72).

Conflicts between drainage and conservation have become particularly acute in the remaining areas of grazing marsh and wet meadow. In this damp terrain is likely to be found reed, sedges, flowering plants and a much greater range of grasses than occur in improved pasture. Grazing, usually by cattle, but sometimes by sheep or horses, helps to maintain the interest and character of many such places and from a conservation point of view it is essential not only to avoid drainage, but also to ensure the continuation of some form of traditional management. This is usually extensive grazing, perhaps with a crop of hay taken in the summer.

Wet pasture and rough grazing of this kind tend to produce a relatively low income for farmers, most of whom take the opportunity of draining and improving it when it becomes practical or economic to do so. Consequently, these wet landscapes are no longer a common part of the lowland scene, and those that remain are under increasing pressure, despite their high amenity value. The advent of a new arterial drainage scheme, or installation of more powerful pumps may change the face of an entire area, as it has done in most of the Fens, while the sale of a farm to a new owner may signal the draining and reseeding of a field or two which the previous occupant was content to leave alone. Drainage is often the focal point of conflict over such sites because it is the single step most likely to destroy them and a decisive element in their future management. Many farmers who have not drained their land feel aggrieved that they are being deprived of an opportunity which most others have already taken advantage of and argue that conservationists are seeking to confine them to a backward and unprofitable form of agriculture. Although conservation depends in practice on voluntary co-operation and large compensation payments, bitterness has emerged in several places, notably in the Somerset Levels. Effigies of the Chairman and a regional staff member of the NCC were burned during negotiations over the designation of a new SSSI at West Sedgemore in 1983.

The largest remaining areas of marshland and wet meadows have become almost household words over the last five years as a result of conflicts over drainage. The Royal Society for the Protection of Birds has stated that "Improvement schemes threaten nearly all of the remaining ornithologically important wet lowland grassland in England and Wales" (73). Their list of such sites includes:

- the Nene Valley in Cambridgeshire, threatened by a comprehensive river improvement scheme
- the North Kent Marshes, threatened by a series of field drainage operations in the area, resulting in grazing marsh being converted to arable land
- the Yare Marshes in Norfolk, parts threatened by pumpdrainage schemes and the possible construction of the Yare Barrier, a major flood control project
- the Somerset Levels, threatened by drainage projects of several kinds
- the Pevensey Levels in Sussex, threatened by local pumping stations designed to reduce flooding and improve control of water levels
- the Derwent Ings in Yorkshire, where the local IDP has proposed a highly controversial pump-drainage project

This is only about half the major sites listed by the RSPB and ignores the much greater number of smaller wetlands potentially affected by drainage schemes. If all the agricultural drainage projects listed in the Water Authority Section 24(5) surveys were carried out, most sites of any size would be eliminated. In practice, this will not occur, and while some threats are imminent, such as a proposal by the Ouse and Derwent IDP to instal a more powerful pump to lower water levels on part of the Derwent Ings, others are much more remote. However, all remaining sites are valuable and conservationists are increasingly reluctant to compromise, especially since many of the larger wetlands, such as the Somerset Levels (60,000 hectares) or North Kent Marshes (14,750 hectares) have already suffered extensive damage and the area of true wildlife interest is much smaller than in the past.

The North Kent Marshes are an example of a site where there has been little arterial work, but extensive field drainage. By

1982, the true area of grazing marsh had shrunk to 7,675 hectares compared with almost double this amount in 1935. About 5,200 hectares has been converted to arable as a result of improved drainage, much of it taking place since 1968 (74). The loss has been even greater in Romney Marsh, in the south of the county, where few truly wet sites now remain as a result of cumulative field drainage and river improvement schemes.

All aspects of the wetland environment have been affected by changes on this scale. The appearance of many lowland valleys has been altered drastically by river improvement schemes and subsequent field drainage. Hedgerows, for example, are often removed in the process of installing underdrainage and enlarging old fields. In extreme cases, a rich river margin scene can be replaced by a straight and rather featureless channel abutted by freshly ploughed fields.

Considerable losses of wetland flora have been observed over the last century and both agricultural drainage and subsequent changes in the management of farmland and water courses have played a major role in this. The use of aquatic herbicides for ditch maintenance has aggravated the effect of channel works and lower water tables. It has been estimated that the distribution of the more commonplace aquatic species was reduced by about 60 per cent between 1930 and 1980 (75), while many plants have become rarer. Over the last three centuries, only seven plants native to fen, marsh or bog have become extinct, but now there are 26 species listed as "vulnerable" and as the survivors are found in a diminishing list of sites, incremental habitat loss is of increasing significance.

A member of the NCC's Chief Scientist's team has summarised the problem. "For the aquatic, bog and fen species, the habitat remaining is all too often the linear drainage channel and its banks. For such "wetland" species to survive, the management of their habitats must be in sympathy with their needs. Unfortunatly this rarely occurs. The relict grazing marsh offers the greatest chance for their survival and it is no coincidence that the vulnerable potamogeton acutifolius is only found on relict grazing marshes, such as the Pevensey Levels, Sussex, the Amberley Wild Brooks, Sussex and Limpenhoe Fen, Norfolk. It is also no coincidence that in 1960 this species was recorded from twenty 10 kilometre squares and is now only found in seven 10 kilometre squares... These losses have to be associated with the attrition on grazing marsh habitats" (76).

Losses of fauna, especially insect life, amphibians, otters and birds have also been marked. Three or four of the 43 species of dragonfly found in Britain have become extinct since 1953 and many others have declined, representing one of the most visible losses of any animal group. Reptiles and amphibians have undergone a parallel decline; frogs, for example, are no longer common in many parts of the country. The otter has become rare in much of England and Wales for a variety of reasons, including poisoning by pesticides and habitat loss. Some fish populations have also suffered, with trout being replaced by coarse fish in a number of streams.

The effects of drainage on breeding and wintering birds were discussed in Chapter 1 and there is plenty of evidence that drainage has reduced the density of breeding waders and waterfowl on marshy sites in Britain. Some rare breeding species, such as the bittern, have been affected by habitat loss. Similarly, it is known that many sites of importance for wintering birds have been destroyed (77). A very thorough recent survey of waders breeding on wet lowland grasslands in England and Wales has shown that populations of several species are lower than expected. Redshank and snipe have become highly unusual breeding birds, largely confined to a few major sites, including the Derwent Ings, North Kent Marshes and Somerset Levels, all of which are threatened by drainage. In Oxfordshire, 112 pairs of redshank were observed in 1939, mostly nesting on grassland; by 1982 this had fallen to 12 pairs (78).

In general terms, it is the plants and animals of habitats vulnerable to agricultural intensification which have declined most in the last 30 years. Notable amongst these are lowland grasslands, heaths and wetlands (79).

The effects of land drainage are as varied as the number of individual schemes, and are not always as visible or as well understood as the impact on wildlife and landscape. In some places, such as the Somerset Levels, lower water tables have damaged interesting archaeological remains and a number of important sites are under threat from drainage. Another problem encountered in Somerset and also in parts of the Norfolk Broads is the existence of acid sulphate soils. Such soils can develop extreme acidity following drainage, reaching a pH of less than four and releasing pollutants in the form of sulphuric acid and soluble iron which is precipitated as ochre in the drainage system. Polluted drainage water can kill aquatic plants, invertebrates and fish and the ochre can cause drains to be blocked (80). Not only does this have important environmental consequences, it can also render drainage uneconomic.

One of the areas of greatest uncertainty is the effect of drainage on the broad ecological and hydrological functions of wetlands. There is particular interest in the question of whether drainage leads to more rapid water run-off from the area concerned, with adverse consequences on flood patterns downstream. There is evidence that this can happen on some soils, but much more work needs to be done in this area (81).

Most individual wetland sites have limited protection unless they are national nature reserves, or are owned by one of the voluntary conservation bodies. Outside these relatively small areas legal protection is confined largely to sites of special scientific interest (SSSIs). There are just over 4,000 such sites in England, Scotland and Wales and none in Northern Ireland where wildlife protection is somewhat weaker, but the equivalent sites are called "Areas of Scientific Interest". SSSIs are designated by the Nature Conservancy Council (NCC), a semi-autonomous authority funded by and responsible to the Department of the Environment.

Since the late 1970s there has been a fierce debate in Britain about the extent to which SSSIs and other important sites should be protected by law. This has not been resolved by the latest legislation, the 1981 Wildlife and Countryside Act, which relies principally on voluntary co-operation for the protection of the countryside. This approach was resisted by many of the leading conservation groups but has a strong appeal to the Conservative government which drew up the legislation.

The 1981 Act did strengthen the arrangements for protecting SSSIs. The NCC now has to advise about 30,000 owners and occu-piers of why their sites are of scientific interest and what kind of operations might harm them. This process is known as "renoti-fication" and is proceeding slowly; only 11 per cent of sites had been renotified by late 1983 and the process is unlikely to be complete before 1986. Owners in turn are required to notify the NCC of their intention to carry out any operations which might be harmful three months in advance. At this point negot-iations can be started, during the course of which both sides often make compromises; it is not uncommon for the NCC to give up part of an SSSI for example. If negotiations fail, the NCC can object to the making of a grant for the proposed development. Where the Ministry withholds grants on these grounds the NCC will normally offer the owner a management agreement, under which compensation is payable on an annual basis for complying with certain stipulations, such as not draining a given area.

Where there is an irretrievable breakdown in negotiations on an important site, the NCC can recommend the use of a Nature Conservation Order, which must be issued by the Secretary of State for the Environment. This extends the period of negot-iation by 12 months, during which time the owner must not damage the site. At the end of this period the NCC is empowered to compulsorily purchase the site, with the consent of the Secretary of State, if no agreement has been reached. These powers, gran-ted under Section 29 of the Act, are regarded as a last resort and only three Nature Conservation Orders had been issued by March 1983 (82). Their effectiveness is rather undermined by the fact that it takes about three weeks for the Department of the Environment to process such an Order, during which time land-owners can destroy the interesting features of a site. This has happened on several occasions and is a major weakness of the Act.

The workings of the Act and its adequacy as a conservation mechanism is a complex subject, but the main principles are voluntary co-operation, and the use of management agreements and compensation on important sites. SSSIs receive no protection until they have been renotified and even then it is only partial. Many important wetlands have not yet been designated as SSSIs or are only partially designated. Only about half the sites meeting

Ramsar criteria for international importance were designated SSSIs by early 1984, although the remainder were likely to become so (83).

SSSIs were being damaged at an alarming rate at the end of the 1970s and it was estimated that 10 per cent of all sites were either damaged or destroyed in 1980 alone. The 1981 Act has certainly not brought this process to a halt. In Norfolk, 22 out of the county's total of 115 SSSIs were damaged or destroyed between 1981 and 1983, while in Northamptonshire it was six out of 44, together with six of the 22 proposed sites in the county (84). Such information is not available for most counties, but a recent report from Wildlife Link identifies 15 SSSIs in different parts of the country and seven proposed sites damaged by agricultural or forestry operations since the passage of the Act (85). Several of these sites were wetlands, damaged by drainage.

Management agreements are now one of the key tools for conservation policy in the countryside, especially for SSSIs. They are not a novel idea, the NCC has had the power to make such agreements since 1968 and 111 were in force over an area of 3,112 hectares by March 1983 (86). However, the number of new agreements being made has increased dramatically since the passage of the Wildlife and Countryside Act. Almost 100 agreements have been concluded since 1981 and 150 more are currently being negotiated, even though site renotification is very far from complete. Such agreements are expensive; those currently under negotiation are expected to cost about £1 million in capital payments and annual payments of around £800,000 (87).

Part of the reason for this expense is that farmers can demand compensation for being denied grants and can base their claims on the higher income which they might have anticipated if they had been allowed to develop their land. In estimating this future income they refer to the likely level of future farm prices under the Common Agricultural Policy. Thus, the present high level of wheat prices is not only an incentive for farmers on marshy land to install drainage if their soils have the potential for growing cereals, but also a factor inflating the cost of the management agreements which the NCC must pay to forestall drainage. Other EC countries emulating this policy are likely to encounter similar problems.

In their 1980-81 Annual Report the NCC estimated that the total cost of protecting SSSIs under this policy could amount to £20 million over 10 years (88). Many outside observers feel that this estimate is unrealistically low and sums several times this figure have been mentioned. There is considerable concern about whether the government will be prepared to meet additional costs on this scale or whether it is right that farmers should receive such generous compensation, which is not available to urban people denied permission to develop their property under the planning system. Some environmental groups, such as Friends of the Earth, are campaigning to change the Act (89) but only small modifications seem likely in the short term.

The NCC has so far been cautious, both in making agreements and in approaching the Department of the Environment for further funds. On the few occasions when they have requested additional funds for site protection, these have been made available. Thus it is not clear whether the NCC have been inhibited in making management agreements because of a fear that money will not be available or whether the government will be prepared to pay if presented with large demands. However, the position has led to a general sense of unease, especially amongst conservation groups, many of which feel that an unworkable system has been established.

The type of conflicts which arise in agricultural areas containing wetlands can be illustrated briefly with one example – the Somerset Levels, an area of about 68,000 hectares of low-lying land in the flood plain of five rivers meeting the sea between the Mendip and the Quantock Hills, a distinctive, largely agricultural landscape containing many individually significant wetland habitats, giving the whole area considerable national importance. It is a key site for breeding waders such as snipe, lapwing and curlew, provides extensive wintering grounds for a range of species and is one of the last strongholds of the otter in England. The flora of the grazing meadows are of particular interest, as are the plants and aquatic invertebrates found in the rhynes, the ditches which separate the fields.

The Levels contain areas of peat and clay, and much of the land, especially the peat, is very productive and could be improved considerably by means of drainage and the reorganisation of fragmented holdings. Over the last decade or so a number of drainage projects have been undertaken, some by the Wessex Water Authority or one of the 16 Internal Drainage Boards in the area, others by individual farmers. Several further schemes have been proposed including major flood alleviation projects for the rivers Brue and Parrett which would lead to lower water tables, considerable investment in field drainage and subsequent agricultural intensification likely to damage many sites. More intensive dairy farming or a switch to arable production is envisaged by many farmers.

While Somerset County Council has been working on an overall plan for the area, sites of wildlife interest have been damaged in a series of incidents usualy involving field drainage. There are nearly 7,000 hectares of SSSI quality on 10 different sites, although less than a third has been designated as such. Those sites which have not been designated as SSSIs have no protection and the NCC does not necessarily object to drainage. On one site, Tealham and Tadham Moors, a proposed SSSI, drainage has been proceeding rapidly in advance of notification, and one farmer drained his land while the NCC was in the process of obtaining a nature conservation order specifically to prevent him from doing so. The area has become a test case for the application of the Wildlife and Countryside Act, and to save a significant number of sites the NCC will have to enter into a considerable number of management agreements.

There are clear advantages in developing special plans for large areas like the Somerset Levels or the Norfolk Broads which are of great conservation value but are not National Parks. However, under present legislation a satisfactory accommodation between drainage and environmental priorities depends largely on voluntary co-operation and the availability of sufficient finance to compensate farmers. As the draft plan for the Somerset Levels points out "It is possible that the costs of improving agriculture, which could destroy important wetland habitats, would be supported by one government department (Ministry of Agriculture, Fisheries and Food) whilst another (Nature Conservancy Council) may be required to compensate those farmers whose methods may be required to remain unchanged or be restricted to only limited improvements" (90). The authors of the plan clearly doubt whether enough money will be forthcoming, even though they suggest that restraints on agricultural improvement will be necessary on only about 10 per cent of the area. More extensive local powers over land use planning are required to give local strategies of this kind real weight.

Conclusions and Impact of the Common Agricultural Policy

In the lowlands of Britain, rather as in the Netherlands, rural land is used intensively and there is a long history of drainage. Although most drainage is now aimed at improving land already in agricultural use and of relatively little wildlife value, a small but significant portion threatens the important pockets of wet pasture, marsh and mire which remain. Many SSSIs are damaged as a result of a farmer draining a single old meadow and small field drainage projects of this kind can be as significant as some of the larger arterial schemes.

If the drainage of environmentally valued sites was to be halted altogether in Britain, it would be of little agricultural significance, affecting the intensification of a relatively small area. The Ministry of Agriculture, which has a decisive role in drainage affairs, has now begun to emphasise to farmers the need to control production and there is a new interest in economising on inputs such as fertilisers and pesticides. This, and the recent small reduction in the rate of grant may reinforce the growth of environmental concern and help to restrain some drainage plans for wetland sites. However, farmers have become accustomed to drainage grants and many now regard them as a right. Loss of freedom to drain and loss of grants are the main issues for them and there is often resentment about "interference" from conservation bodies, even where sites are of national importance and generous compensation is being offered. Consequently, questions of land use priorities have become entangled with arguments about property rights and compensation and the fate of many wetlands now depends on the somewhat unpredictable outcome of the NCC's efforts to negotiate management agreements. Those wetlands which are not SSSIs, including many sites of a

Ramsar standard, are the most vulnerable of all, especially now that drainage grants can be obtained without prior approval.

The environmental effects of arterial schemes are extremely varied and partly reflect the practice of individual Water Authorities and their willingness to listen to conservation bodies, which have no formal representation on the decision making committees. The Ministry of Agriculture also has a strong influence on Water Authority schemes and they are not prepared to grant aid expenditure required for environmental reasons above a rather modest level. The Ministry is the body ultimately concerned with assessing arterial schemes and deciding whether or not they are economically worthwhile and from an environmental point of view, reform of cost-benefit appraisal methods and potential reforms in the administration of drainage are both vital issues.

Small but significant sums of EC money have been channeled into drainage work in Britain, with the most notable impact being in Northern Ireland, in the Western Isles of Scotland and in parts of the Fens. Threats to the machair in the Western Isles are relatvely well known, but Northern Ireland also contains a wealth of small wetlands, especially damp unploughed meadows, some of which will have been drained as a result of EC supported schemes. However, as in other countries, the major effect of the CAP on drainage has been via agricultural prices, which have provided farmers with an incentive to up-grade and convert land. The sharp rise in farm land prices in the 1970s can be attributed partly to the CAP as well as to inflation and other factors and this certainly acted as a spur to drainage. In some parts of the country, such as the Halvergate Marshes, it is the prospect of being able to grow wheat which attracts farmers to drainage schemes and it is quite clear that the CAP has pushed up wheat prices beyond their previous levels in the UK.

The price of wheat and other agricultural produce is now an important element, not only in the economics of drainage schemes, but also in the negotiation of management agreements. The price of saving wetlands is partly determined in Brussels.

References

1. Ministry of Agriculture, Fisheries and Food, 1983, Annual Review of Agriculture 1983, London
2. Royal Society for the Protection of Birds, 1983, Land Drainage and Birds in England and Wales: An Interim Report, Sandy, England
3. Trafford, B. D., 1970, "Field drainage, The Journal of the Royal Agricultural Society of England 137: 129-152
4. Ibid
5. Green, F. H. W., 1980, "Field Under-drainage Before and After 1940", The Agricultural History Review, Vol 28, Part

II, pp 120–123

6. Personal communication, Department of Agriculture and Fisheries for Scotland

7. Ibid

8. Department of Agriculture for Northern Ireland, 1982, Northern Ireland Agriculture, Belfast

9. Trafford, B. D., 1982, The Background to Land Drainage Policies and Practices in England and Wales, paper presented to a seminar "Assainissement agricole, economic et environnement" at L'Ecole Polytechnique, Paris, February 1982

10. Trafford, B. D., 1983, The Background to Land Drainage in England and Wales, paper for an Institute of Biology Symposium "Wetlands Under Threat?", London 1983

11. Ibid

12. Ibid

13. Ibid

14. Chatterton, J. B., 1983 Gauging the Economic Viability of Agricultural Land Drainage Schemes in England and Wales, paper presented to seminar at the Ecole Polytechnique, Paris

15. Department of Agriculture, Northern Ireland, personal communication

16. Bowers, J., 1984, "Running Soar", Ecos, Vol 5 No 1, winter 1984, pp 2–5

17. From the foreword included in several ADAS pamphlets in the series "Getting down to drainage", MAFF, London (circa 1975–81)

18. Trafford, B. D., 1977, "Recent progress in field drainage: Part I", Journal of the Royal Agricultural Society, Vol 138

19. Armstrong, A. C., 1978 A Digest of Drainage Statistics, Field Drainage Experimental Unit Technical Report 78/7, Cambridge, UK

20. Personal communication, Department of Agriculture, Northern Ireland

21. Personal communication, Department of Agriculture and Fisheries for Scotland

22. Personal communication, Department of Agriculture, Northern Ireland

23. Armstrong, A. C., 1981, Drainage Statistics 1978–80, Field Drainage Experimental Unit Technical Report 80/1, Cambridge, UK

24. Cole, G., 1976, "Land Drainage in England and Wales", Journal of the Institution of Water Engineers and Scientists 30, pp 345–367

25. Parker, D. J., and Penning-Rowsell, E., 1980, Water Planning in Britain, London

26. Trafford, 1982, op. cit.

27. Ministry of Agriculture, Fisheries and Food, 1977, Drainage in the Economy of the Farm, ADAS Technical Management Note No 23, London

28. Armstrong, 1981, op. cit.

29. Ibid

30. Ibid

31. Ibid

32. Carter, E., 1982, "Land Drainage", Farming and Wildlife Advisory Group Newsletter, Spring/Summer 1982

33. House of Lords Select Committee on the European Communities, 1982, <u>Socio-structural Policy</u>, second report, session 1982-83
34. Trafford, 1983, op. cit.
35. Parker and Penning-Rowsell, 1980, op. cit.
36. See, for example, Royal Society for the Protection of Birds, 1983, op. cit.
37. Ibid
38. Penning-Rowsell, E. C., and Chatterton, J. B., 1983 <u>Assessing Wetland Values</u>, paper presented for an Institute of Biology Symposium "Wetlands Under Threat?", London
39. Trafford, 1982, op. cit.
40. Ibid
41. Ibid
42. Ibid
43. Caufield, C., 1981, "Britain's Heritage of Wildlife Drains Away", <u>New Scientist</u>, 3rd September 1981, pp 583-586
44. Parker and Penning-Rowsell, 1980, op. cit.
45. <u>Birds</u>, spring 1984, page 7
46. Water Space Amenity Commission, 1980, <u>Conservation and Land Drainage Guidelines</u>, London
47. <u>Farmer's Weekly</u>, 20th January 1984, p 60
48. See evidence submitted by the Ministry of Agriculture, Fisheries and Food and the Countryside Commission to the House of Lords Sub-Committee Inquiry on Agriculture and the Environment, expected to be published summer 1984
49. Trafford, 1983, op. cit.
50. Ibid
51. Chatterton, 1983, op. cit.
52. Trafford, 1982, op. cit.
53. Trafford, 1983, op. cit.
54. Ministry of Agriculture, Fisheries and Food, press release, 1st July 1983
55. Ministry of Agriculture, Fisheries and Food, press release, 17th November 1983
56. Department of Agriculture, Northern Ireland, personal communication
57. Waterman, J., 1984, "How the Agriculture Fund is helping to Drain the Fens", <u>Europe 84</u>, Nos 1/2, pp 16/17
58. Ministry of Agriculture, Fisheries and food, 1984, written evidence submitted to House of Lords Select Committee on the European Communities for their report on agriculture and the environment, expected to be published summer 1984
59. Ibid
60. <u>Farmer's Weekly</u>, 3rd June 1982
61. Information supplied by the Department of Agriculture, Northern Ireland
62. Reed, T.M., "The IDP A Year On", <u>Ecos</u> 5(1), 1984, pp 23-26
63. RSPB, 1983, op. cit.
64. National report by the United Kingdom to the Groningen meeting of the Convention on Wetlands of International Importance, 1984, mimeo
65. Ibid
66. <u>ENDS</u>, Report 106, p8
67. <u>Guardian</u>, 21st July 1983

68. North, R., 1983, Wild Britain, London
69. Nature Conservancy Council, 1984, written evidence submitted to the House of Lords Select Committee on the European Communities for their report on agriculture and the environment expected to be published summer 1984
70. Ibid
71. National report by the UK to the 1984 meeting of the Convention on Wetlands of International Importance, op. cit.
72. Relton, J., 1972, "Disappearance of Farm Ponds", Monks Wood Experimental Station Report 1969-71, 32
73. RSPB, 1983, op. cit.
74. Ibid
75. Newbold, C., 1981, "The decline of aquatic plants and associated wetland wildlife in Britain - causes and perspectives on management techniques", paper for Proceedings on Aquatic Weeds and their Control, 1981
76. Ibid
77. RSPB, 1983, op. cit.
78. Smith, K.W., 1983, "The status and distribution of waders breeding on wet lowland grasslands in England and Wales", Bird Study 30: 177-192
79. Nature Conservancy Council, 1984, op. cit.
80. Environmental Resource Management Ltd, 1981, Acid Sulphate Soils in Broadland, Broads Authority, Norwich
81. "Too much drainage spells trouble on t'farm", New Scientist, 21st January 1982, 159
82. Nature Conservancy Council, 1984(a), Ninth Report, London
83. National report by the UK to the 1984 meeting of the Convention on Wetlands of International Importance, op. cit.
84. Wildlife Link, 1983, Habitat Report No 2, London
85. Ibid
86. Nature Conservancy Council, 1984(a), op. cit.
87. Parliamentary answers by Mr Waldegrave to questions by Mr Hunter, 2nd May 1984
88. Nature Conservancy Council, 1982, Seventh Report, London
89. Friends of the Earth, 1983, Proposals for a National Heritage Bill, London
90. Somerset County Council, 1983, Draft Somerset Levels and Moors Plan, Taunton
91. Green, F.H.W., 1979, Field Drainage in Europe: A Quantitative Survey, Institute of Hydrology, Wallingford, UK

CHAPTER 6 : CONCLUSIONS

The evidence reviewed here, which is far from complete, confirms the widespread view that wetlands are amongst the most threatened of European habitats and that drainage is one of the prime causes of this. The large scale of current works in France and Ireland is particularly alarming. In looking more closely at drainage and the way in which it is organised and financed, a multitude of differences become apparent, but there are still many common factors to be distinguished. It is the purpose of this concluding chapter to identify some of them.

The Threat to Wetlands

Wetlands take many shapes and forms, from coastal mudflats to upland mires. Amongst those most threatened by agricultural drainage are marshes, wet meadows, small ponds and lakes, ditches, streams and rivers, some peat bogs and certain areas of salt marsh. In Ireland, turloughs have been almost entirely eliminated.

The era of large-scale land reclamation for agriculture is largely over in the four countries covered here, although there remain some significant threats, for example to coastal marshes in France or the Markerwaard in the Netherlands. Small scale reclamation remains common however. Farmland is created by nibbling away at the edges of poorly protected sites, filling in farm ponds and draining small areas of marsh which may be of local significance even if they are not internationally important sites.

River improvement works have a variety of different objectives, but most arterial schemes designed to benefit agriculture involve a lowering of neighbouring watertables and better provision for field drainage, as well as affecting the river and its banks. In all four countries wetlands are being damaged or destroyed by improvements in arterial drainage. The impact of large catchment drainage schemes is particularly evident in Ireland, while in the Netherlands comprehensive land development schemes have resulted in major hydrological changes and the creation of "standard landscapes". Insensitive maintenance work, involving the unnecessary clearance of bankside vegetation, for example, is also a threat.

It is certainly possible to lessen the destructive impact of improvement works by sensitive scheme design and careful execution, thus retaining a richer river landscape. This approach has been practised in parts of West Germany and the Netherlands for some years and is now becoming more common in Britain. However, the essence of many schemes is to reduce seasonal flooding and permit the effective drainage of surrounding fields, marsh or bogland, thus eliminating the habitat required by wetland fauna and flora. Compromise is difficult in such circumstances and there is often a straight choice between conservation and agricultural improvement.

Field drainage is varied in its environmental impact. It may be undertaken by farmers individually or in groups, in isolated patches or in complex land consolidation schemes, it may involve installing underdrainage or constructing surface ditches, but in most cases it involves lowering water levels or at least eliminating wet patches. On land which is already intensively farmed or where the water level is no longer near the surface, field drainage will generally have little effect on wildlife although it may involve important landscape changes such as hedge and ditch removal.

On the other hand, where the land is wet enough to support fauna and flora of some interest, even for short periods of the year, the consequences of drainage may be more serious, resulting in the total disappearance of wet habitats. The declining area of wet pasture available to breeding waders is of serious concern in both the Netherlands and the UK, for example. It is not only wet fields that are at risk; field drainage may also result in the elimination of old drainage ditches, now valued as wildlife refuges in extensively farmed landscapes, and this is a common feature of land consolidation schemes. In general, the impact of field drainage is usually greatest when land is being drained for the first time, or where an old system is being sharply upgraded, perhaps to allow pasture to be converted to arable.

It is difficult to distinguish the proportion of field drainage which is environmentally damaging from that which is not. In the UK, the proportion of "new" drainage affecting relatively wet land is probably around 5-8 per cent; in France, where much less land has been drained in the past, it is almost certainly much higher. The effects of individual drainage schemes are varied, but they share a common overall aim - an improvement in agricultural productivity. This may be achieved by improving soil conditions for plants, by increasing inputs of fertilisers and agrochemicals and by allowing heavier machinery to be brought on the land at an earlier date, etc. Drainage often removes a major barrier to intensification and thus opens the way for a set of practices which may themselves threaten wetlands through eutrophication, the run-off of pesticides etc. Pollution from agricultural sources is an important threat to lakes, rivers and other wetlands in all four countries and it is long-term, indirect effects of this kind which create the conditions in which it is harder to conserve individual sites.

The loss of wetlands in the four countries is difficult to quantify in any remotely satisfactory way. In the UK it has been estimated that about half the lowland fens and the valley and basin mires have been significantly destroyed or damaged since the end of the Second World War, with the prime causes being drainage, reclamation for agriculture and chemical enrichment of drainage water. In Ireland, major arterial schemes have affected large areas and about a quarter of the country's farmland has been subject to field drainage during the same period. In France, drainage has progressed much more slowly until recently, but has expanded rapidly over the last decade and more than half the wetlands of major importance for wildfowl are now affected by drainage or are at some risk. If the decline of wetlands continues on the present scale, we can expect very substantial losses and a serious impoverishment of the European environment within a few decades.

In the six other EC countries, wetlands are also under pressure from both agricultural drainage and other quarters. The IUCN's "Wetland Directory", published in 1980, notes that drainage is a threat to several sites of international importance within the Community (1), and the same impression can be gained from other sources. The Evros Delta, for example, is one Ramsar site known to be threatened by agricultural reclamation, although it may still be the most important wetland for waterfowl in Greece.

One measure of the problem is the number of threatened or endangered species which depend on wetlands. About three-quarters of the endangered or vulnerable European bird species are in decline, and of these about 47 per cent are wetland species threatened by destruction of habitat (2). A recent report by the Nature Conservancy Council suggests that all 111 of the EC's breeding species of reptiles or amphibians are endangered to some degree, along with 2000 plant species (3). In all the countries considered here, the protection of both species and sites depends on the maintenance of some traditional farming practices as well as high water tables.

Drainage is by no means the only threat to wetlands and the species which inhabit them. Urban and industrial development, flood protection schemes, pollution from a variety of sources, recreation and tourist development, and the shooting of wildfowl all appear to be significant pressures in the countries considered here. Nonetheless, drainage is considered either a primary or the single greatest threat to wetlands in all four countries.

Land Drainage

Most drainage works in north-west Europe are undertaken wholly or partly for agricultural purposes. Schemes applying to river valleys or whole catchments commonly have an urban component and drainage is frequently associated with flood control projects, particularly in the UK and the Netherlands, but the single most important reason for drainage is undoubtedly the improvement of agricultural land. The pace of new work has been slowest in France. By the end of the 1970s around 10 per cent of the agricultural area had been drained in France and over 60 per cent in the Netherlands and the UK.

Field drainage is one of the most widely practised forms of agricultural improvement and is taking place on a considerable scale, currently around 140,000 hectares a year in France, around 120,000 hectares a year in the UK, around 30,000 hectares a year in Ireland and 25,000 hectares a year in the Netherlands. There has been a rapid expansion in France in recent years, but more stability in the other three countries. Some of this effort is taking place on previously undrained fields, especially in France and the west of Ireland, but most of it is on land which has been drained in the past.

In the UK and the Netherlands most field drainage work is intended to upgrade or replace previous drains and improve productivty. In the Netherlands, water level management is increasingly sophisticated. In pursuing optimal soil moisture conditions, schemes may be designed to lower the water table sufficiently to improve trafficability for farm vehicles in the spring, even if this entails irrigation or controlled flooding to prevent excessive drying out in the summer. This probably indicates the future direction of farm drainage on some of the better soils in the Community, assuming adequate finance and no major change in policy.

Nearly all drainage works in the four countries considered here receive some form of public subsidy. In Ireland arterial works are entirely state funded and field drainage is heavily subsidised, especially in the west. Two-thirds of the cost of land consolidation projects in the Netherlands is provided by the government. In France, the level of public support varies, but is generally in the range of 25-70 per cent. In the UK the position is broadly similar. Subsidies for arterial works tend to be higher than for field drainage everywhere and there is a tendency for group projects to be supported more generously than those of individual farmers.

Subsidies for field drainage are usually greater in less favoured areas than elsewhere and are particularly high in the west of Ireland. In poorer agricultural areas drainage is often seen as an important form of infrastructure improvement and means of raising farm incomes, although the costs tend to be higher and the returns less good than on better agricultural land. Most field drainage takes place on fertile lowland soils, especially those devoted to arable cropping. Often this is in relatively dry areas, for example the eastern half of the UK.

Finance for Drainage

The majority of public funds for supporting drainage come from national budgets rather than from the European Community. However, the EC has made available considerable funds for drainage through a variety of channels. The major source of these has been the guidance sector of the Community's agricultural fund, FEOGA. Field drainage and land consolidation schemes have been supported under the farm modernisation Directive 72/159 and the Less Favoured Areas Directive 75/268. Selected schemes throughout the Community have been partly financed under Regulation 17/64 for individual capital projects, a scheme which has now been phased out.

In recent years there have been a number of special regional aid programmes which have provided assistance for drainage. Most significant of these have been measures aimed specifically at assisting drainage in the west of Ireland, Directive 78/628 and Regulation 2195/81. Indeed Community funds for drainage have been particularly concentrated in Ireland. There have been schemes to assist drainage along the border with Northern Ireland, small grants from the Regional Development Fund towards arterial projects, and substantial loans from the European Investment Bank to help the government finance its share of drainage costs.

Under the Western Drainage Scheme in Ireland, FEOGA meets half the costs of arterial projects and around a third of the cost of field drainage, but outside Ireland the scale of the Community's contribution is more typically in the range of 5-15 per cent. In France, the Netherlands and the UK, finance from the Community has helped to support national drainage programmes, but has probably not had a decisive influence on the level of expenditure. In Ireland, however, the Community's financial assistance appears to have stimulated more ambitious drainage programmes than otherwise would have existed. In all four countries, Community finance has played an important part in the viability of a number of individual schemes, some of them of environmental significance, such as the draining of areas of machair in the Western Isles of Scotland.

The influence of the Common Agricultural Policy on national drainage programmes extends considerably beyond the direct payment of grants. By establishing a broadly free market in agricultural produce in the Community, the CAP has increased competitive pressures on farmers in many parts of Europe, perhaps felt most keenly in the "less favoured" areas. In general, CAP prices have been secure and rather high relative to those on the world market, which has attracted capital into agriculture and helped sustain high land prices. The cost of maintaining traditional forms of agriculture and leaving wetland undrained has risen accordingly.

In this economic climate, there has been a strong incentive to farmers to increase production, particularly of cereals and milk, which are now in permanent surplus. Consequently, they have intensified almost all aspects of production and, on a lesser scale, have transferred pasture into arable land and taken over previously uncultivated land, including marshes and other wetlands. Improved drainage has a role in all these routes to higher output and is likely to remain cost-effective for many farmers while CAP prices continue at broadly their present levels and generous subsidies from national and Community sources remain available. Arterial schemes are more dependent on central government grants, but they too are often justified by reference to projected agricultural benefits, the value of which much depends on CAP price levels.

In the United Kingdom, where the protection of important sites from drainage now depends heavily on management agreements, the cost of compensating farmers for income foregone depends greatly on CAP price levels. If a similar approach is adopted elsewhere, the CAP could come to determine the cost of conservation directly instead of indirectly. The dangers of this are all too obvious and need to be considered carefully before this kind of compensation becomes more widely used.

If CAP prices are lowered over time, or the level of national grants is reduced, some of the present incentives for drainage will be weakened. However, there is little doubt that drainage would still be cost-effective on some wetland sites, and the need for effective conservation policies would still remain.

Drainage Policies and the Environment

In principle, cost-benefit analysis offers a useful means of evaluating arterial drainage schemes and other relatively large projects, such as land consolidation. Indeed, it is used, at least for some schemes, in each of the four countries. In practice, its usefulness has been greatly diminished by the methodologies used, the tendency to choose assumptions favourable to the proposed scheme and the practice of either ignoring environmental costs or giving them little weight. This is a crucial weakness in present policy and the recent steps towards a more rigorous approach in the UK and the Netherlands are to be welcomed.

The common economic rationale behind drainage schemes is to increase agricultural output and raise farm incomes, but at present it is far from clear whether drainage represents the best available investment for this purpose. Drainage investments are sustained by historical momentum, strong institutional support and a predisposition by governments and the EC for "infrastructure improvement" projects, especially in less favoured areas. More careful appraisal of their economic value and the merits of alternative investments is overdue.

Conservation policies exist in each of the four Member States and a variety of protective measures are available. Some of these are utilised and enforced with much more vigour than others; however, in general they are not being operated in such a way as to provide adequate protection at the moment. The approach to conservation is most sophisticated in the Netherlands and least developed in Ireland and this stems partly from institutional factors.

In general, agricultural drainage is administered and grant aided by Ministries primarily concerned with either agriculture or public works. Usually they are responsible for the key decisions at a local level where environmental authorities are often poorly represented. In the Netherlands, there is greater integration of agricultural and environmental responsibility within a single Ministry and unofficial bodies are better represented in local decisions over drainage. This appears to have many advantages over the arrangements in the other three countries.

The Role of the European Community

The weaknesses of nature conservation legislation in particular countries have to be tackled at a national level, but the EC Bird Directive has created a role for the Community in setting an overall framework for habitat protection. The significance of this Directive is not that it has been enforced vigorously in all the Member States, some of which appear to be moving very slowly, but that it has established an important new principle. Member States have agreed to ensure sufficient diversity and area of habitats so as to maintain the population of a substantial list of species. In seeking some kind of accord between agriculture and the environment at the EC level, the balance of legislation is no longer tipped quite so heavily in favour of production.

To provide adequate protection for wetlands, some specific and urgent action is required. Measures to improve the economic evaluation of new schemes, to assess environmental impacts in advance, to strengthen conservation legislation, to fund the required initiatives, to reform institutions, to heighten awareness of the value of wetlands and so forth, must be instituted largely at the local and national level. However, it is the European Community as a whole which has responsibility for the CAP and its broad implications for the environment.

The present indications are that production limits are beginning to assume a larger role within the CAP and that quotas will be used for this purpose rather than substantial price cuts. At the same time, structural policies and special aid measures for poorer regions are likely to grow in importance. Indeed, an amended farm structure policy has been in the process of emerging since 1982, but with little consideration of its environmental implications until a late stage in the drafting. Even modest reforms offer some opportunity for implanting environmental considerations into policy and they should not be ignored.

One of the most crucial arenas for integrating agricultural and environmental policy is regional farm aid, of the kind available to Ireland, the Western Isles of Scotland, Lozère, Greece, the Mezzogiorno and on an increasing scale to the Mediterranean. The Community's usual approach is to channel additional finance into farming in order to intensify production, and particularly to accelerate infrastructure improvements, such as drainage, irrigation and farm roads. In consequence, Community funds are managed largely by agricultural institutions which may have little appreciation of environmental factors and little money is available for conservation or, indeed, for alternative methods of raising local incomes.

There is little doubt that these regions need assistance, although the focus on agriculture may not always be helpful. It is more questionable whether they will be able to compete in the long term with the main centres of agricultural production, particularly as Community output becomes subject to increasing controls. Developments which damage the natural environment may prove a poor investment, deterring tourists as well as undermining conservation. Greater effort should be devoted to finding ways to support more extensive traditional forms of agriculture - which are often critical to the maintenance of grazing marsh and other habitats.

If the Community is to employ a more discriminating agricultural policy, it must have much more precise data on the environmental consequences of particular projects and farming practices. At present it is often extremely difficult to distinguish environmentally damaging drainage projects from acceptable ones, either at a national or a Community level. Information about the design and cost of schemes is collected systematically, but there is no consistent effort to compile and evaluate data on the environmental effect of works, even though some schemes do receive close scrutiny.

To rectify this requires a better wetland data base, an effective prior notification system for drainage works, adequate evaluation procedures and some long-term monitoring of selected sites. This would not need to cover every individual field drainage operation, but at least projects of a significant size and those in particularly sensitive areas. Appropriate systems of prior notification and evaluation are the responsibility of Member States, but the Community has a role in encouraging such developments, especially where it is providing direct aid for particular projects or regions. It could also help to establish and finance a European inventory of wetlands, covering sites of local and national as well as international importance. Such an inventory would be an invaluable tool for directing policy and could be built up quite rapidly from the survey work which has been undertaken in the past.

There already exists a proposal for the establishment of an information system on the state of the environment in the Community, which is intended to include a register of sites of major importance for nature conservation. An inventory of wetlands should be a priority under this programme, but it should be comprehensive in coverage rather than a replication of the existing lists of internationally significant sites.

Finally, the Community must consider carefully the case for future funding of new agricultural drainage work. Relatively few projects are financed with the help of large contributions from Brussels, but in such cases it is important to demand an adequate environmental evaluation and to have the power to reject unacceptable schemes.

Stronger protection for wetlands is justified, not only because of the continued threats to a diminishing area of habitat and the obligations of the Bird Directive and international agreements, such as the Ramsar Convention, but also because the need for greater agricultural production in the EC is increasingly dubious. In conservation terms, the cost of wetland drainage is rising, while for the Community as a whole the agricultural benefits are diminishing.

References

1. Carp, E., 1980, "A Directory of Western Paleartic Wetlands", IUCN/UNEP, Gland, Switzerland
2. de Molenaar, J.G., 1981, "Agriculture and Birdlife in Europe", lecture given to the International Council for Bird Preservation, mimeo, 1981
3. A major study soon to be published by the European Commission, reported in Europe 84 No 3, March 1984. 13

FREE BOOKS OFFER

To get you started, we'll send you
2 FREE books and a FREE gift

- -

There's no catch, everything is **FREE**

Accepting your 2 **FREE** books and **FREE** mystery gift
places you under no obligation to buy anything.

Be part of the Mills & Boon® Book Club™ and receive your favourite
Series books up to 2 months before they are in the shops and delivered
straight to your door. Plus, enjoy a wide range of **EXCLUSIVE** benefits!

- Best new women's fiction – delivered right to
  your door with FREE P&P
- Avoid disappointment – get your books up to
  2 months before they are in the shops
- No contract – no obligation to buy

2 **FREE** books
and a
FREE gift

We hope that after receiving your free books you'll
want to remain a member. But the choice is yours.
So why not give us a go? You'll be glad you did!

Visit **millsandboon.co.uk** to stay up to date
with offers and to sign-up for our newsletter

H0HIA

Mrs/Miss/Ms/Mr   Initials

BLOCK CAPITALS PLEASE

Surname

Address

Postcode

Email

MILLS & BOON®
Book Club

FREE BOOK OFFER
FREEPOST NAT 10298
RICHMOND
TW9 1BR

NO STAMP
NECESSARY
IF POSTED IN
THE U.K. OR N.I.